TANK GIRL GOLD

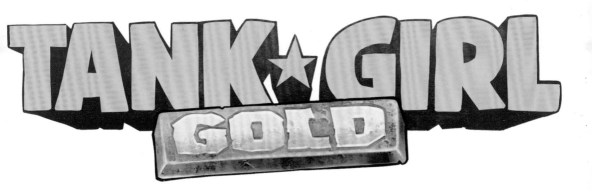

WRITTEN BY
ALAN MARTIN

DRAWN & LETTERED BY
BRETT PARSON

ADDITIONAL COLORS BY
NED IVORY

Cover By
CHRIS WAHL

Forbidden Planet Cover By
ANDREW ROBINSON

TITAN COMICS

EDITOR
TOM WILLIAMS

SENIOR DESIGNER
ANDREW LEUNG

SENIOR EDITOR
ANDREW JAMES

TITAN COMICS EDITORIAL
**JONATHAN STEVENSON,
LAUREN MCPHEE,
AMOONA SAOHIN**

SENIOR PRODUCTION CONTROLLER
JACKIE FLOOK

PRODUCTION SUPERVISOR
MARIA PEARSON

PRODUCTION CONTROLLER
PETER JAMES

ART DIRECTOR
OZ BROWNE

SENIOR SALES MANAGER
STEVE TOTHILL

PRESS OFFICER
WILL O'MULLANE

MARKETING MANAGER
RICKY CLAYDON

ADVERTISING MANAGER
MICHELLE FAIRLAMB

ADS & MARKETING ASSISTANT
TOM MILLER

HEAD OF RIGHTS
JENNY BOYCE

PUBLISHING MANAGER
DARRYL TOTHILL

PUBLISHING DIRECTOR
CHRIS TEATHER

OPERATIONS DIRECTOR
LEIGH BAULCH

EXECUTIVE DIRECTOR
VIVIAN CHEUNG

PUBLISHER
NICK LANDAU

TANK GIRL: GOLD
ISBN: 9781785855252

FORBIDDEN PLANET EDITION
ISBN: 9781785863301

PUBLISHED BY TITAN COMICS,
A DIVISION OF TITAN PUBLISHING GROUP, LTD.
144 SOUTHWARK STREET,
LONDON, SE1 0UP

WWW.TITAN-COMICS.COM
BECOME A FAN ON FACEBOOK.COM/COMICSTITAN
FOLLOW US ON TWITTER @COMICSTITAN
VISIT THE OFFICIAL TANK GIRL WEBSITE AT WWW.TANK-GIRL.COM

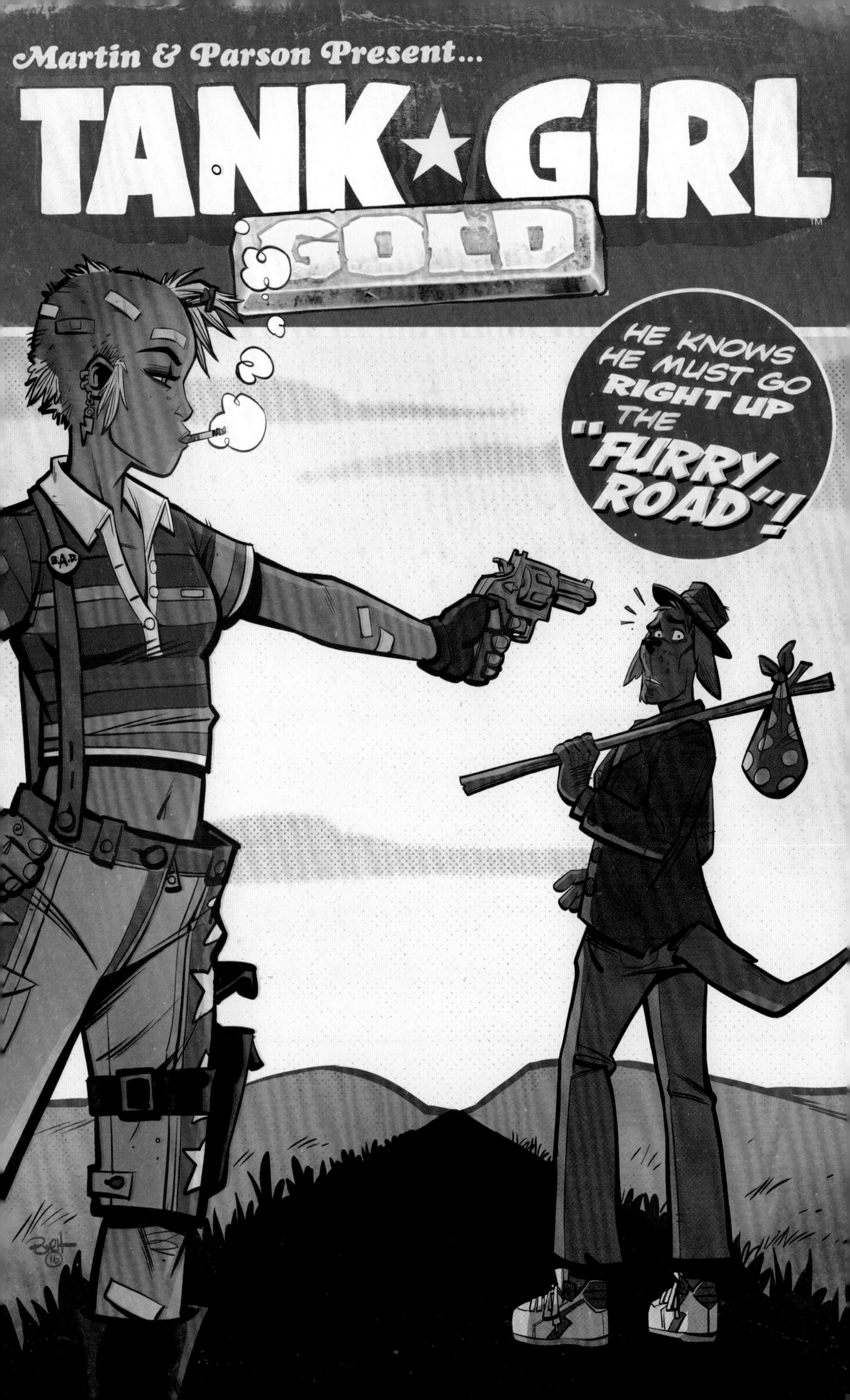
Martin & Parson Present...
TANK GIRL
GOLD
HE KNOWS HE MUST GO RIGHT UP THE "FURRY ROAD"!
B.A.D.
BRETT '16

THE GIRL WHO SLEPT WITH ELVIS

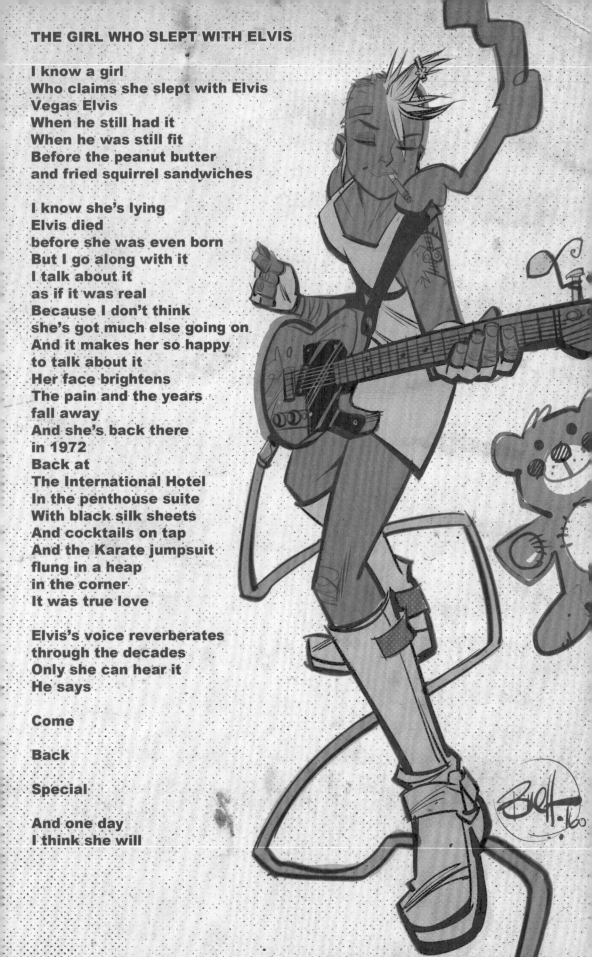

I know a girl
Who claims she slept with Elvis
Vegas Elvis
When he still had it
When he was still fit
Before the peanut butter
and fried squirrel sandwiches

I know she's lying
Elvis died
before she was even born
But I go along with it
I talk about it
as if it was real
Because I don't think
she's got much else going on
And it makes her so happy
to talk about it
Her face brightens
The pain and the years
fall away
And she's back there
in 1972
Back at
The International Hotel
In the penthouse suite
With black silk sheets
And cocktails on tap
And the Karate jumpsuit
flung in a heap
in the corner
It was true love

Elvis's voice reverberates
through the decades
Only she can hear it
He says

Come

Back

Special

And one day
I think she will

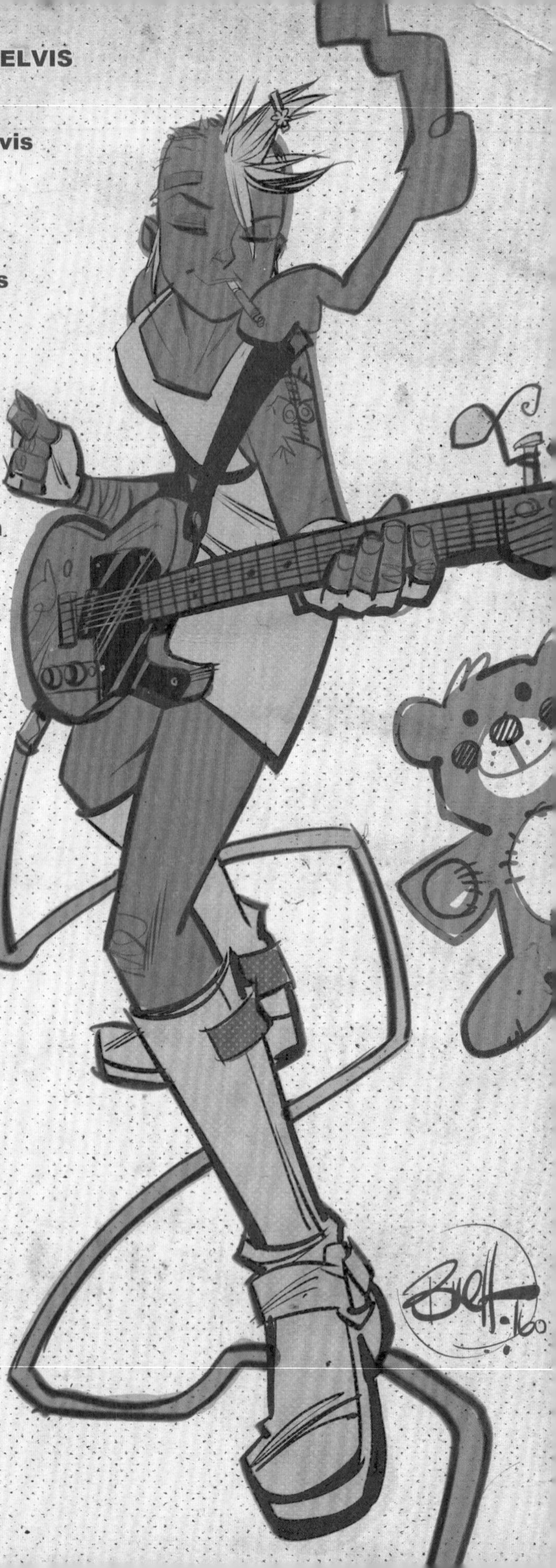

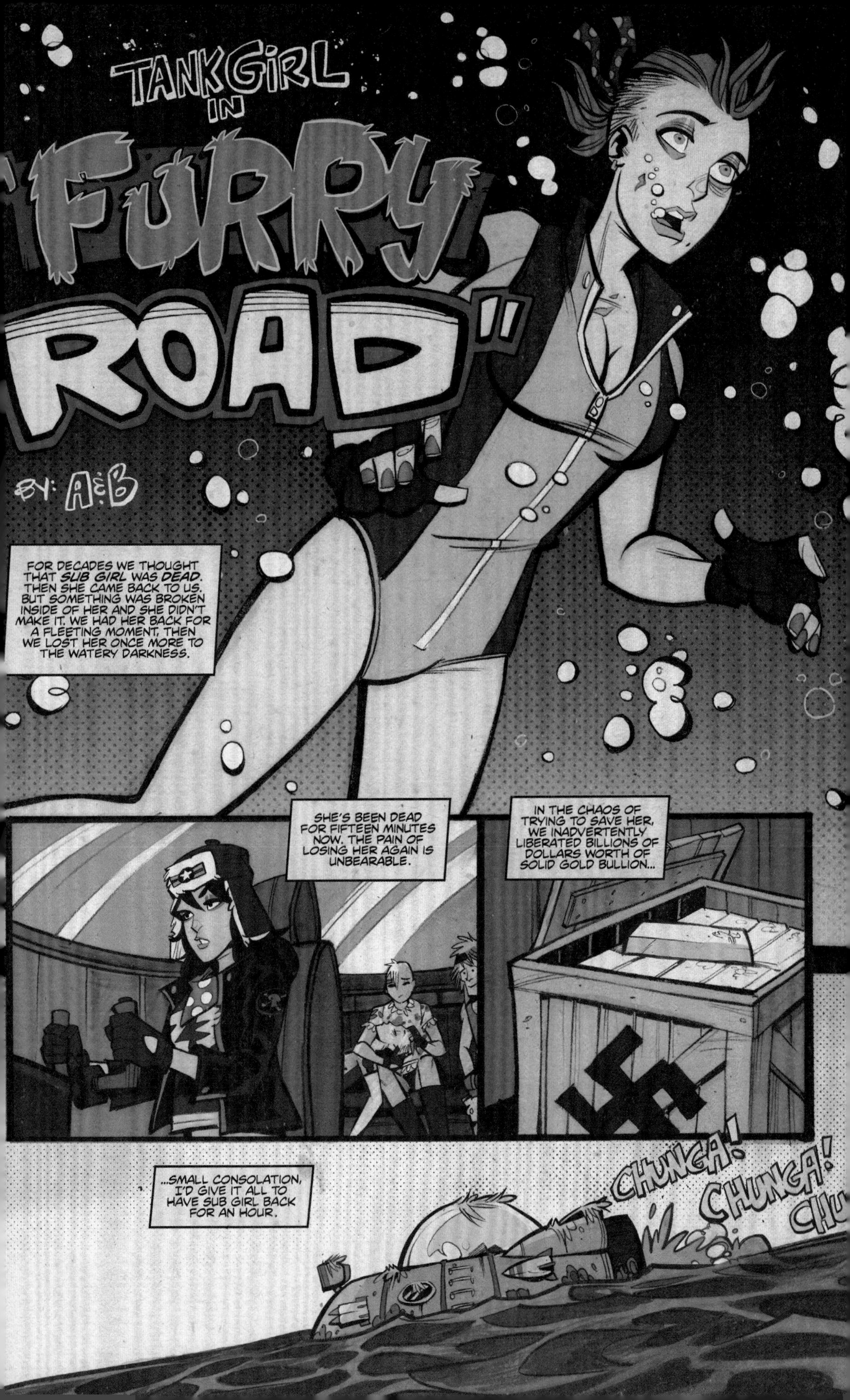

TANK GIRL IN
"FURRY ROAD"
BY: A&B
FOR DECADES WE THOUGHT THAT SUB GIRL WAS DEAD. THEN SHE CAME BACK TO US. BUT SOMETHING WAS BROKEN INSIDE OF HER AND SHE DIDN'T MAKE IT. WE HAD HER BACK FOR A FLEETING MOMENT, THEN WE LOST HER ONCE MORE TO THE WATERY DARKNESS.
SHE'S BEEN DEAD FOR FIFTEEN MINUTES NOW. THE PAIN OF LOSING HER AGAIN IS UNBEARABLE.
IN THE CHAOS OF TRYING TO SAVE HER, WE INADVERTENTLY LIBERATED BILLIONS OF DOLLARS WORTH OF SOLID GOLD BULLION...
...SMALL CONSOLATION, I'D GIVE IT ALL TO HAVE SUB GIRL BACK FOR AN HOUR.
CHUNGA! CHUNGA! CHU

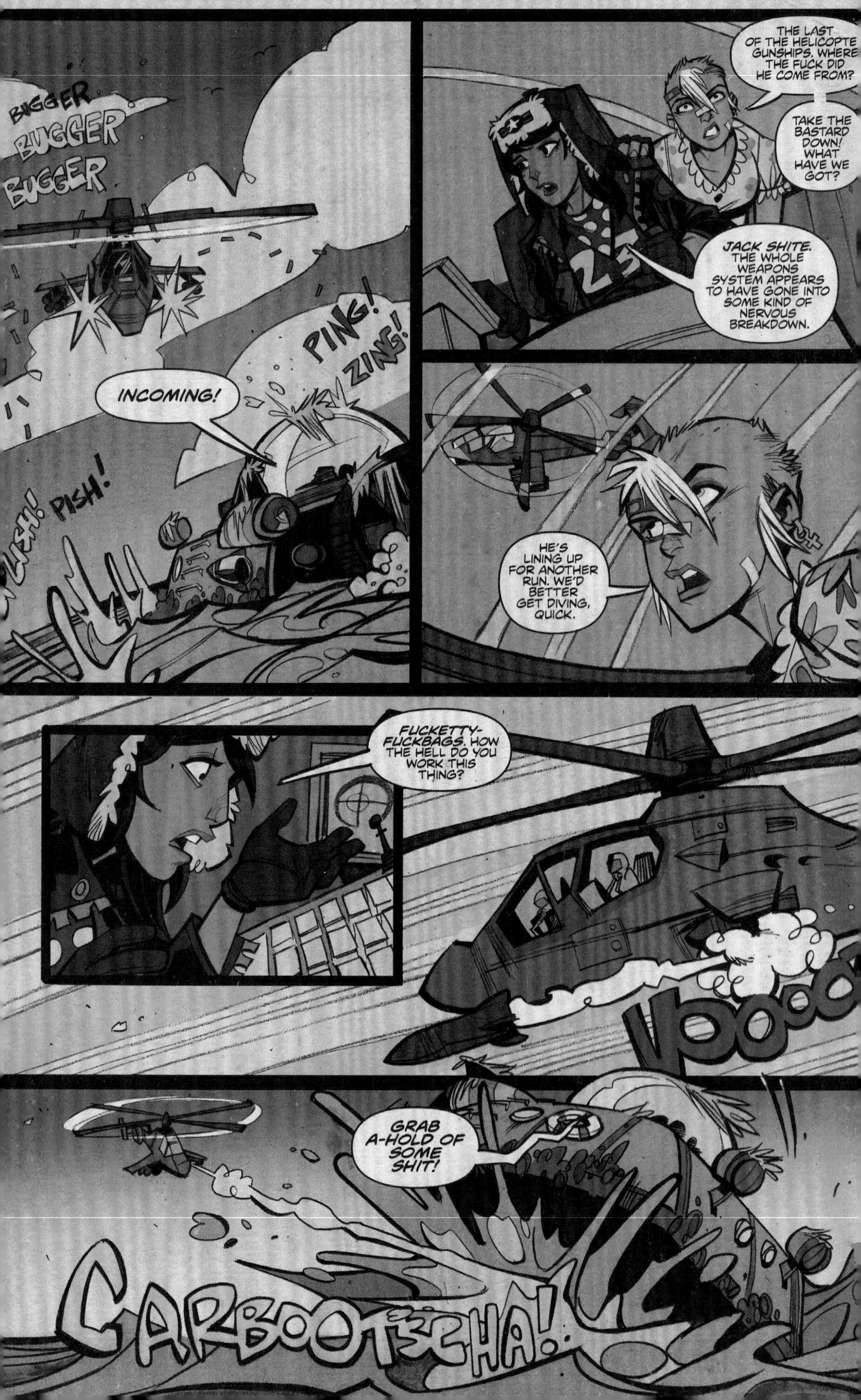
BUGGER
BUGGER
BUGGER
PING!
ZING!
INCOMING!
PISH!
THE LAST OF THE HELICOPTE GUNSHIPS. WHERE THE FUCK DID HE COME FROM?
TAKE THE BASTARD DOWN! WHAT HAVE WE GOT?
JACK SHITE. THE WHOLE WEAPONS SYSTEM APPEARS TO HAVE GONE INTO SOME KIND OF NERVOUS BREAKDOWN.
HE'S LINING UP FOR ANOTHER RUN. WE'D BETTER GET DIVING, QUICK.
FUCKETTY-FUCKBAGS. HOW THE HELL DO YOU WORK THIS THING?
GRAB A-HOLD OF SOME SHIT!
CARBOOTSCHA!

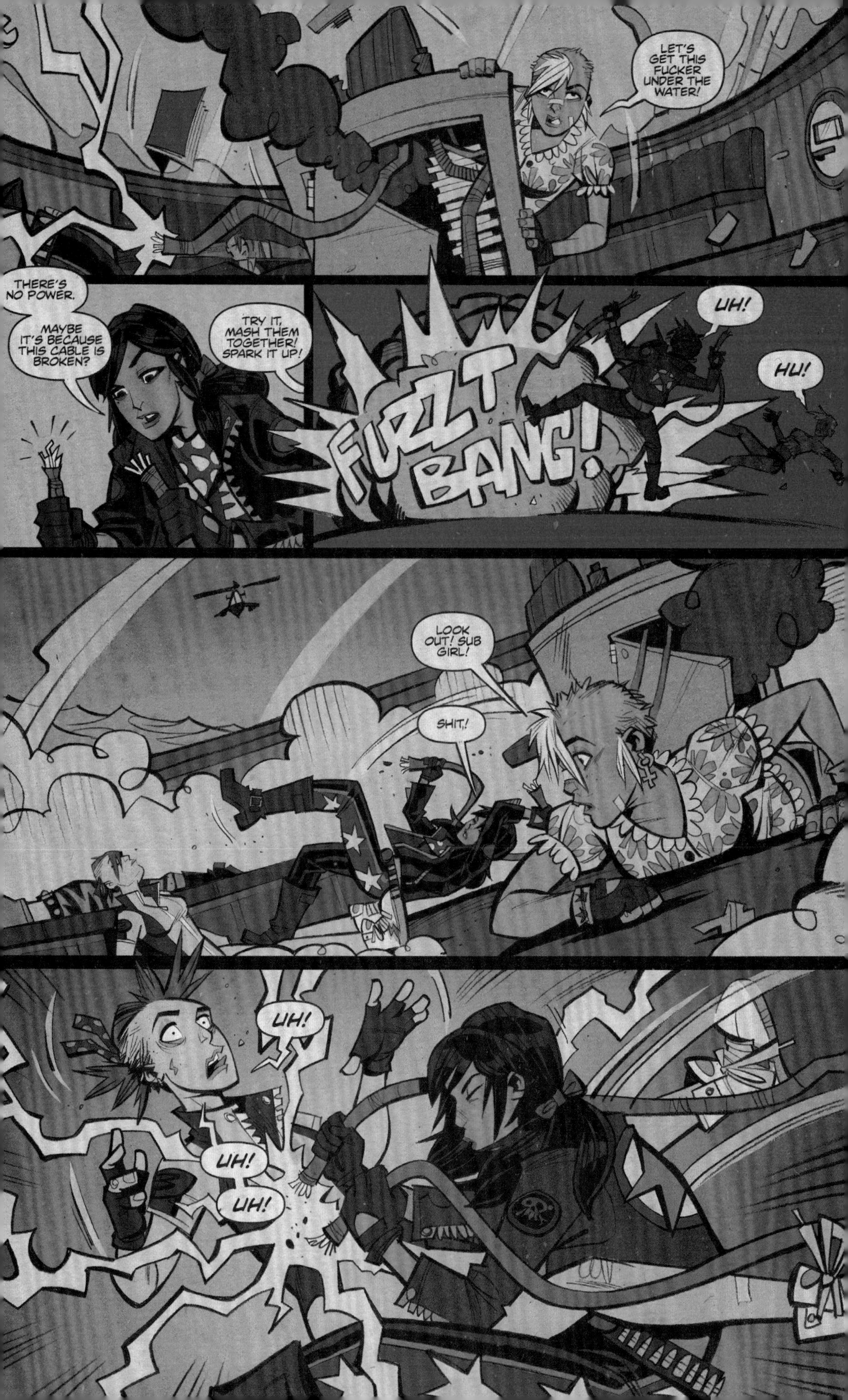
LET'S GET THIS FUCKER UNDER THE WATER!
THERE'S NO POWER.
MAYBE IT'S BECAUSE THIS CABLE IS BROKEN?
TRY IT, MASH THEM TOGETHER! SPARK IT UP!
FURZLT BANG!
UH!
HU!
LOOK OUT! SUB GIRL!
SHIT!
UH!
UH!
UH!

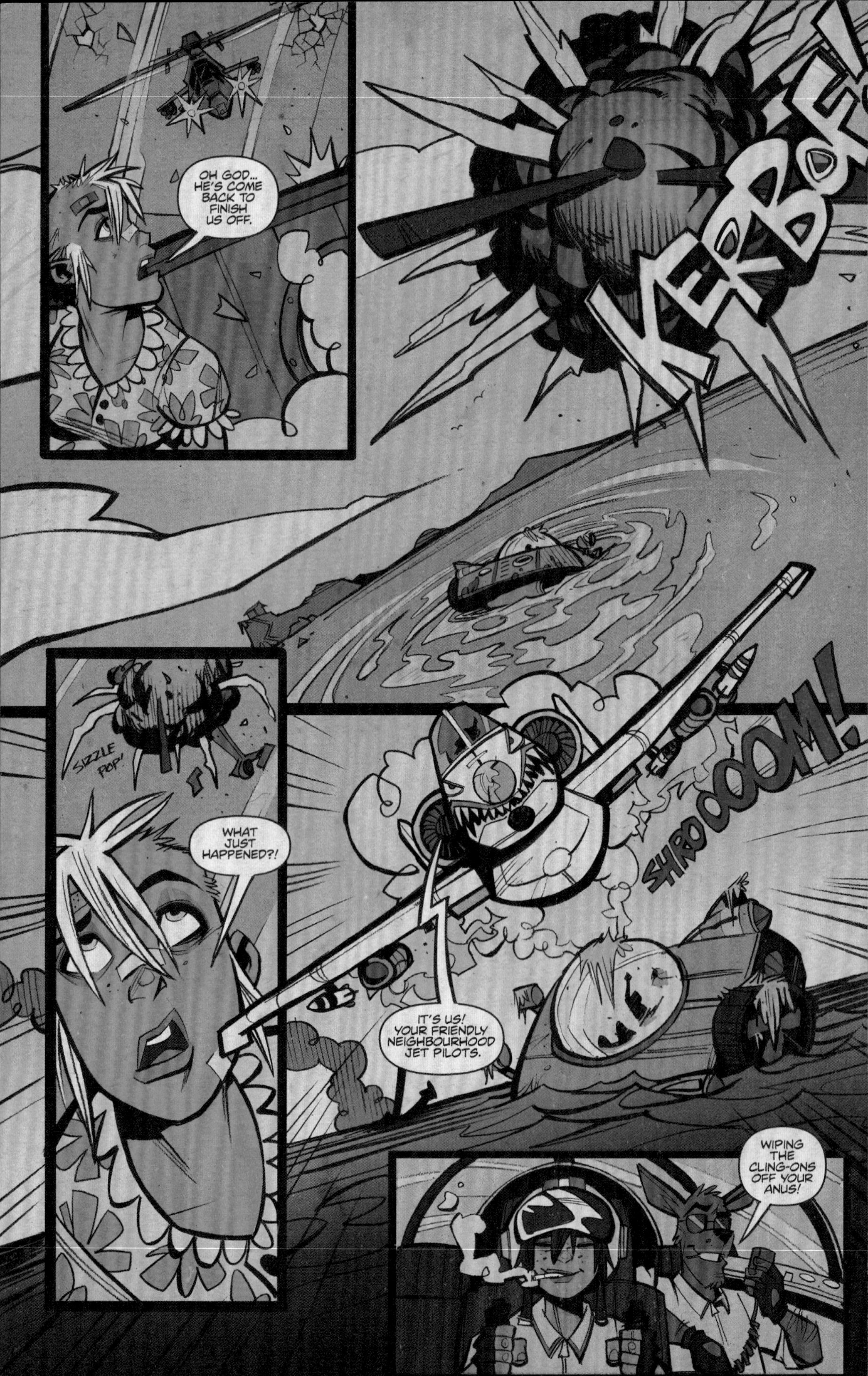
OH GOD... HE'S COME BACK TO FINISH US OFF.
KERBOOM!
SIZZLE POP!
WHAT JUST HAPPENED?!
SHROOOOM!
IT'S US! YOUR FRIENDLY NEIGHBOURHOOD JET PILOTS.
WIPING THE CLING-ONS OFF YOUR ANUS!

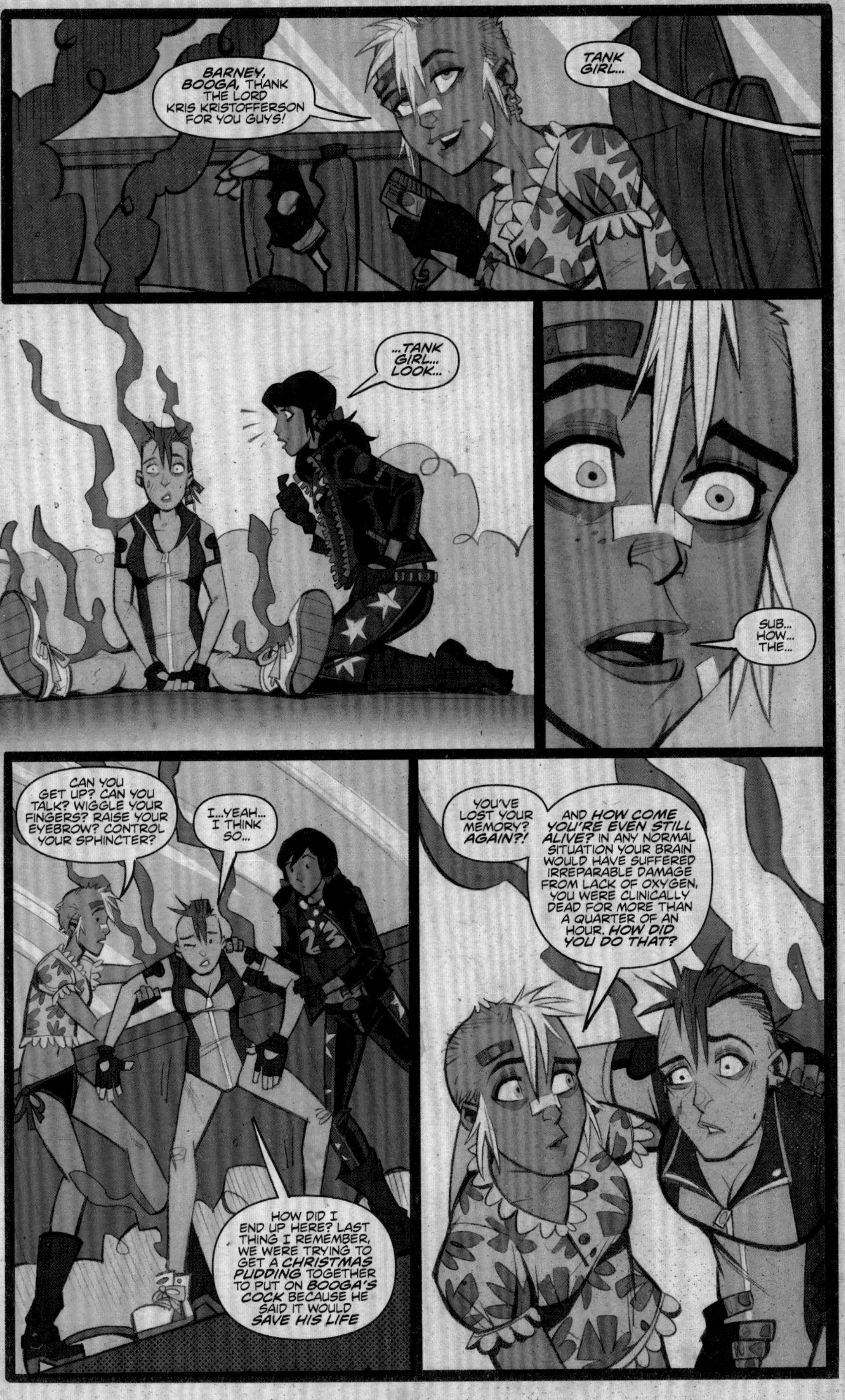

BARNEY, BOOGA, THANK THE LORD KRIS KRISTOFFERSON FOR YOU GUYS!
TANK GIRL...
...TANK GIRL... LOOK...
SUB... HOW... THE...
CAN YOU GET UP? CAN YOU TALK? WIGGLE YOUR FINGERS? RAISE YOUR EYEBROW? CONTROL YOUR SPHINCTER?
I...YEAH... I THINK SO...
HOW DID I END UP HERE? LAST THING I REMEMBER, WE WERE TRYING TO GET A CHRISTMAS PUDDING TOGETHER TO PUT ON BOOGA'S COCK BECAUSE HE SAID IT WOULD SAVE HIS LIFE
YOU'VE LOST YOUR MEMORY? AGAIN?!
AND HOW COME YOU'RE EVEN STILL ALIVE? IN ANY NORMAL SITUATION YOUR BRAIN WOULD HAVE SUFFERED IRREPARABLE DAMAGE FROM LACK OF OXYGEN, YOU WERE CLINICALLY DEAD FOR MORE THAN A QUARTER OF AN HOUR. HOW DID YOU DO THAT?

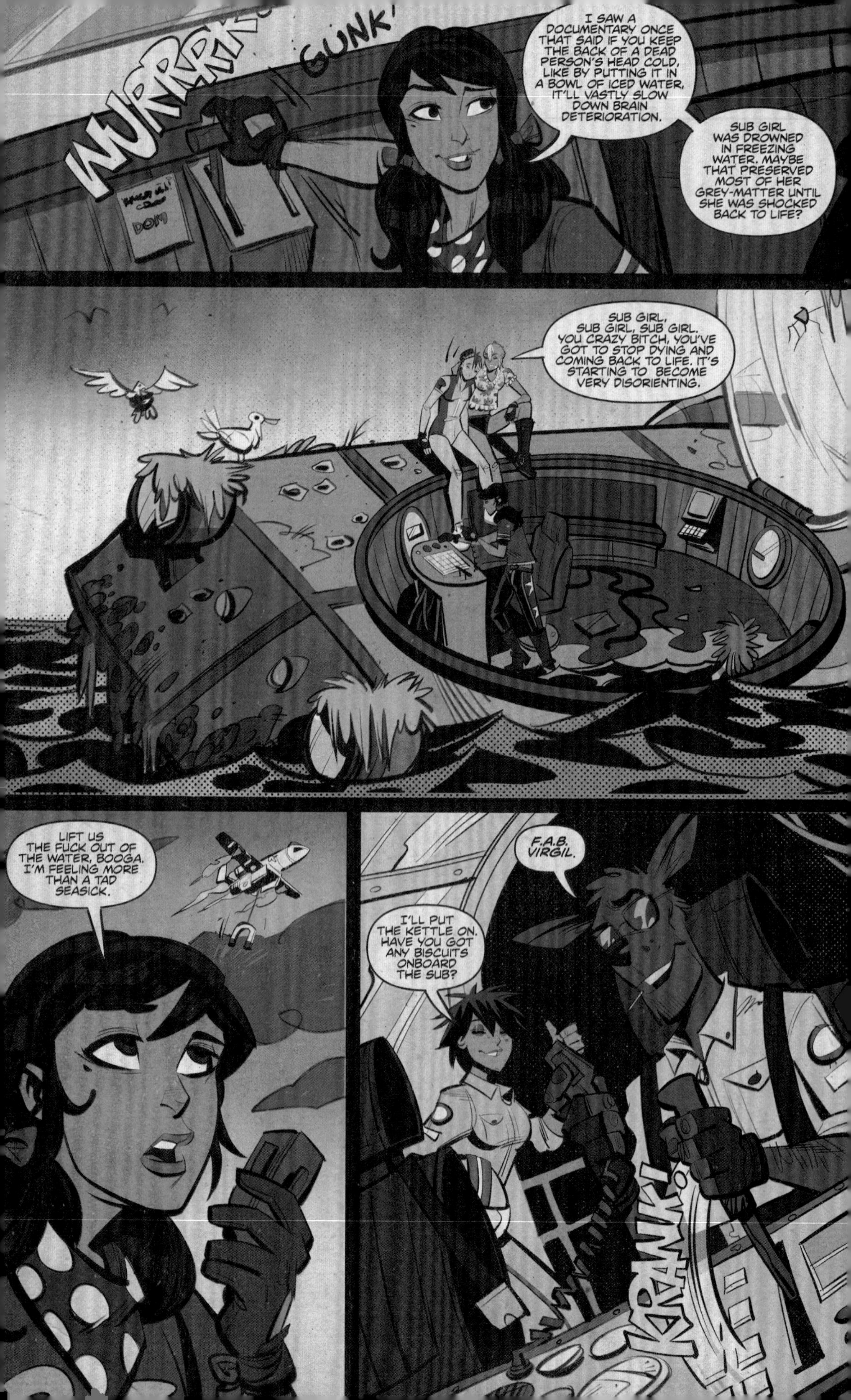
WURRRK!
GUNK!
I SAW A DOCUMENTARY ONCE THAT SAID IF YOU KEEP THE BACK OF A DEAD PERSON'S HEAD COLD, LIKE BY PUTTING IT IN A BOWL OF ICED WATER, IT'LL VASTLY SLOW DOWN BRAIN DETERIORATION.
SUB GIRL WAS DROWNED IN FREEZING WATER. MAYBE THAT PRESERVED MOST OF HER GREY-MATTER UNTIL SHE WAS SHOCKED BACK TO LIFE?
SUB GIRL, SUB GIRL, SUB GIRL. YOU CRAZY BITCH, YOU'VE GOT TO STOP DYING AND COMING BACK TO LIFE. IT'S STARTING TO BECOME VERY DISORIENTING.
LIFT US THE FUCK OUT OF THE WATER, BOOGA. I'M FEELING MORE THAN A TAD SEASICK.
F.A.B. VIRGIL.
I'LL PUT THE KETTLE ON. HAVE YOU GOT ANY BISCUITS ONBOARD THE SUB?
KRANK!

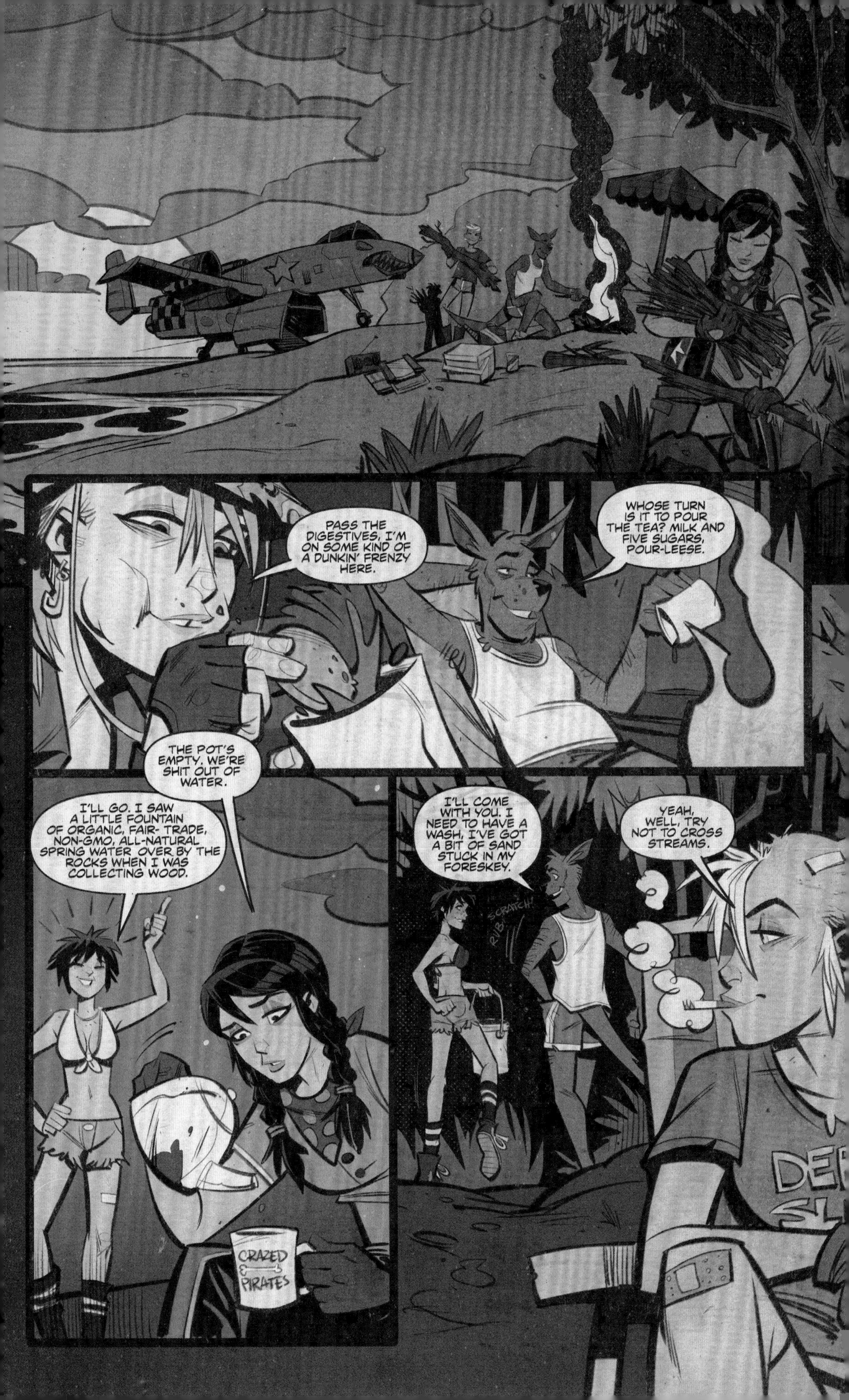

PASS THE DIGESTIVES, I'M ON SOME KIND OF A DUNKIN' FRENZY HERE.
WHOSE TURN IS IT TO POUR THE TEA? MILK AND FIVE SUGARS, POUR-LEESE.
THE POT'S EMPTY. WE'RE SHIT OUT OF WATER.
I'LL GO. I SAW A LITTLE FOUNTAIN OF ORGANIC, FAIR- TRADE, NON-GMO, ALL-NATURAL SPRING WATER OVER BY THE ROCKS WHEN I WAS COLLECTING WOOD.
CRAZED PIRATES
I'LL COME WITH YOU. I NEED TO HAVE A WASH, I'VE GOT A BIT OF SAND STUCK IN MY FORESKEY.
YEAH, WELL, TRY NOT TO CROSS STREAMS.
SCRATCH!
RUB.

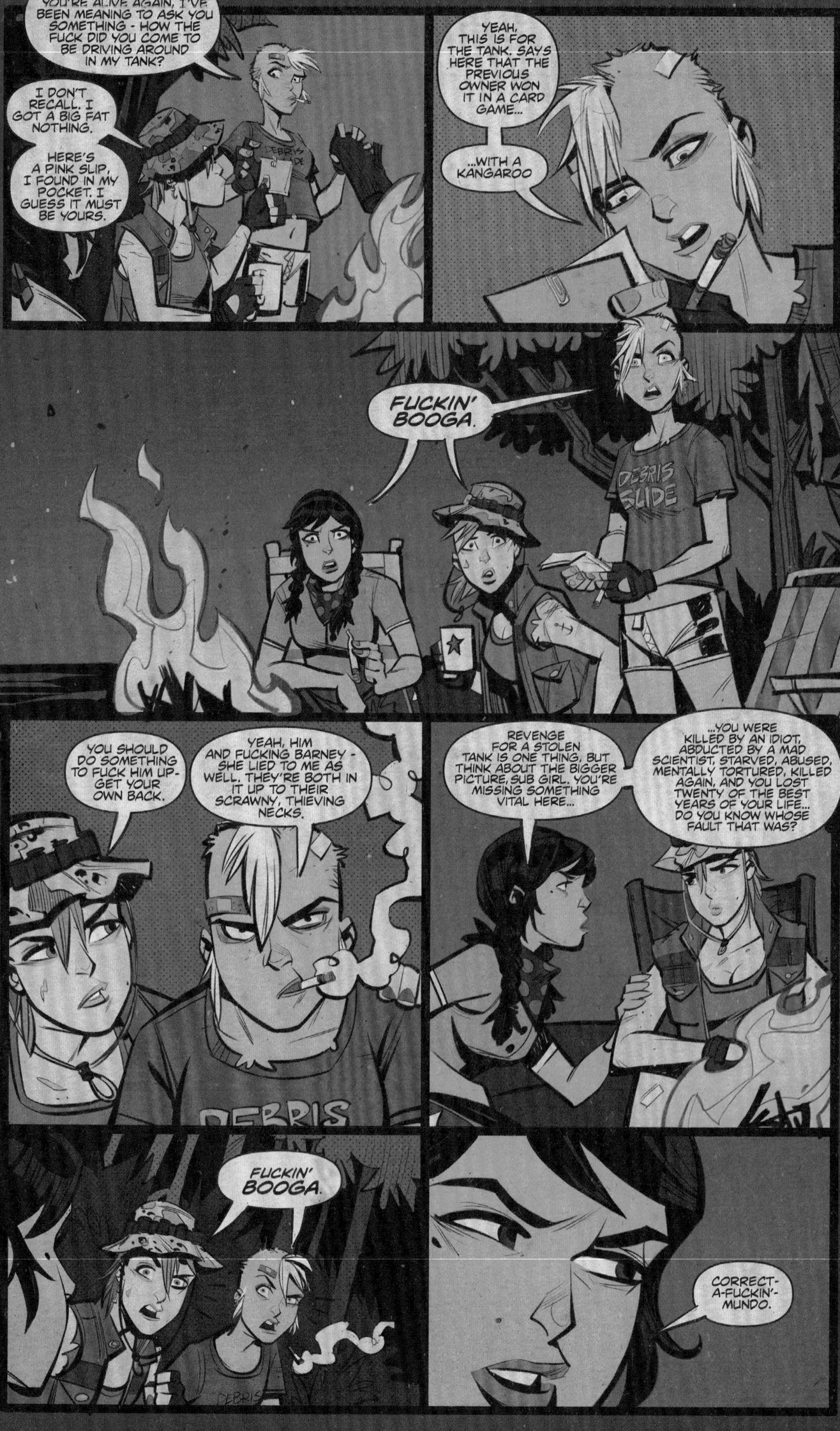
SO, SUB GIRL, NOW THAT YOU'RE ALIVE AGAIN, I'VE BEEN MEANING TO ASK YOU SOMETHING - HOW THE FUCK DID YOU COME TO BE DRIVING AROUND IN MY TANK?
I DON'T RECALL. I GOT A BIG FAT NOTHING.
HERE'S A PINK SLIP, I FOUND IN MY POCKET. I GUESS IT MUST BE YOURS.
YEAH, THIS IS FOR THE TANK. SAYS HERE THAT THE PREVIOUS OWNER WON IT IN A CARD GAME...
...WITH A KANGAROO
FUCKIN' BOOGA.
YOU SHOULD DO SOMETHING TO FUCK HIM UP- GET YOUR OWN BACK.
YEAH, HIM AND FUCKING BARNEY - SHE LIED TO ME AS WELL. THEY'RE BOTH IN IT UP TO THEIR SCRAWNY, THIEVING NECKS.
REVENGE FOR A STOLEN TANK IS ONE THING, BUT THINK ABOUT THE BIGGER PICTURE, SUB GIRL. YOU'RE MISSING SOMETHING VITAL HERE...
...YOU WERE KILLED BY AN IDIOT, ABDUCTED BY A MAD SCIENTIST, STARVED, ABUSED, MENTALLY TORTURED, KILLED AGAIN, AND YOU LOST TWENTY OF THE BEST YEARS OF YOUR LIFE... DO YOU KNOW WHOSE FAULT THAT WAS?
FUCKIN' BOOGA.
CORRECT-A-FUCKIN'-MUNDO.

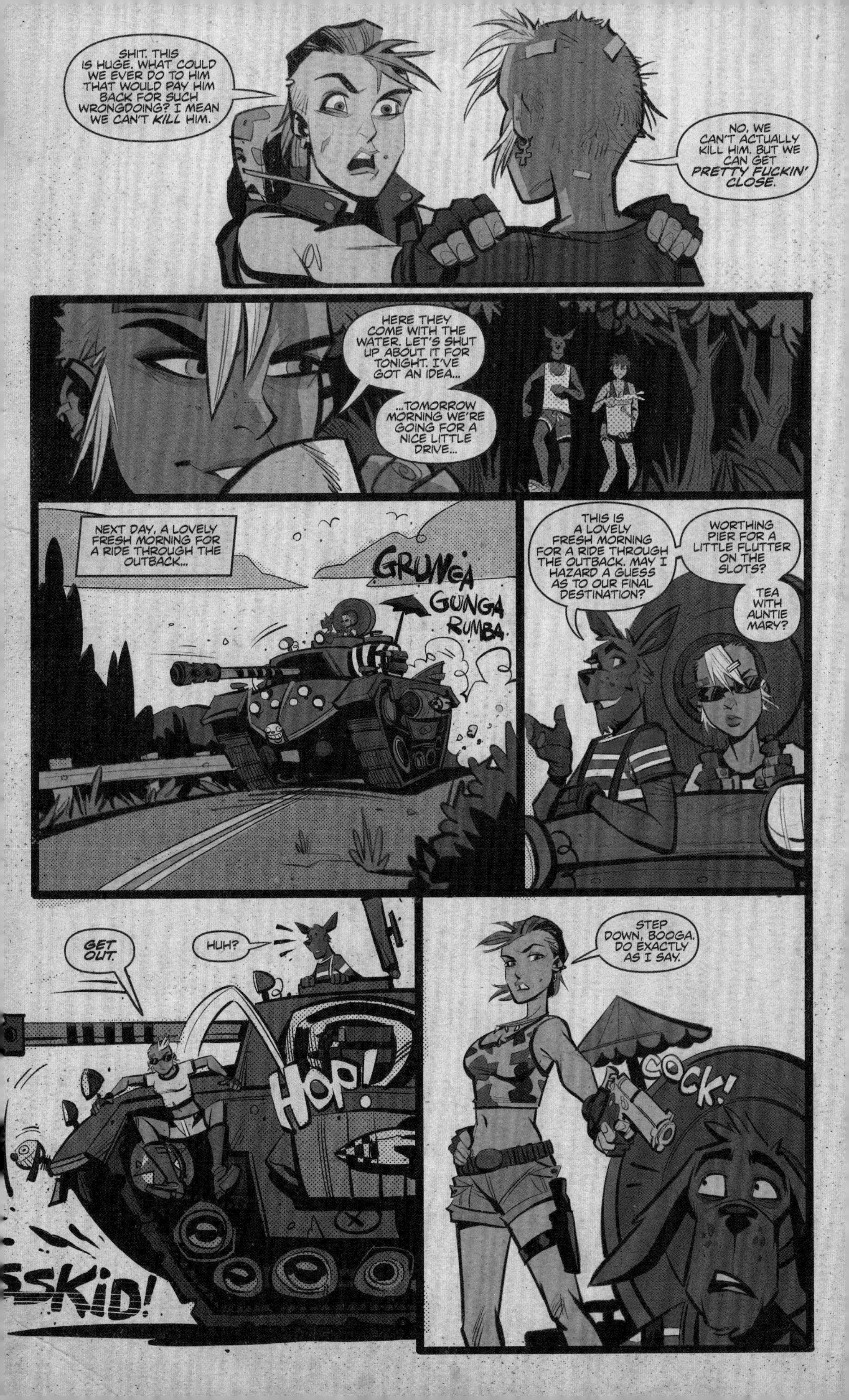
SHIT. THIS IS HUGE. WHAT COULD WE EVER DO TO HIM THAT WOULD PAY HIM BACK FOR SUCH WRONGDOING? I MEAN WE CAN'T KILL HIM.
NO, WE CAN'T ACTUALLY KILL HIM. BUT WE CAN GET PRETTY FUCKIN' CLOSE.
HERE THEY COME WITH THE WATER. LET'S SHUT UP ABOUT IT FOR TONIGHT. I'VE GOT AN IDEA...
...TOMORROW MORNING WE'RE GOING FOR A NICE LITTLE DRIVE...
NEXT DAY, A LOVELY FRESH MORNING FOR A RIDE THROUGH THE OUTBACK...
GRUNGA
GUNGA
RUMBA
THIS IS A LOVELY FRESH MORNING FOR A RIDE THROUGH THE OUTBACK. MAY I HAZARD A GUESS AS TO OUR FINAL DESTINATION?
WORTHING PIER FOR A LITTLE FLUTTER ON THE SLOTS?
TEA WITH AUNTIE MARY?
GET OUT.
HUH?
HOP!
SSKID!
STEP DOWN, BOOGA. DO EXACTLY AS I SAY.
COCK!

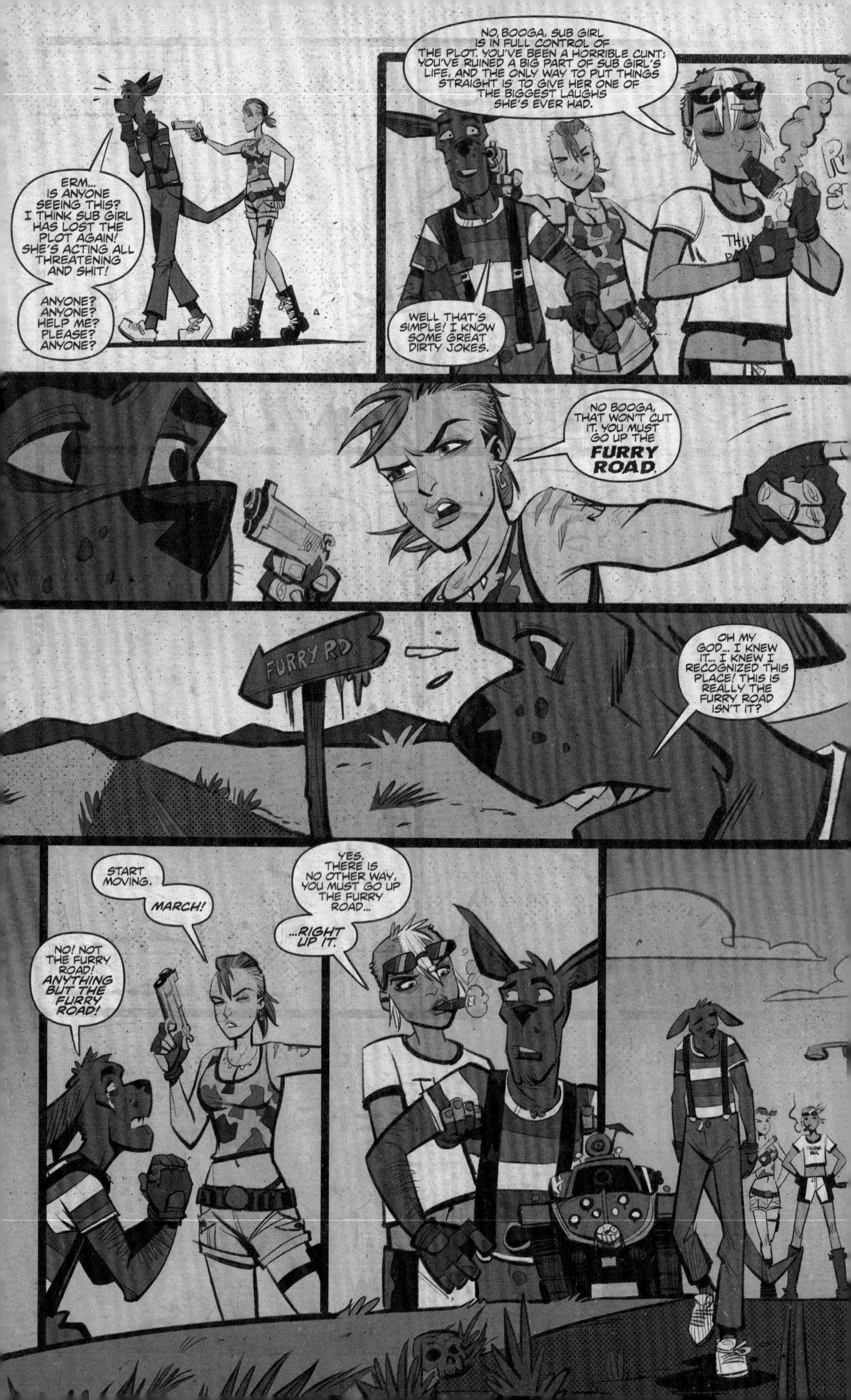
ERM... IS ANYONE SEEING THIS? I THINK SUB GIRL HAS LOST THE PLOT AGAIN! SHE'S ACTING ALL THREATENING AND SHIT!
ANYONE? ANYONE? HELP ME? PLEASE? ANYONE?
NO, BOOGA, SUB GIRL IS IN FULL CONTROL OF THE PLOT. YOU'VE BEEN A HORRIBLE CUNT; YOU'VE RUINED A BIG PART OF SUB GIRL'S LIFE, AND THE ONLY WAY TO PUT THINGS STRAIGHT IS TO GIVE HER ONE OF THE BIGGEST LAUGHS SHE'S EVER HAD.
WELL THAT'S SIMPLE! I KNOW SOME GREAT DIRTY JOKES.
NO BOOGA, THAT WON'T CUT IT. YOU MUST GO UP THE FURRY ROAD.
FURRY RD.
OH MY GOD... I KNEW IT... I KNEW I RECOGNIZED THIS PLACE! THIS IS REALLY THE FURRY ROAD ISN'T IT?
START MOVING.
MARCH!
NO! NOT THE FURRY ROAD! ANYTHING BUT THE FURRY ROAD!
YES. THERE IS NO OTHER WAY, YOU MUST GO UP THE FURRY ROAD...
...RIGHT UP IT.

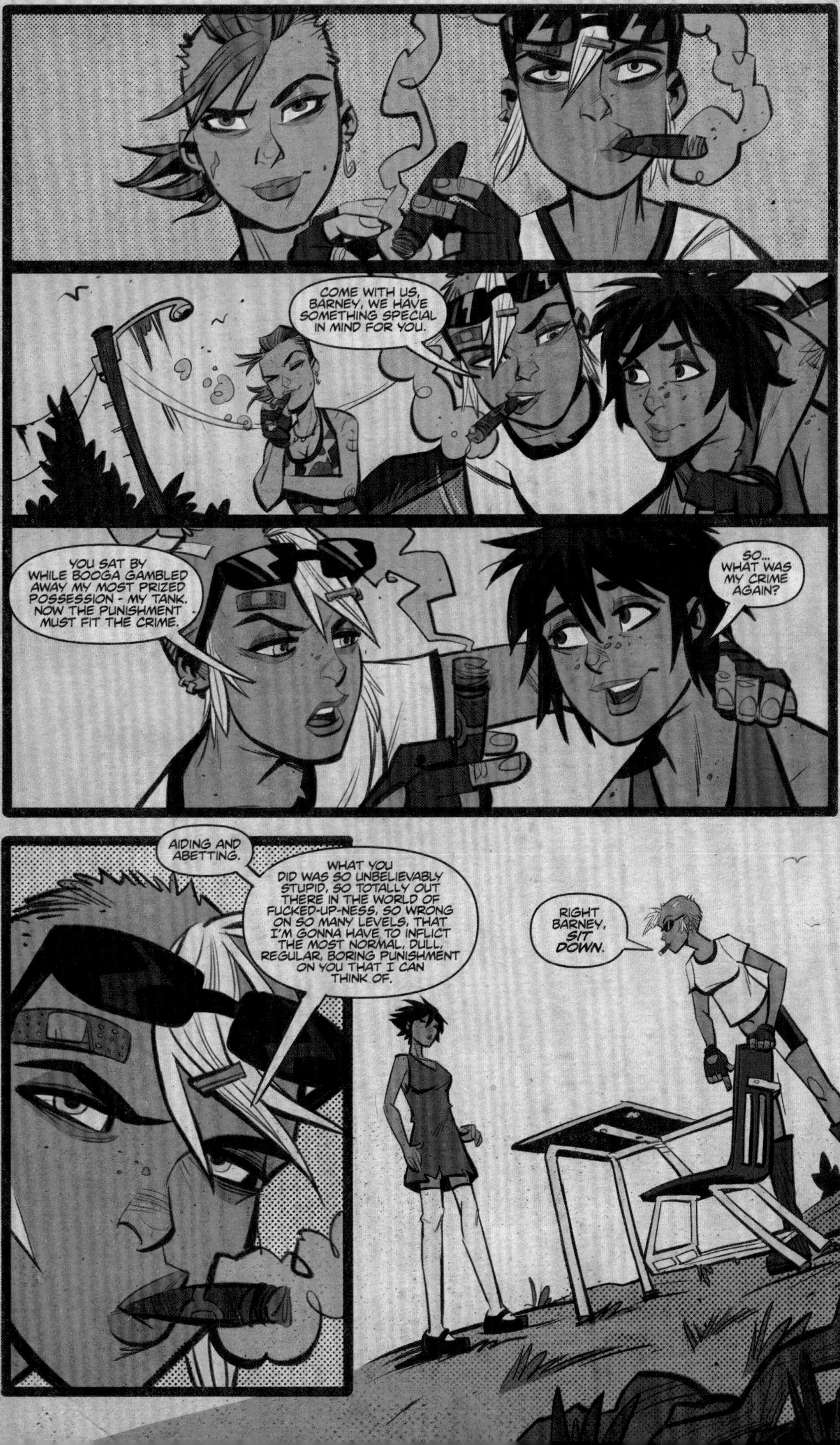

COME WITH US, BARNEY, WE HAVE SOMETHING SPECIAL IN MIND FOR YOU.
YOU SAT BY WHILE BOOGA GAMBLED AWAY MY MOST PRIZED POSSESSION - MY TANK. NOW THE PUNISHMENT MUST FIT THE CRIME.
SO... WHAT WAS MY CRIME AGAIN?
AIDING AND ABETTING.
WHAT YOU DID WAS SO UNBELIEVABLY STUPID, SO TOTALLY OUT THERE IN THE WORLD OF FUCKED-UP-NESS, SO WRONG ON SO MANY LEVELS, THAT I'M GONNA HAVE TO INFLICT THE MOST NORMAL, DULL, REGULAR, BORING PUNISHMENT ON YOU THAT I CAN THINK OF.
RIGHT BARNEY, SIT DOWN.

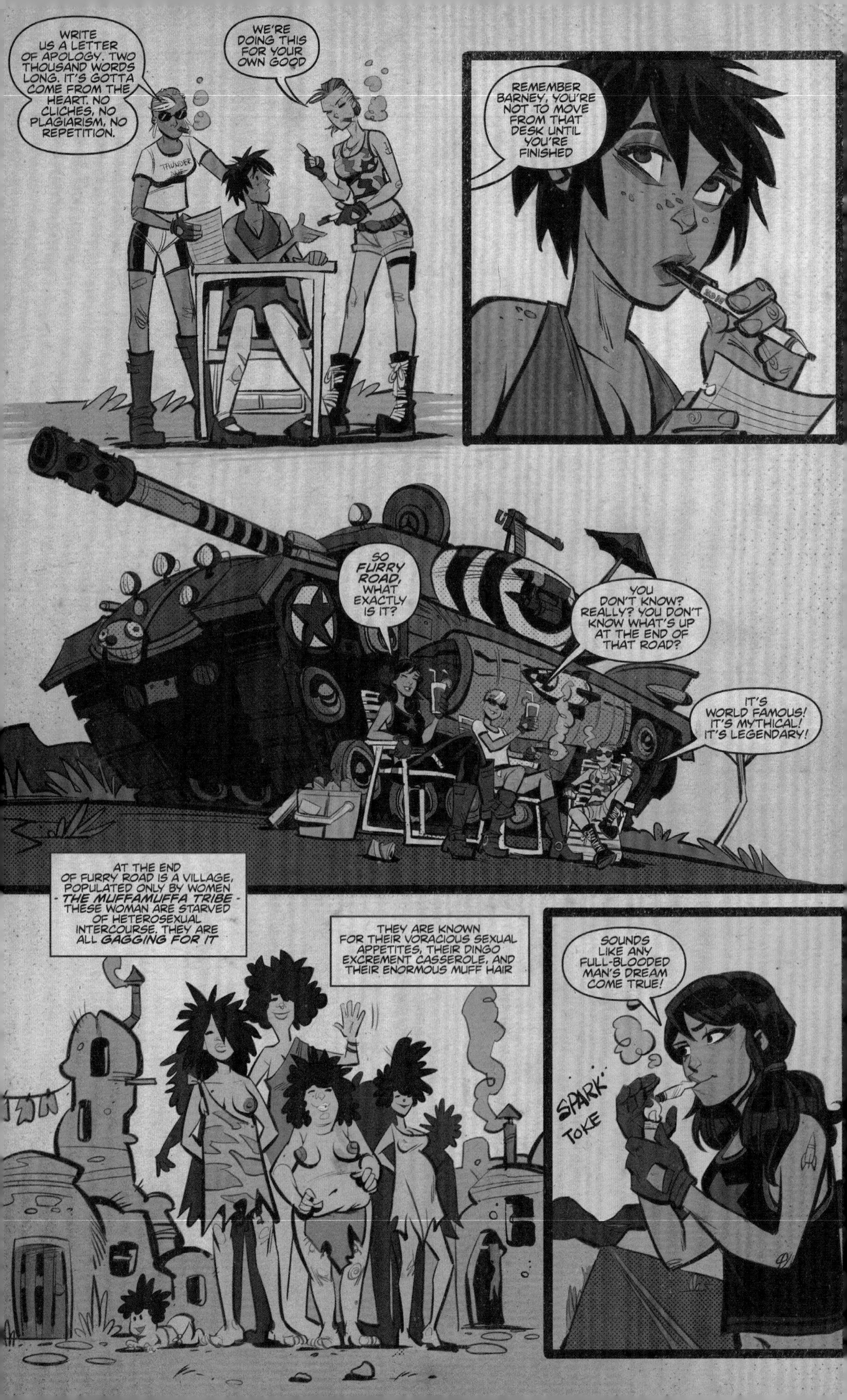
WRITE US A LETTER OF APOLOGY. TWO THOUSAND WORDS LONG. IT'S GOTTA COME FROM THE HEART. NO CLICHES, NO PLAGIARISM, NO REPETITION.
WE'RE DOING THIS FOR YOUR OWN GOOD
THUNDER
REMEMBER BARNEY, YOU'RE NOT TO MOVE FROM THAT DESK UNTIL YOU'RE FINISHED
SO *FURRY ROAD*, WHAT EXACTLY IS IT?
YOU DON'T KNOW? REALLY? YOU DON'T KNOW WHAT'S UP AT THE END OF THAT ROAD?
IT'S WORLD FAMOUS! IT'S MYTHICAL! IT'S LEGENDARY!
AT THE END OF FURRY ROAD IS A VILLAGE, POPULATED ONLY BY WOMEN - *THE MUFFAMUFFA TRIBE* - THESE WOMAN ARE STARVED OF HETEROSEXUAL INTERCOURSE. THEY ARE ALL *GAGGING FOR IT*
THEY ARE KNOWN FOR THEIR VORACIOUS SEXUAL APPETITES, THEIR DINGO EXCREMENT CASSEROLE, AND THEIR ENORMOUS MUFF HAIR
SOUNDS LIKE ANY FULL-BLOODED MAN'S DREAM COME TRUE!
SPARK
TOKE

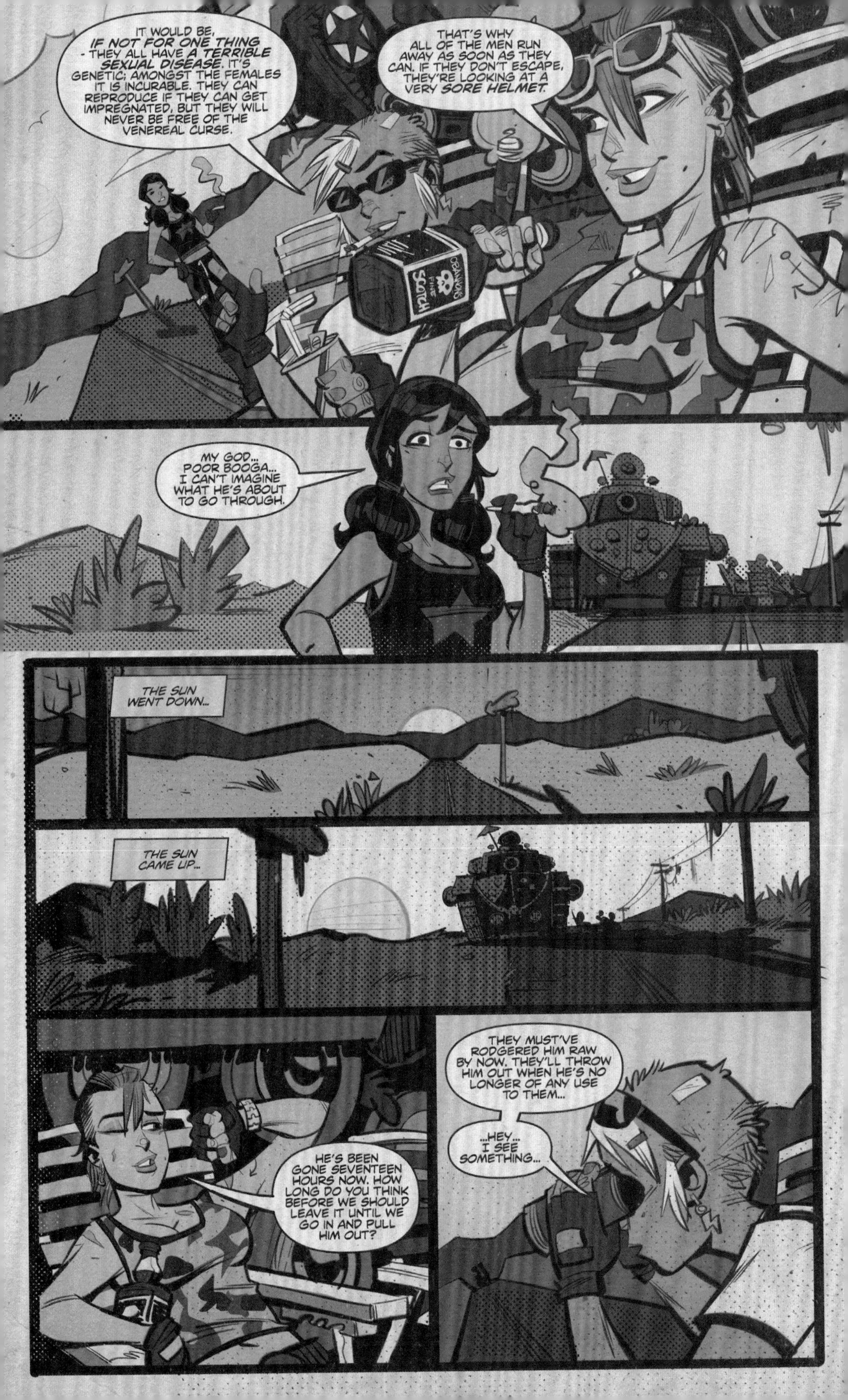
IT WOULD BE, IF NOT FOR ONE THING - THEY ALL HAVE A TERRIBLE SEXUAL DISEASE. IT'S GENETIC; AMONGST THE FEMALES IT IS INCURABLE. THEY CAN REPRODUCE IF THEY CAN GET IMPREGNATED, BUT THEY WILL NEVER BE FREE OF THE VENEREAL CURSE.
THAT'S WHY ALL OF THE MEN RUN AWAY AS SOON AS THEY CAN. IF THEY DON'T ESCAPE, THEY'RE LOOKING AT A VERY SORE HELMET.
FINE SCOTCH
MY GOD... POOR BOOGA... I CAN'T IMAGINE WHAT HE'S ABOUT TO GO THROUGH.
THE SUN WENT DOWN...
THE SUN CAME UP...
HE'S BEEN GONE SEVENTEEN HOURS NOW. HOW LONG DO YOU THINK BEFORE WE SHOULD LEAVE IT UNTIL WE GO IN AND PULL HIM OUT?
THEY MUST'VE RODGERED HIM RAW BY NOW. THEY'LL THROW HIM OUT WHEN HE'S NO LONGER OF ANY USE TO THEM...
...HEY... I SEE SOMETHING...

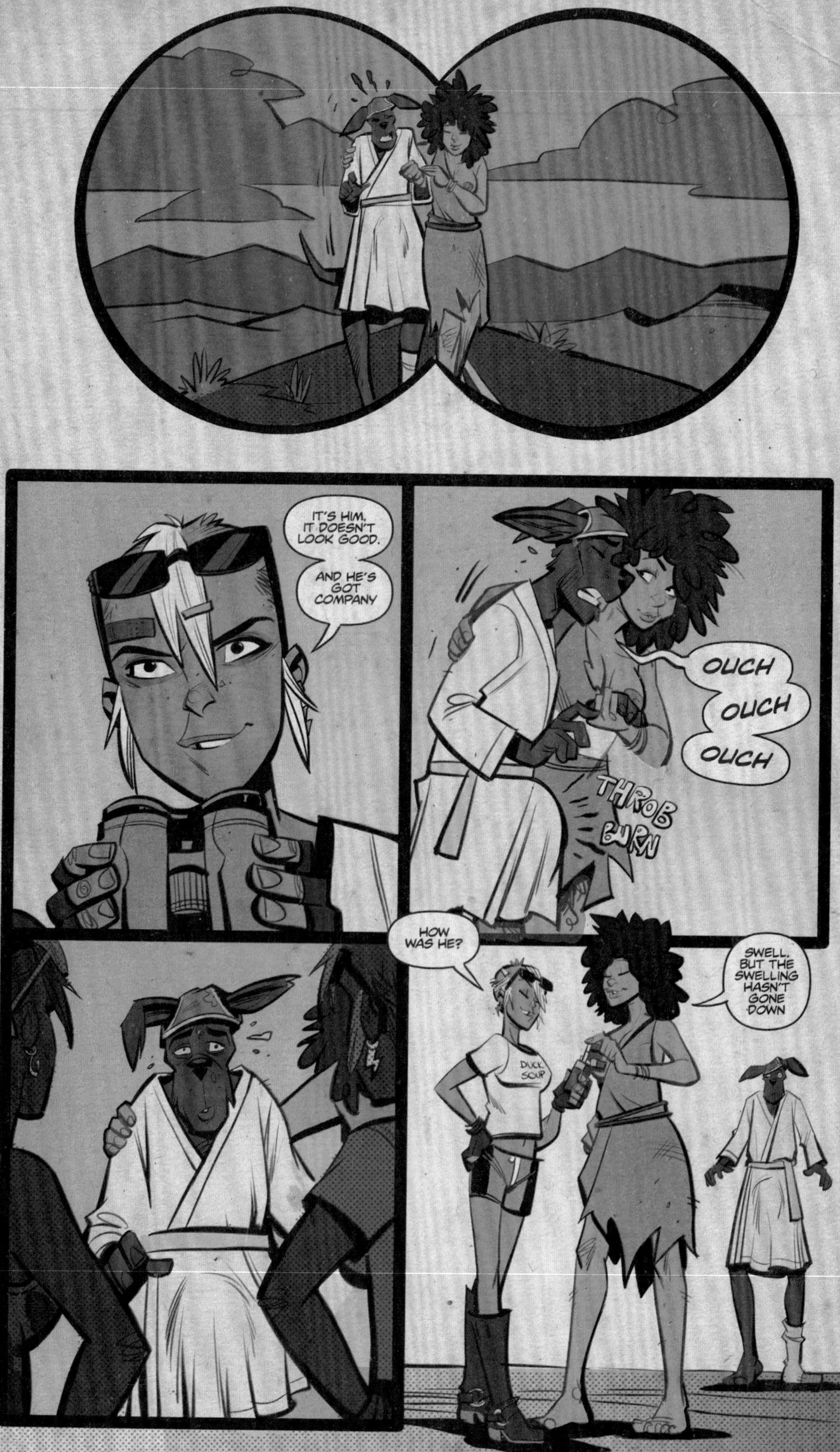

IT'S HIM. IT DOESN'T LOOK GOOD.
AND HE'S GOT COMPANY
OUCH
OUCH
OUCH
THROB
BURN
HOW WAS HE?
SWELL. BUT THE SWELLING HASN'T GONE DOWN
DUCK SOUP

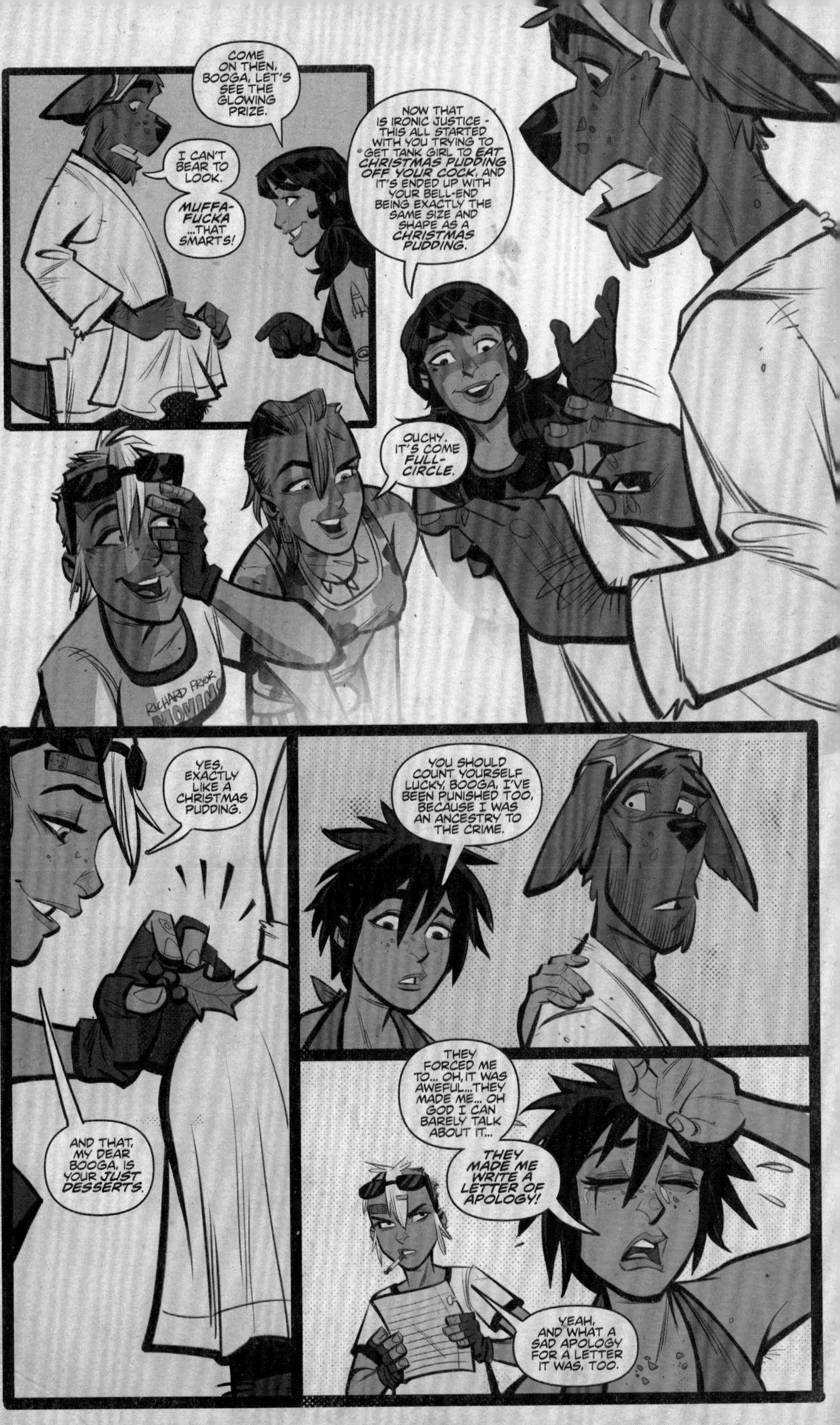
COME ON THEN, BOOGA, LET'S SEE THE GLOWING PRIZE.
I CAN'T BEAR TO LOOK.
MUFFA-FUCKA ...THAT SMARTS!
NOW THAT IS IRONIC JUSTICE - THIS ALL STARTED WITH YOU TRYING TO GET TANK GIRL TO EAT CHRISTMAS PUDDING OFF YOUR COCK, AND IT'S ENDED UP WITH YOUR BELL-END BEING EXACTLY THE SAME SIZE AND SHAPE AS A CHRISTMAS PUDDING.
OUCHY. IT'S COME FULL-CIRCLE.
RICHARD PRYOR
YES, EXACTLY LIKE A CHRISTMAS PUDDING.
AND THAT, MY DEAR BOOGA, IS YOUR JUST DESSERTS.
YOU SHOULD COUNT YOURSELF LUCKY, BOOGA, I'VE BEEN PUNISHED TOO, BECAUSE I WAS AN ANCESTRY TO THE CRIME.
THEY FORCED ME TO... OH, IT WAS AWEFUL... THEY MADE ME... OH GOD I CAN BARELY TALK ABOUT IT...
THEY MADE ME WRITE A LETTER OF APOLOGY!
YEAH, AND WHAT A SAD APOLOGY FOR A LETTER IT WAS, TOO.

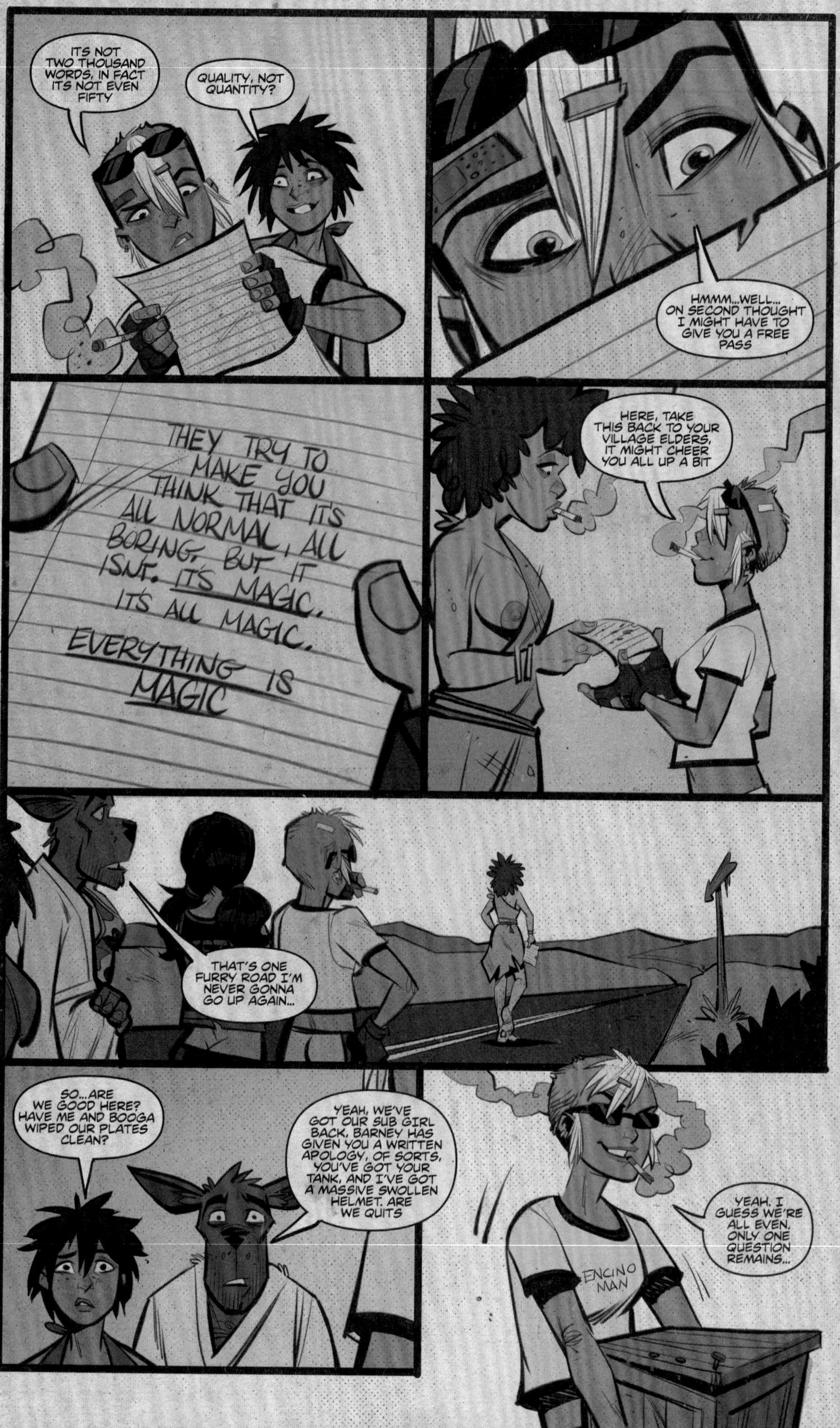
ITS NOT TWO THOUSAND WORDS, IN FACT ITS NOT EVEN FIFTY
QUALITY, NOT QUANTITY?
HMMM...WELL... ON SECOND THOUGHT I MIGHT HAVE TO GIVE YOU A FREE PASS
THEY TRY TO MAKE YOU THINK THAT IT'S ALL NORMAL, ALL BORING, BUT IT ISN'T. IT'S MAGIC. IT'S ALL MAGIC. EVERYTHING IS MAGIC
HERE, TAKE THIS BACK TO YOUR VILLAGE ELDERS, IT MIGHT CHEER YOU ALL UP A BIT
THAT'S ONE FURRY ROAD I'M NEVER GONNA GO UP AGAIN...
SO...ARE WE GOOD HERE? HAVE ME AND BOOGA WIPED OUR PLATES CLEAN?
YEAH, WE'VE GOT OUR SUB GIRL BACK, BARNEY HAS GIVEN YOU A WRITTEN APOLOGY, OF SORTS, YOU'VE GOT YOUR TANK, AND I'VE GOT A MASSIVE SWOLLEN HELMET. ARE WE QUITS
ENCINO MAN
YEAH. I GUESS WE'RE ALL EVEN, ONLY ONE QUESTION REMAINS...

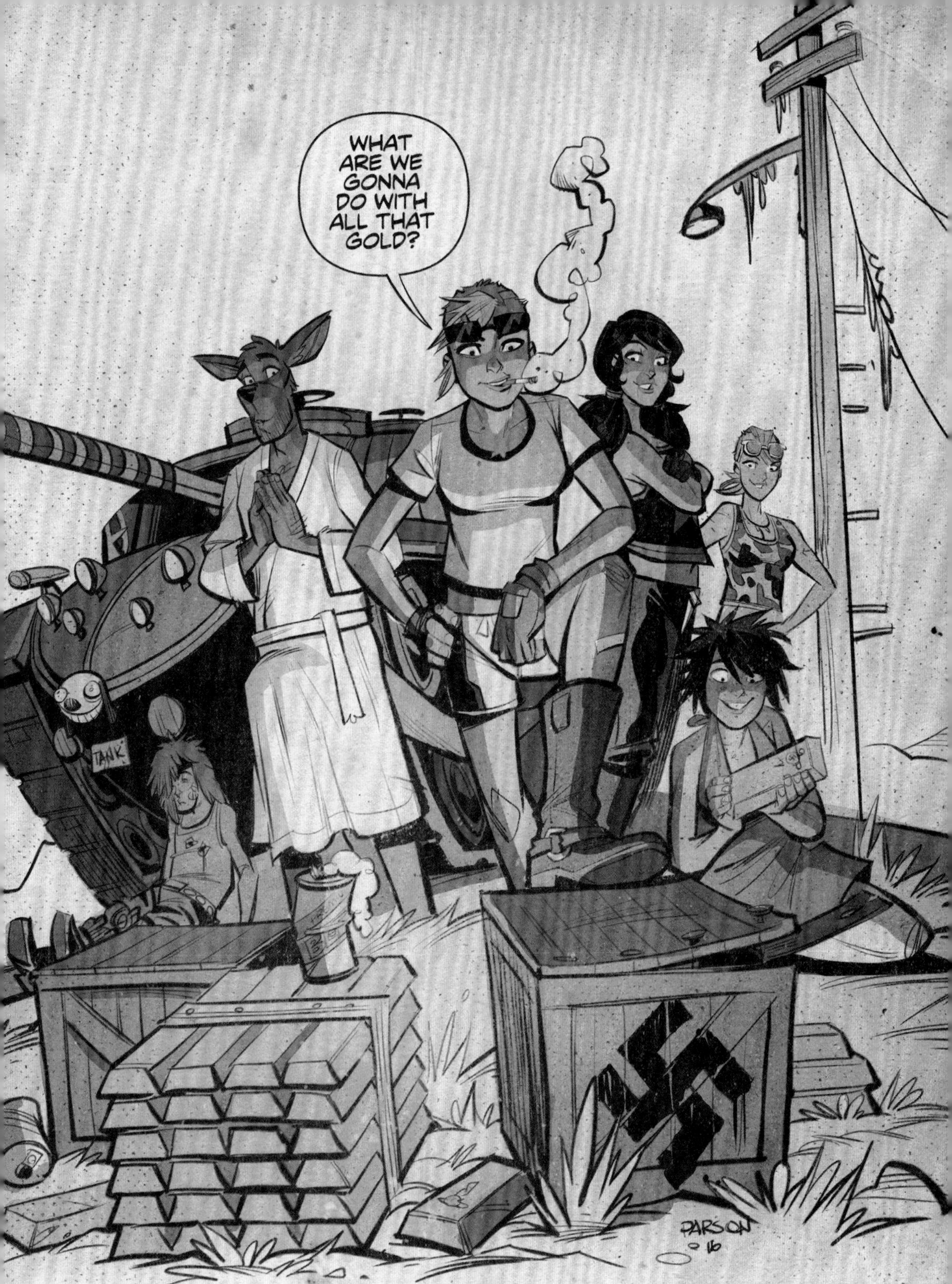
WHAT ARE WE GONNA DO WITH ALL THAT GOLD?
TANK

NEXT:

What They're Gonna Do With All That Gold

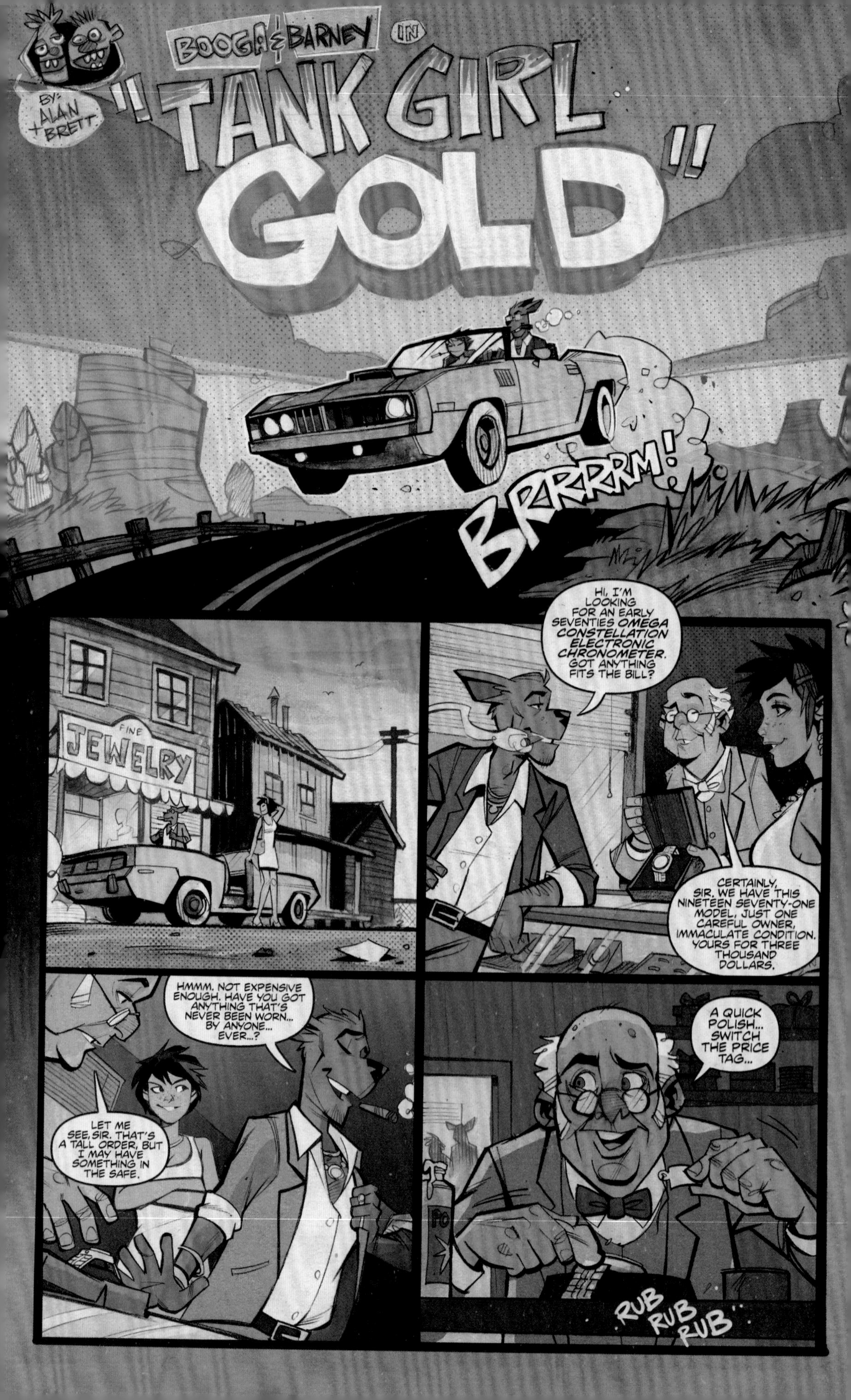
BOOGA & BARNEY IN
BY: ALAN + BRETT
"TANK GIRL GOLD"!
BRRRRRM!
FINE JEWELRY
HI, I'M LOOKING FOR AN EARLY SEVENTIES OMEGA CONSTELLATION ELECTRONIC CHRONOMETER. GOT ANYTHING FITS THE BILL?
CERTAINLY, SIR. WE HAVE THIS NINETEEN SEVENTY-ONE MODEL, JUST ONE CAREFUL OWNER, IMMACULATE CONDITION. YOURS FOR THREE THOUSAND DOLLARS.
HMMM. NOT EXPENSIVE ENOUGH. HAVE YOU GOT ANYTHING THAT'S NEVER BEEN WORN... BY ANYONE... EVER...?
LET ME SEE, SIR. THAT'S A TALL ORDER, BUT I MAY HAVE SOMETHING IN THE SAFE.
A QUICK POLISH... SWITCH THE PRICE TAG...
RUB RUB RUB

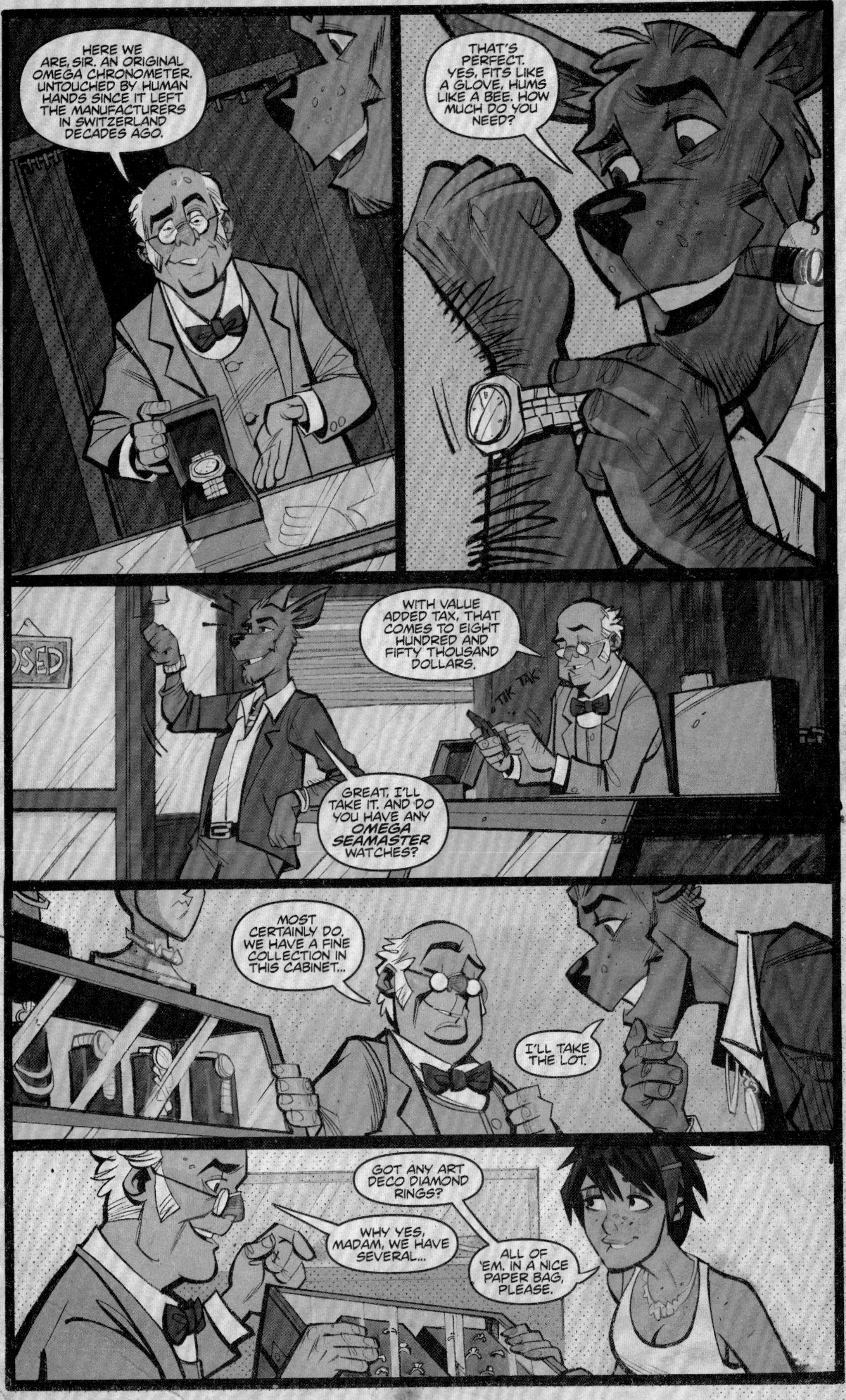
HERE WE ARE, SIR. AN ORIGINAL OMEGA CHRONOMETER. UNTOUCHED BY HUMAN HANDS SINCE IT LEFT THE MANUFACTURERS IN SWITZERLAND DECADES AGO.
THAT'S PERFECT. YES, FITS LIKE A GLOVE, HUMS LIKE A BEE. HOW MUCH DO YOU NEED?
OSED
WITH VALUE ADDED TAX, THAT COMES TO EIGHT HUNDRED AND FIFTY THOUSAND DOLLARS.
TIK TAK
GREAT, I'LL TAKE IT. AND DO YOU HAVE ANY *OMEGA SEAMASTER* WATCHES?
MOST CERTAINLY DO. WE HAVE A FINE COLLECTION IN THIS CABINET...
I'LL TAKE THE LOT.
GOT ANY ART DECO DIAMOND RINGS?
WHY YES, MADAM, WE HAVE SEVERAL...
ALL OF 'EM. IN A NICE PAPER BAG, PLEASE.

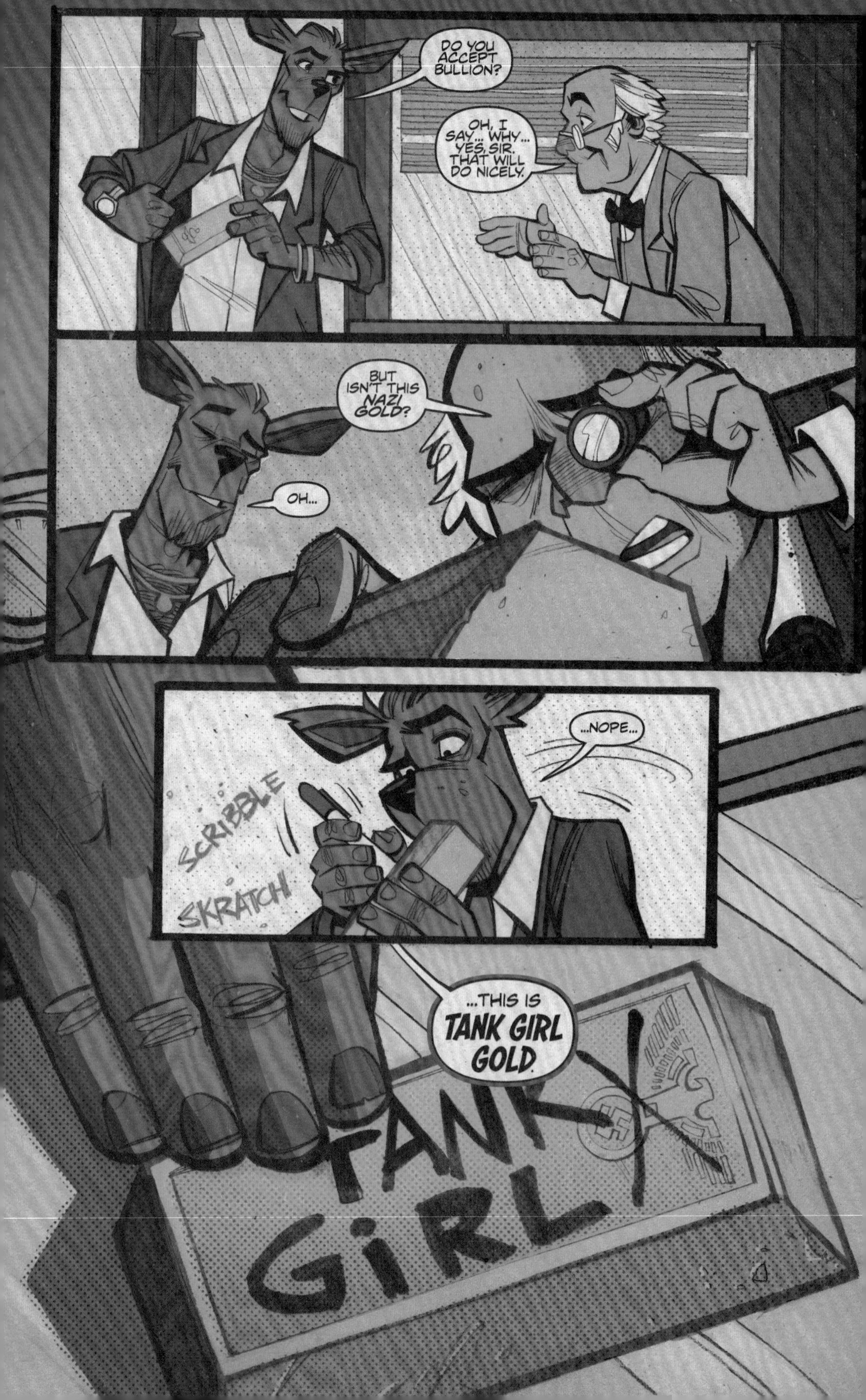
DO YOU ACCEPT BULLION?
OH, I SAY... WHY... YES, SIR. THAT WILL DO NICELY.
BUT ISN'T THIS NAZI GOLD?
OH...
...NOPE...
SCRIBBLE
SKRATCH
...THIS IS TANK GIRL GOLD.
TANK GIRL

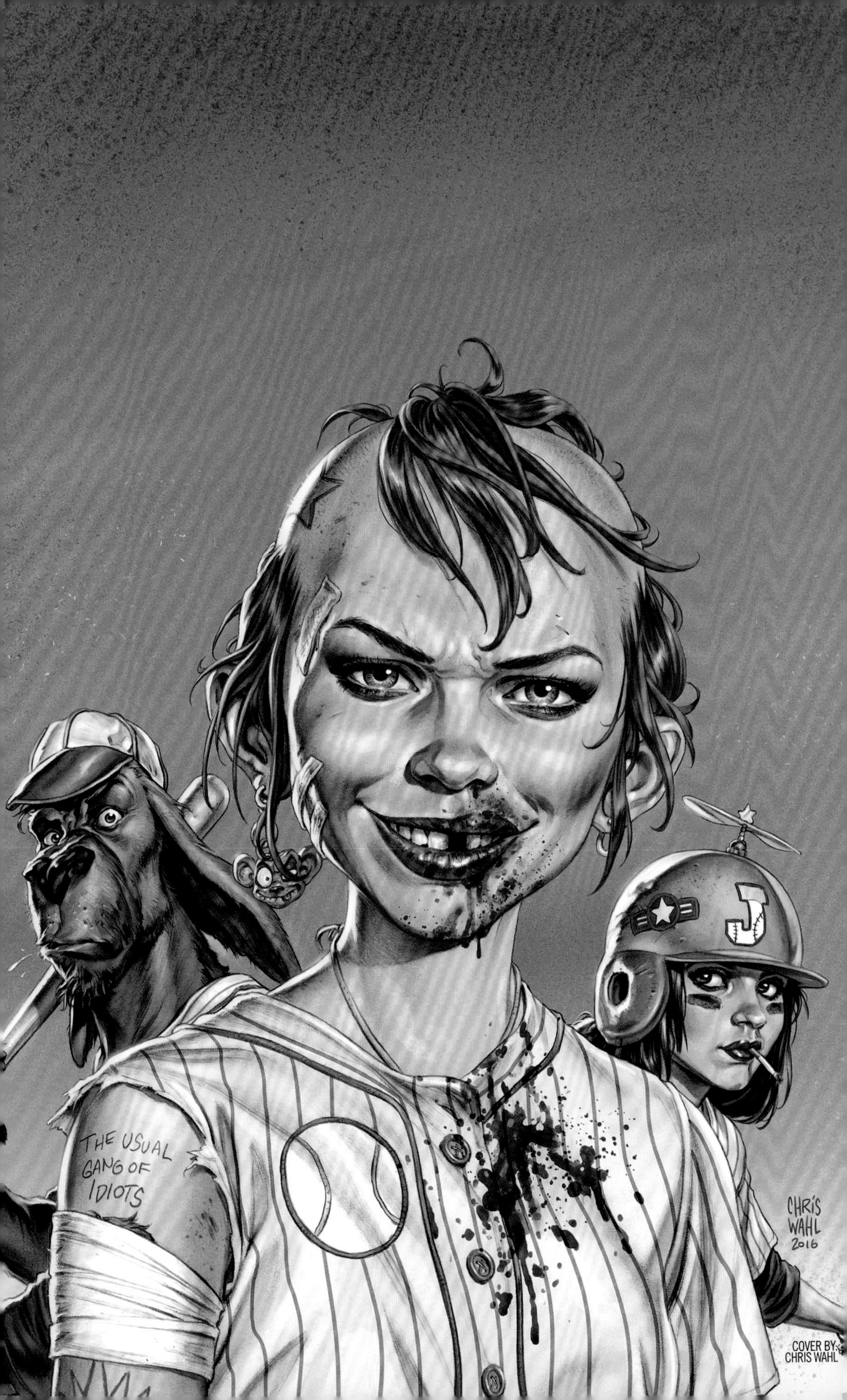
THE USUAL GANG OF IDIOTS
J
CHRIS WAHL 2016
COVER BY: CHRIS WAHL

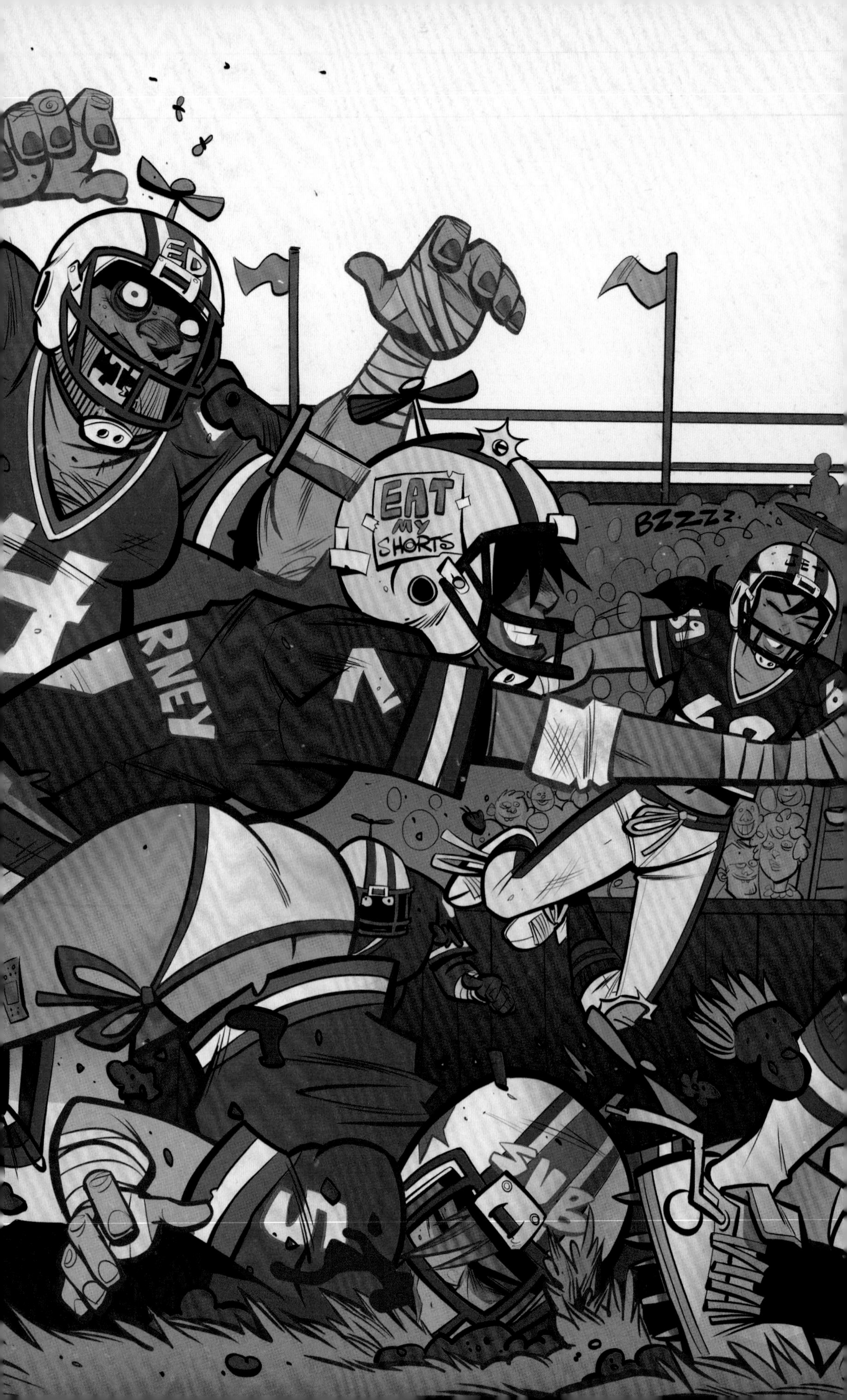
ED
EAT MY SHORTS
BZZZzz
RNEY
SUB

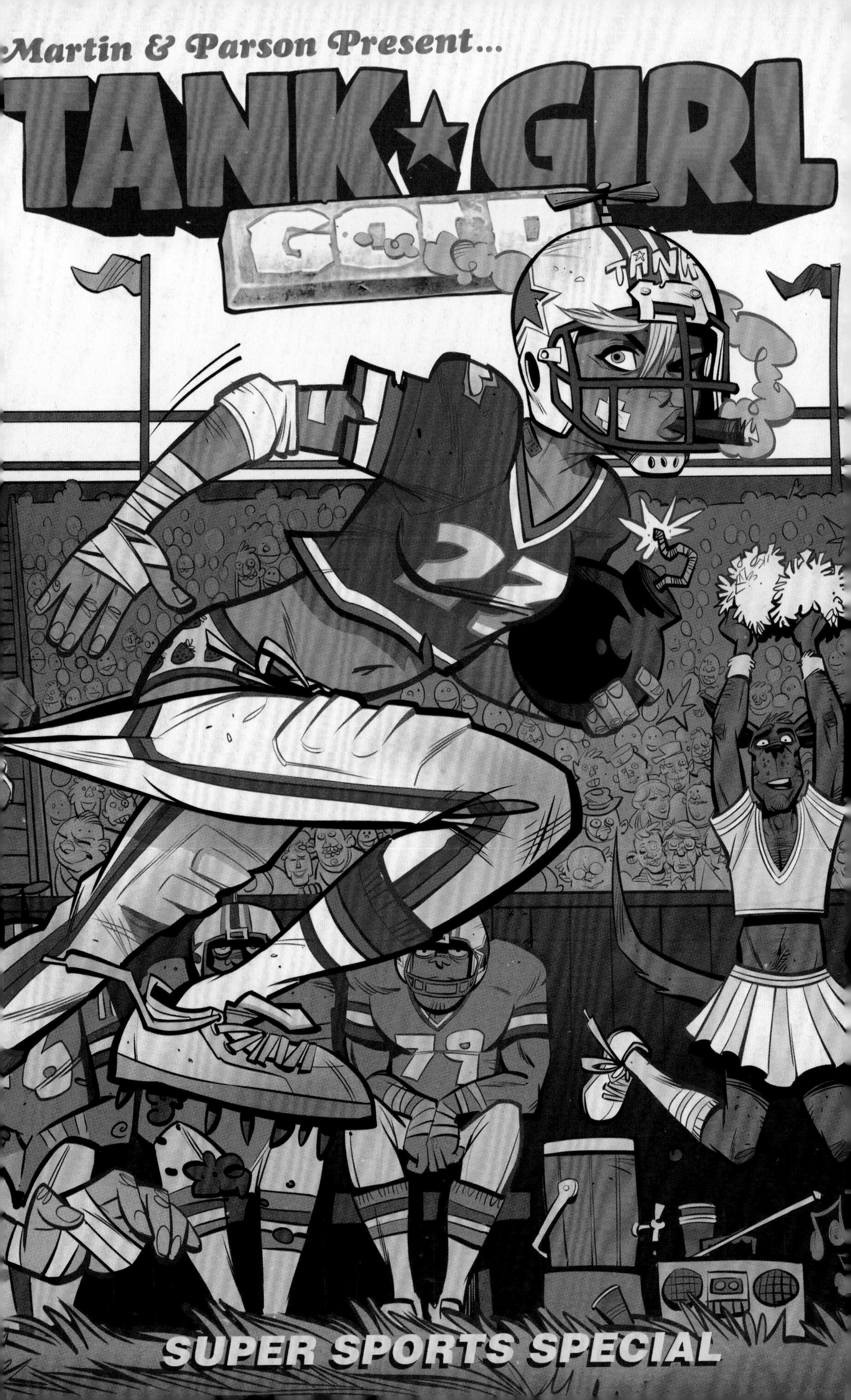
Martin & Parson Present...
TANK GIRL
GOLD
TANK
SUPER SPORTS SPECIAL

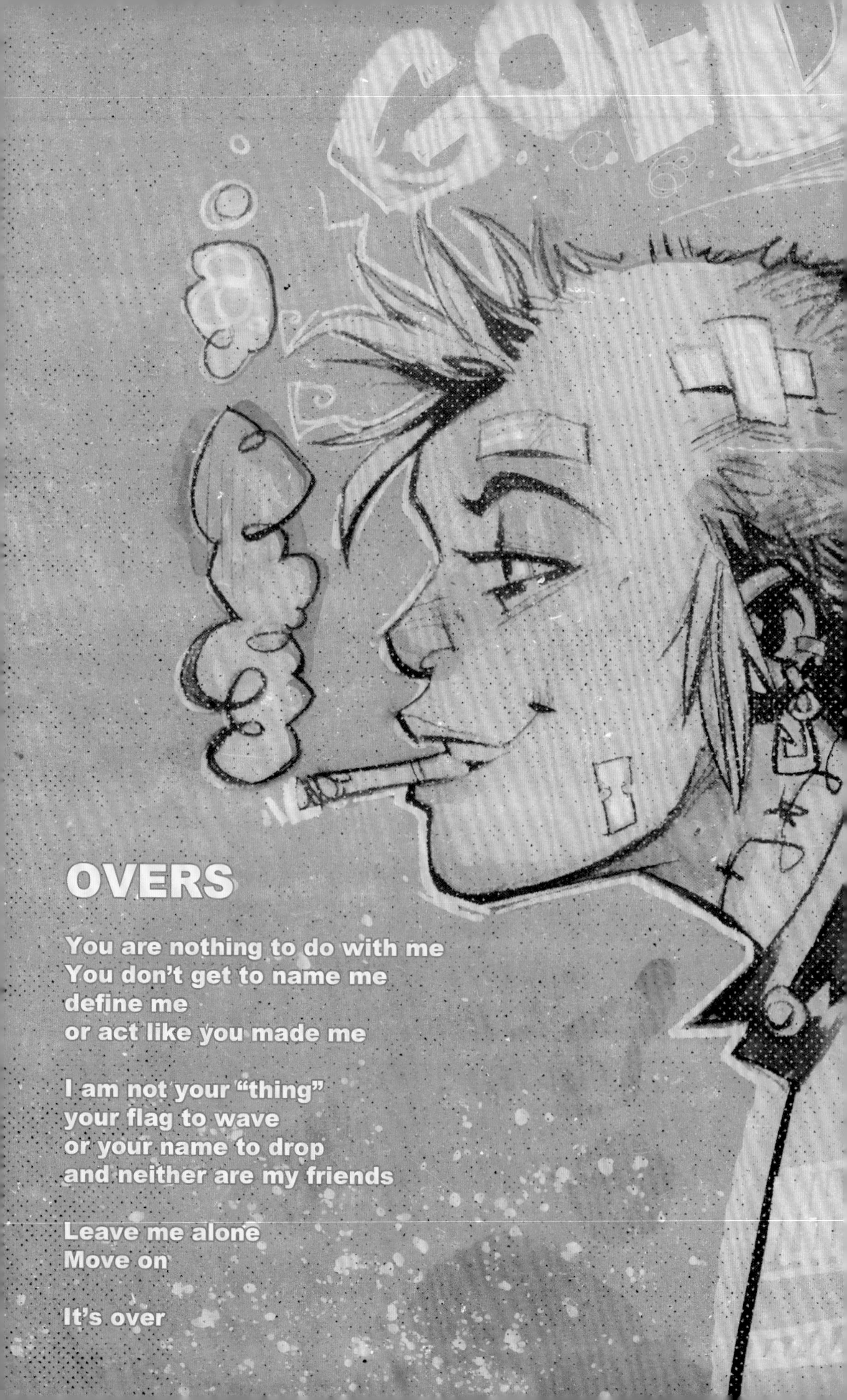

OVERS

You are nothing to do with me
You don't get to name me
define me
or act like you made me

I am not your "thing"
your flag to wave
or your name to drop
and neither are my friends

Leave me alone
Move on

It's over

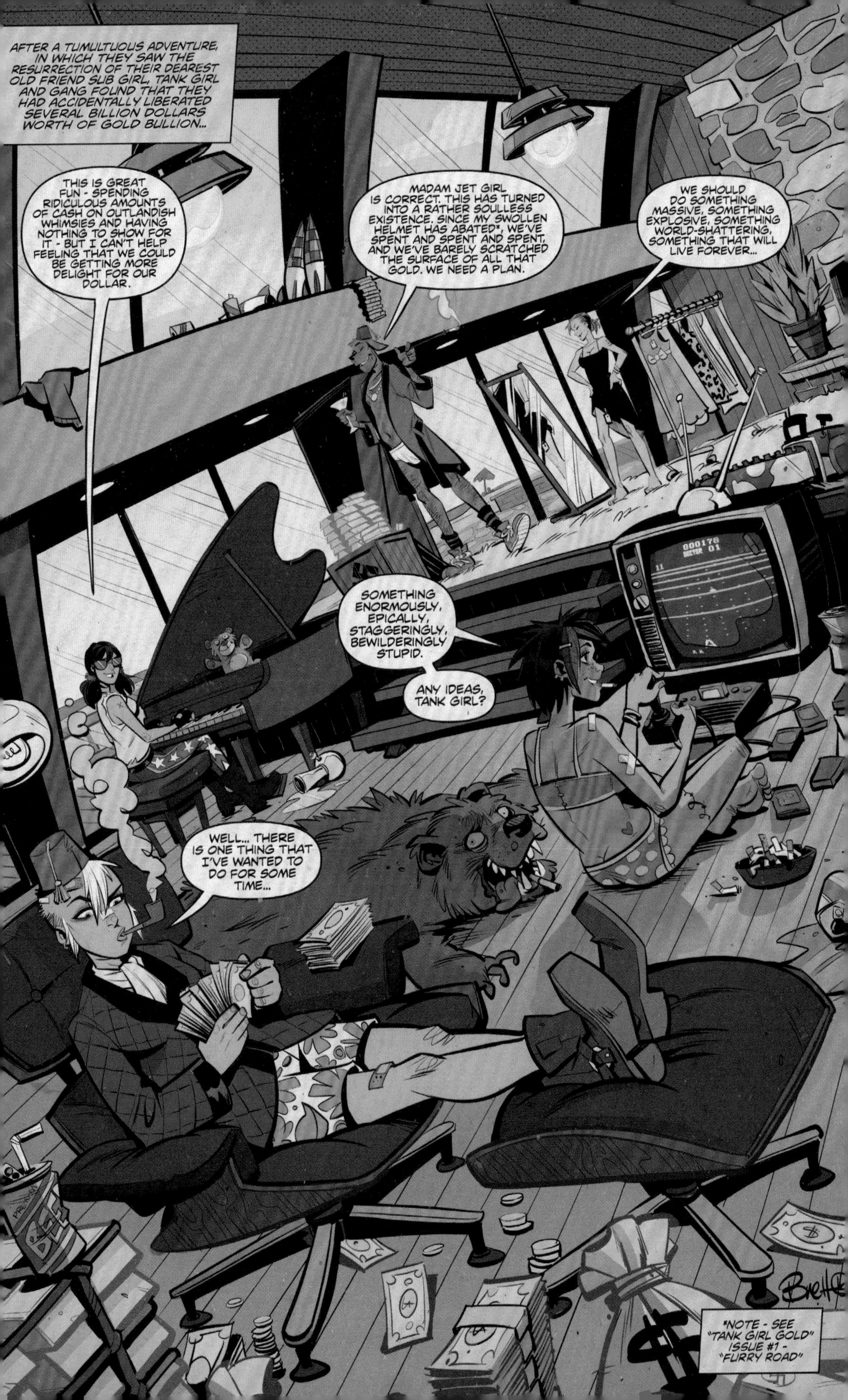
AFTER A TUMULTUOUS ADVENTURE, IN WHICH THEY SAW THE RESURRECTION OF THEIR DEAREST OLD FRIEND SUB GIRL, TANK GIRL AND GANG FOUND THAT THEY HAD ACCIDENTALLY LIBERATED SEVERAL BILLION DOLLARS WORTH OF GOLD BULLION...
THIS IS GREAT FUN - SPENDING RIDICULOUS AMOUNTS OF CASH ON OUTLANDISH WHIMSIES AND HAVING NOTHING TO SHOW FOR IT - BUT I CAN'T HELP FEELING THAT WE COULD BE GETTING MORE DELIGHT FOR OUR DOLLAR.
MADAM JET GIRL IS CORRECT. THIS HAS TURNED INTO A RATHER SOULLESS EXISTENCE. SINCE MY SWOLLEN HELMET HAS ABATED*, WE'VE SPENT AND SPENT AND SPENT, AND WE'VE BARELY SCRATCHED THE SURFACE OF ALL THAT GOLD. WE NEED A PLAN.
WE SHOULD DO SOMETHING MASSIVE, SOMETHING EXPLOSIVE, SOMETHING WORLD-SHATTERING, SOMETHING THAT WILL LIVE FOREVER...
SOMETHING ENORMOUSLY, EPICALLY, STAGGERINGLY, BEWILDERINGLY STUPID.
ANY IDEAS, TANK GIRL?
WELL... THERE IS ONE THING THAT I'VE WANTED TO DO FOR SOME TIME...
*NOTE - SEE "TANK GIRL GOLD" ISSUE #1 - "FURRY ROAD"

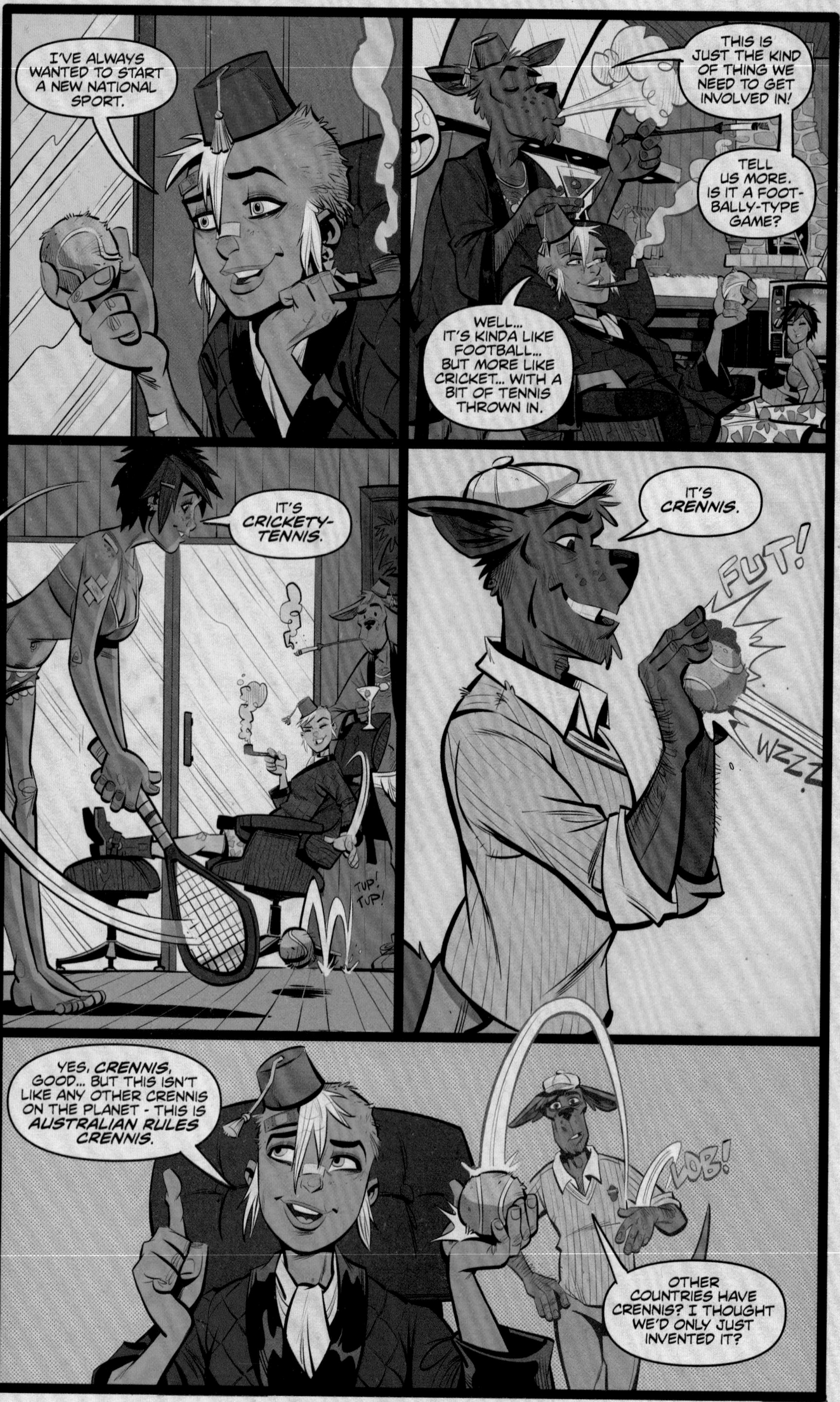
I'VE ALWAYS WANTED TO START A NEW NATIONAL SPORT.
THIS IS JUST THE KIND OF THING WE NEED TO GET INVOLVED IN!
TELL US MORE. IS IT A FOOT-BALLY-TYPE GAME?
WELL... IT'S KINDA LIKE FOOTBALL... BUT MORE LIKE CRICKET... WITH A BIT OF TENNIS THROWN IN.
IT'S CRICKETY-TENNIS.
TUP! TUP!
IT'S CRENNIS.
FUT!
WZZZ
YES, CRENNIS, GOOD... BUT THIS ISN'T LIKE ANY OTHER CRENNIS ON THE PLANET - THIS IS AUSTRALIAN RULES CRENNIS.
LOB!
OTHER COUNTRIES HAVE CRENNIS? I THOUGHT WE'D ONLY JUST INVENTED IT?

Most sports evolve through decades of trial and error, slowly honing the rules, regulations, and hardware, while audiences patiently wait for the best athletes with the right skill-sets to emerge as champions of the game. Tank Girl claims that she has been dreaming up the rules for her sport since she was twelve, but, to any casual onlooker, it would appear that she'd thought it all up in five minutes whilst sat on a lavatory in a drunken stupor. Please come along and join us for the inaugural ceremony and opening match, as…

TANK GIRL introduces AUSTRALIAN RULES CRENNIS

ARTIST : BREAD PARSLEY WRITER : ALFRED MARTINI

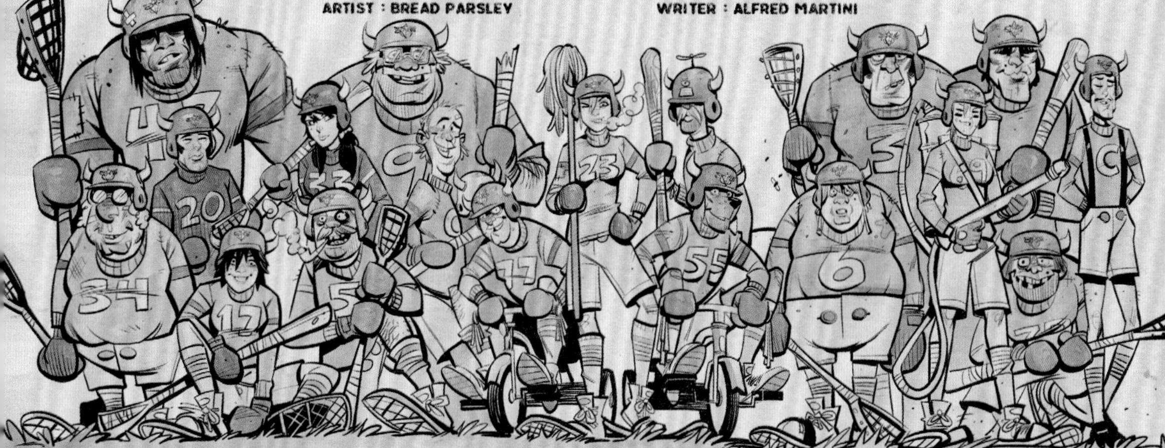

A Crennis Brigade (team) consists of either seventeen or eighteen players: four Square Pegs, two Bikers, one Third Eye, two Overlords, four Big Babies, two Toadstools, one Belcher, one Charlady, and an optional Crooner. There is no referee or umpire in Crennis, and all disputes are resolved by arguing and fighting.

The Gonad is a small ball, usually about five inches in diameter, made from the untreated lining of a beaver's stomach, which has been ceremonially pumped full of fresh custard until it is firm and tight - this happens before each game and is the responsibility of the visiting team.

The double-ended Tallywacker serves as a dual-action catching-and-hitting device. This is the most important component of the player's kit - only one Tallywacker may be used for the entire duration of a Crennis Player's career, so they are guarded with a jealous fervor. Suitable for catching high-speed Gonads, and for removing smiles, teeth, wind, and kneecaps.

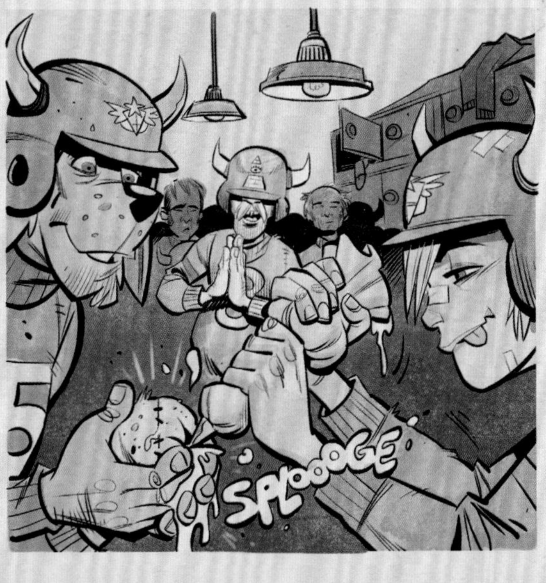
SPLOOOGE

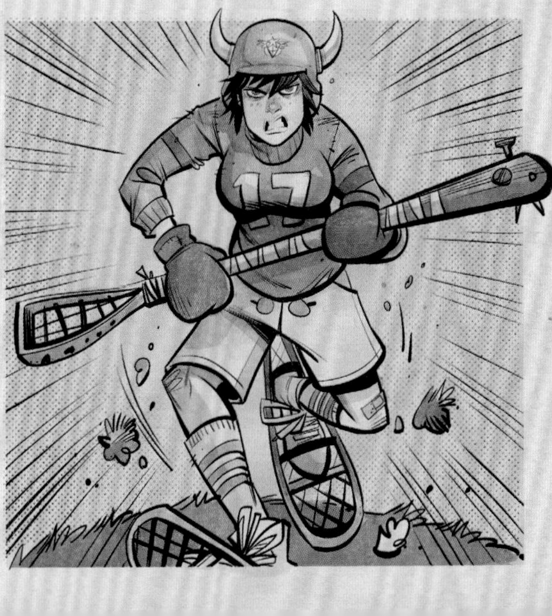

The visitors are known as **The Presuming Team**, and the home squad are **The Offending Team**. The playing field is called **The Oblong**; it resembles a soccer pitch with a tennis net stretching part-way across the centre. It has two half-size goals at one end, and a single full-size goal at the other.

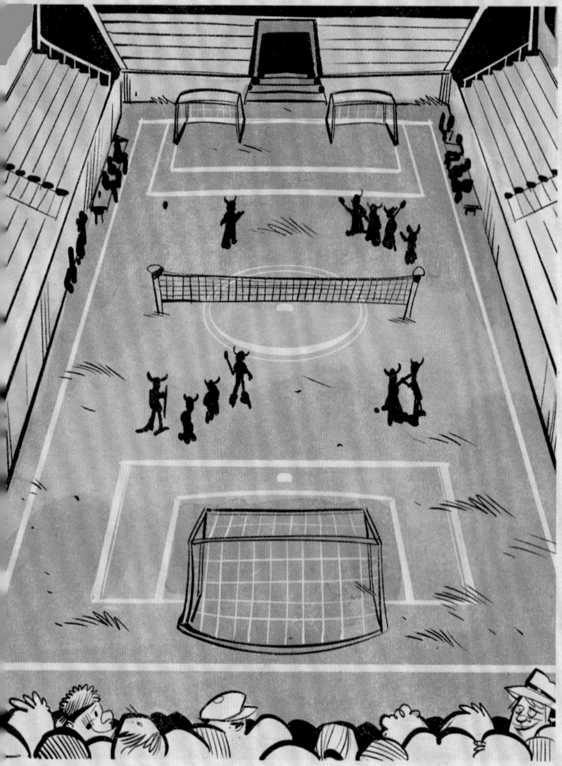

The aim of **Crennis** is to score the most **Jack Horners**. A **Jack Horner** occurs when a player from your Brigade gets to stand in a specific corner of the playing field, with his head bowed and his back to the game. Once in the corner, he can only be removed by a **Carry-Out**.

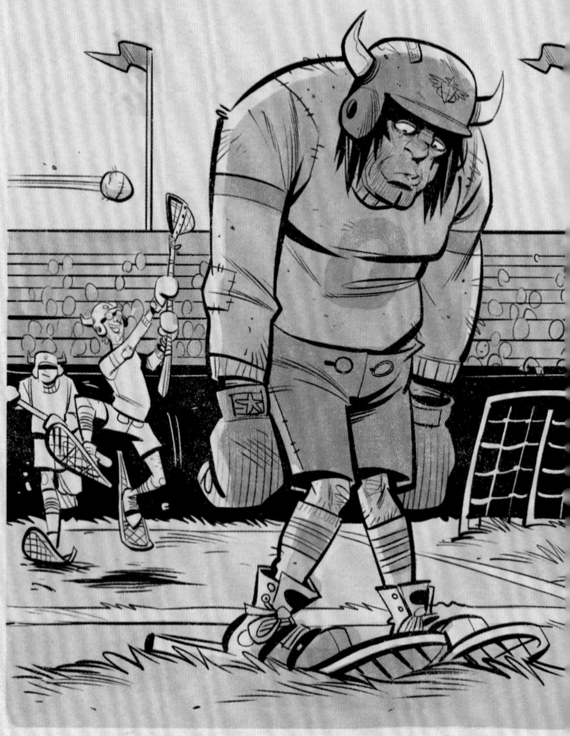

To claim a Jack Horner, your Brigade needs to get the Gonad into the opposing Brigade's goal, and keep it there for at least twenty-three seconds.

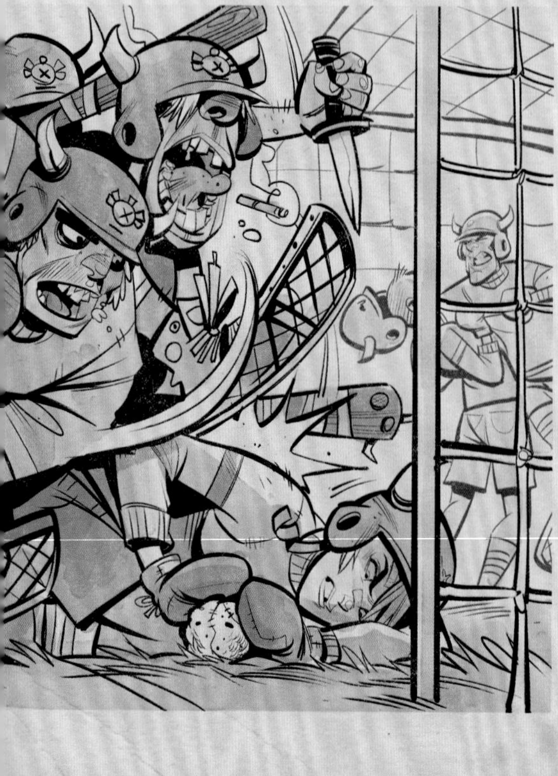

Bikers have the added avantage of being mounted on state-of-the-art, pedal-powered vehicles. No speed restrictions apply, and collisions with other Bikers are not counted as fouls.

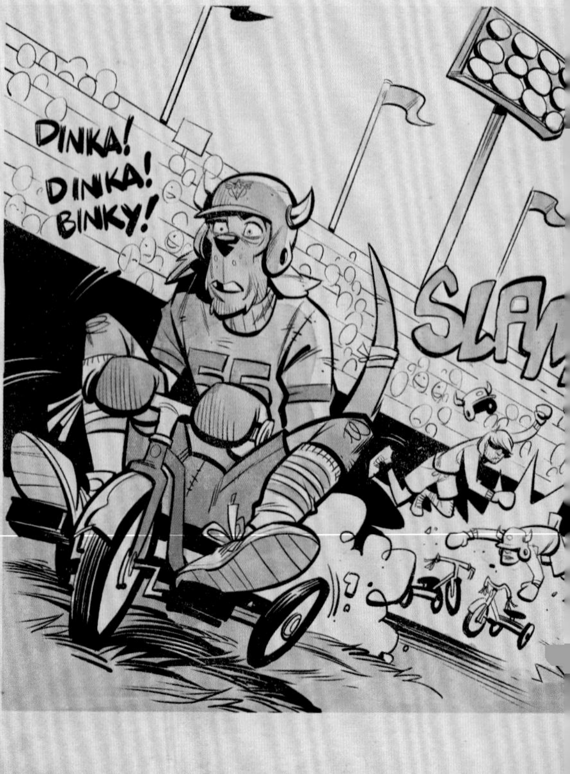
DINKA!
DINKA!
BINKY!

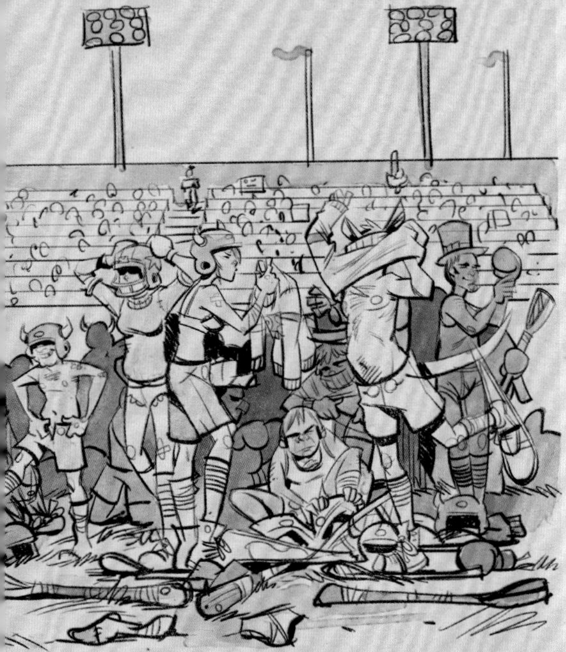

Crennis is a game of three halves. At the end of each half, the Brigades switch ends and swap shirts, causing mild disorientation on the playing field, and utter bewilderment in the audience.

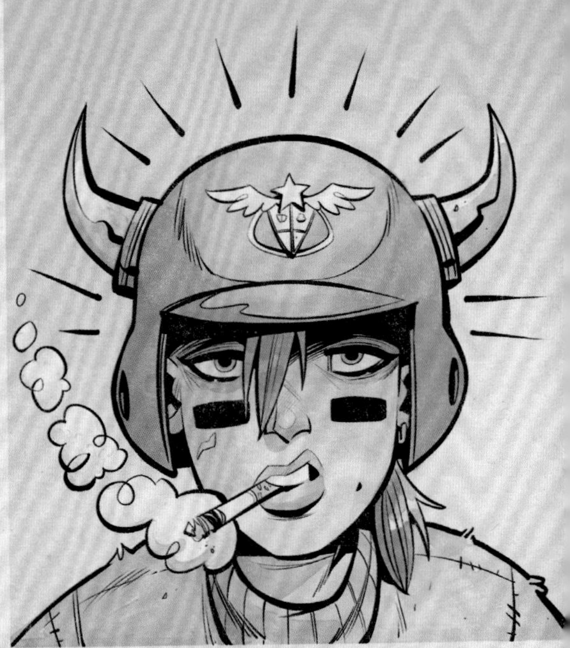

The only thing that differentiates Brigades from each other is the small crest on the front of their **Gufneys** - the hard helmets worn by Crennis players.

Your team may include an optional **Crooner**. The Crooner is not allowed to touch the Gonad, but he is allowed to sing dirty sports songs, as loud as he likes, into the faces of the opposing Brigade.

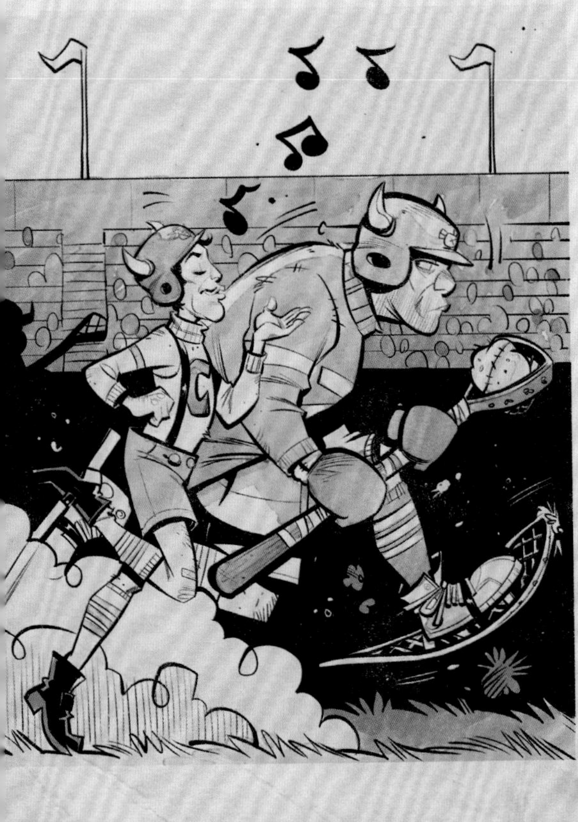

The scoring player must remain in the corner until his Brigade score again. To remove him by a **Carry-Out**, all bikers from the opposing Brigade carry him aloft to the diagonally opposite corner.

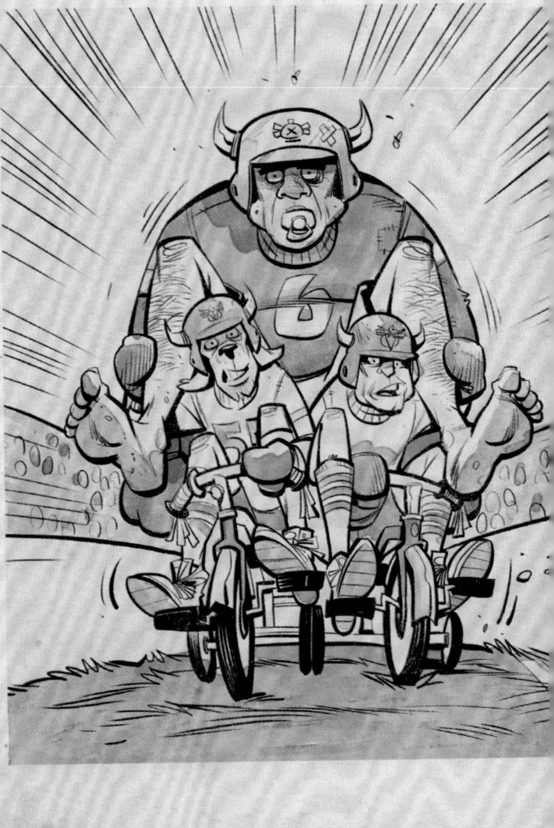

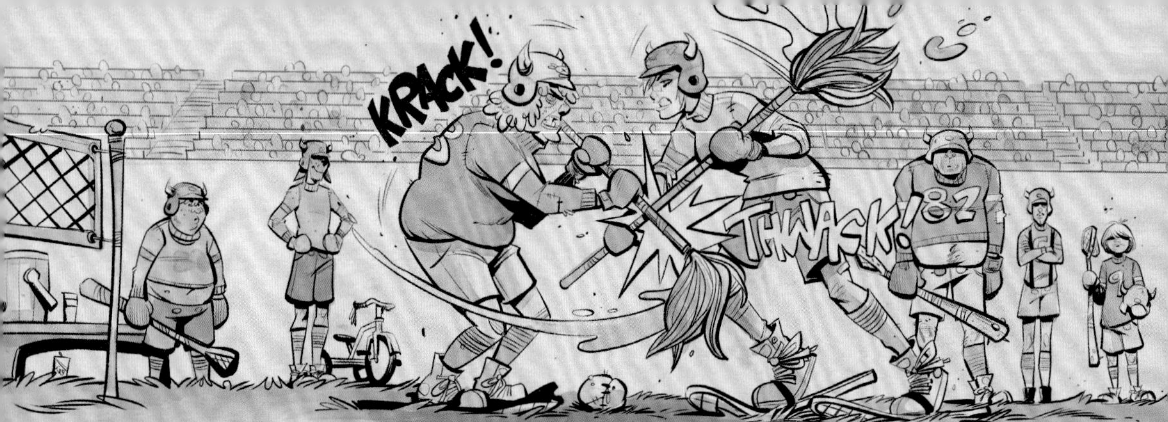
KRACK!
THWACK!

The three halves of the game are divided into one hour, half an hour, and two minutes. During the final two-minute half (known as the Clean-Up), only the Charladies are allowed to score.

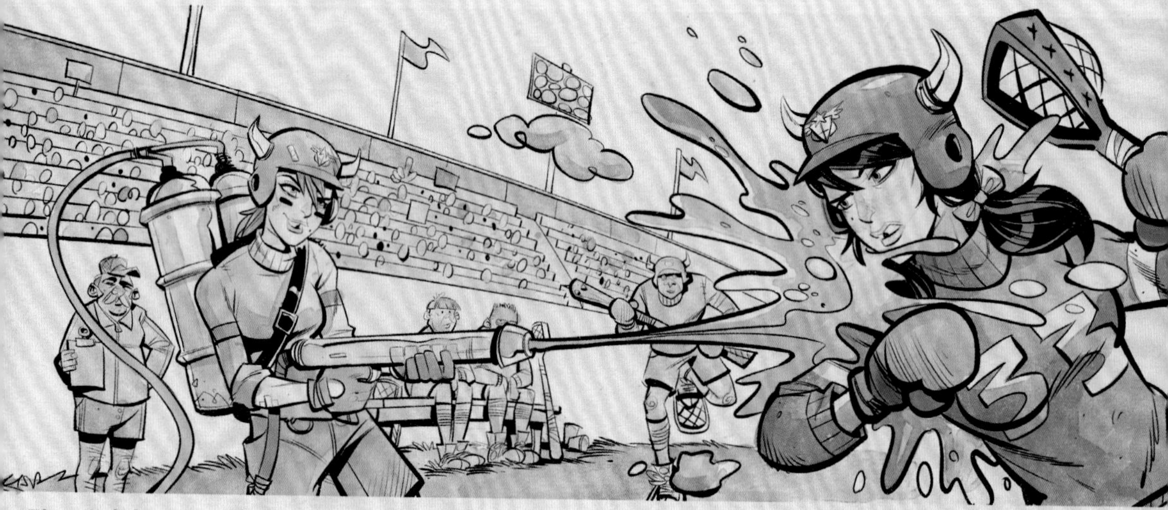

The Belchers operate independently of the rest of the Brigade, randomly soaking any member of either team with delicious fizzy beer from their two high pressure tanks.

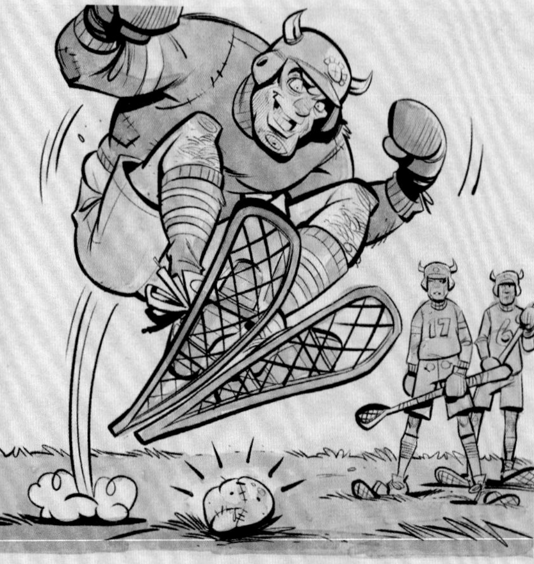

If the Gonad has remained untouched and stationary for more than thirty seconds, the Presuming team can call **Stampsies**, and stomp on it in an attempt to split it open. When Stampsies is called, all players must immediately freeze.

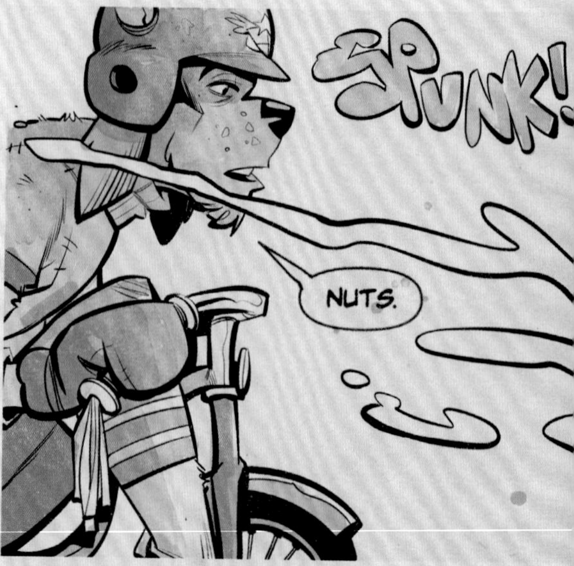
SPUNK!
NUTS.

If the Presuming Brigade are successful with their Stampsy, and if a member of the Offending team is caught by the ensuing issue, this is called a **Splash-Back**. The game finishes instantly, with the Presuming team winning.

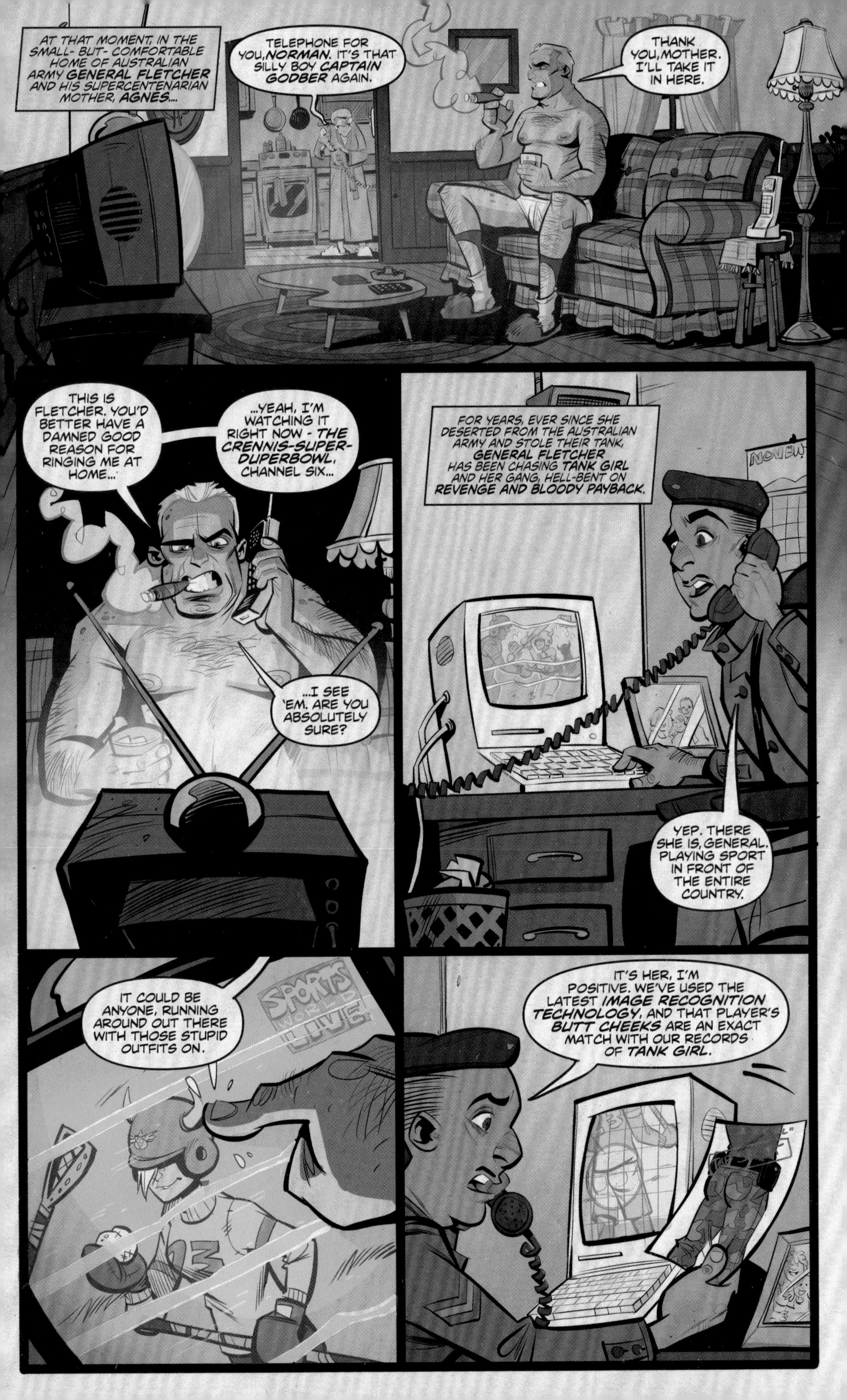
AT THAT MOMENT, IN THE SMALL-BUT-COMFORTABLE HOME OF AUSTRALIAN ARMY GENERAL FLETCHER AND HIS SUPERCENTENARIAN MOTHER, AGNES...
TELEPHONE FOR YOU, NORMAN. IT'S THAT SILLY BOY CAPTAIN GODBER AGAIN.
THANK YOU, MOTHER. I'LL TAKE IT IN HERE.
THIS IS FLETCHER. YOU'D BETTER HAVE A DAMNED GOOD REASON FOR RINGING ME AT HOME...
...YEAH, I'M WATCHING IT RIGHT NOW - THE CRENNIS-SUPER-DUPERBOWL, CHANNEL SIX...
...I SEE 'EM. ARE YOU ABSOLUTELY SURE?
FOR YEARS, EVER SINCE SHE DESERTED FROM THE AUSTRALIAN ARMY AND STOLE THEIR TANK, GENERAL FLETCHER HAS BEEN CHASING TANK GIRL AND HER GANG, HELL-BENT ON REVENGE AND BLOODY PAYBACK.
YEP. THERE SHE IS, GENERAL. PLAYING SPORT IN FRONT OF THE ENTIRE COUNTRY.
IT COULD BE ANYONE, RUNNING AROUND OUT THERE WITH THOSE STUPID OUTFITS ON.
SPORTS WORLD LIVE
IT'S HER, I'M POSITIVE. WE'VE USED THE LATEST IMAGE RECOGNITION TECHNOLOGY, AND THAT PLAYER'S BUTT CHEEKS ARE AN EXACT MATCH WITH OUR RECORDS OF TANK GIRL.

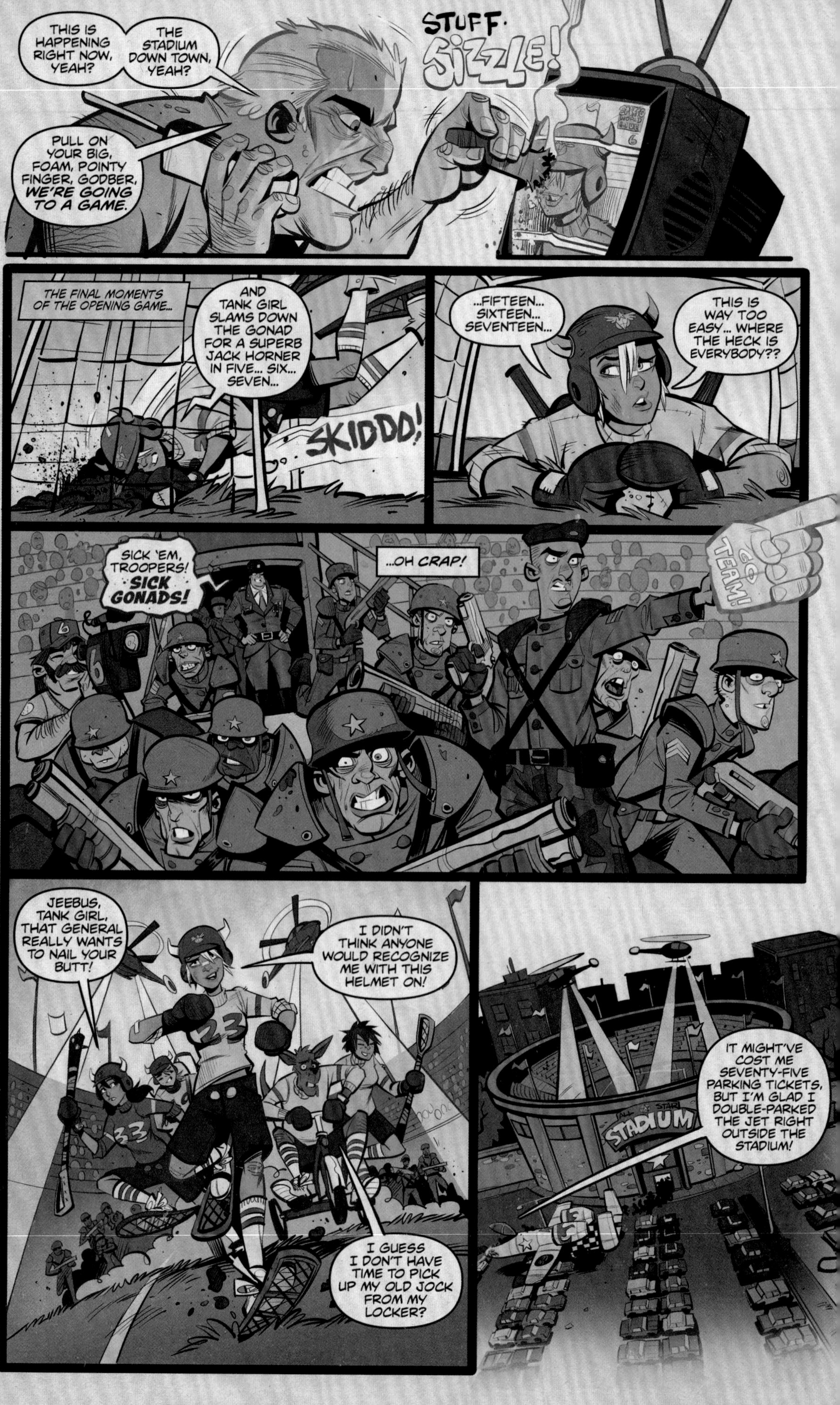

THIS IS HAPPENING RIGHT NOW, YEAH?
THE STADIUM DOWN TOWN, YEAH?
STUFF- SIZZLE!
PULL ON YOUR BIG, FOAM, POINTY FINGER, GODBER, *WE'RE GOING TO A GAME.*
THE FINAL MOMENTS OF THE OPENING GAME...
AND TANK GIRL SLAMS DOWN THE GONAD FOR A SUPERB JACK HORNER IN FIVE... SIX... SEVEN...
SKIDDD!
...FIFTEEN... SIXTEEN... SEVENTEEN...
THIS IS WAY TOO EASY... WHERE THE HECK IS EVERYBODY??
SICK 'EM, TROOPERS! **SICK GONADS!**
...OH *CRAP!*
GO TEAM!
JEEBUS, TANK GIRL, THAT GENERAL REALLY WANTS TO NAIL YOUR BUTT!
I DIDN'T THINK ANYONE WOULD RECOGNIZE ME WITH THIS HELMET ON!
I GUESS I DON'T HAVE TIME TO PICK UP MY OLD JOCK FROM MY LOCKER?
ALL STAR STADIUM
IT MIGHT'VE COST ME SEVENTY-FIVE PARKING TICKETS, BUT I'M GLAD I DOUBLE-PARKED THE JET RIGHT OUTSIDE THE STADIUM!

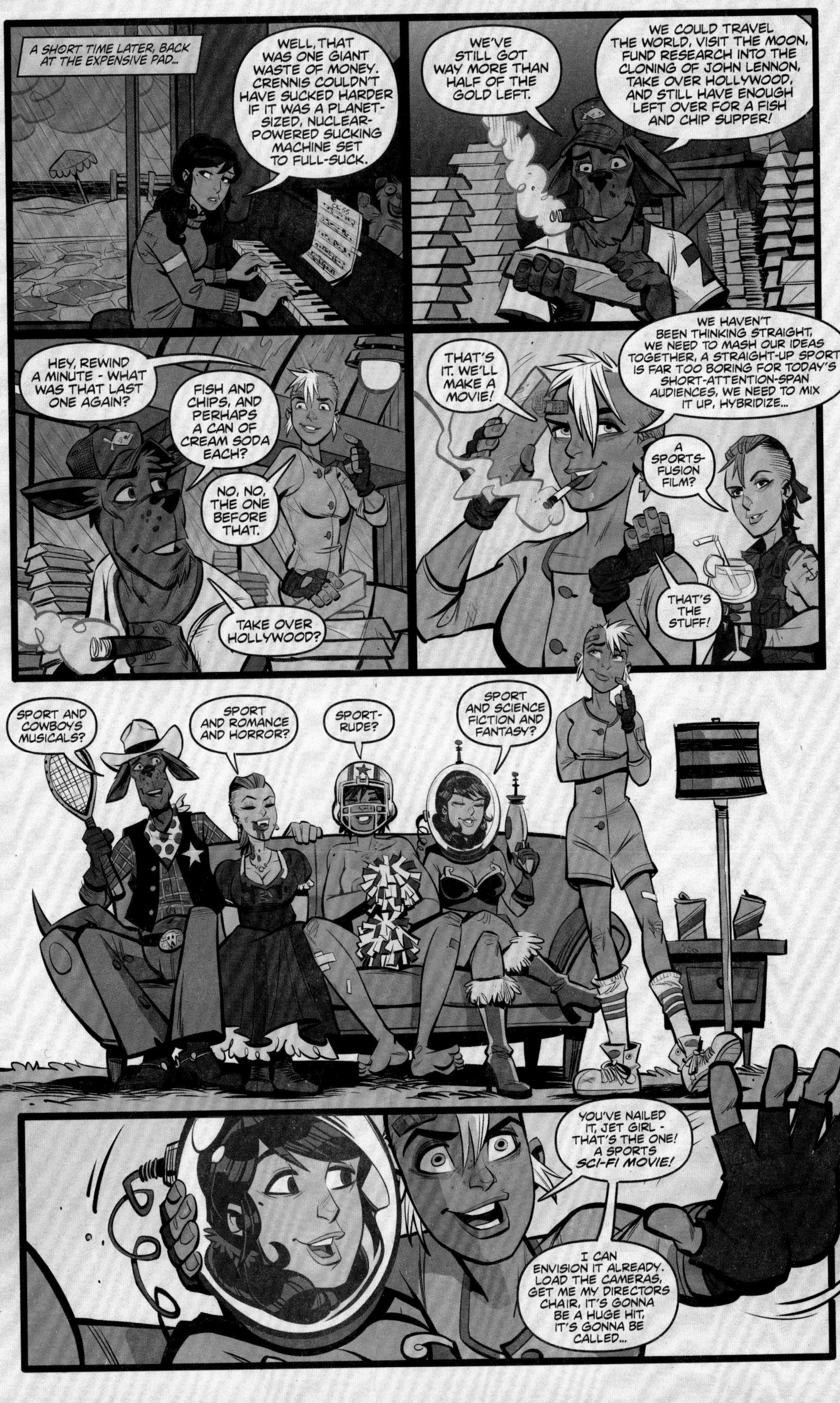
A SHORT TIME LATER, BACK AT THE EXPENSIVE PAD...
WELL, THAT WAS ONE GIANT WASTE OF MONEY. CRENNIS COULDN'T HAVE SUCKED HARDER IF IT WAS A PLANET-SIZED, NUCLEAR-POWERED SUCKING MACHINE SET TO FULL-SUCK.
WE'VE STILL GOT WAY MORE THAN HALF OF THE GOLD LEFT.
WE COULD TRAVEL THE WORLD, VISIT THE MOON, FUND RESEARCH INTO THE CLONING OF JOHN LENNON, TAKE OVER HOLLYWOOD, AND STILL HAVE ENOUGH LEFT OVER FOR A FISH AND CHIP SUPPER!
HEY, REWIND A MINUTE - WHAT WAS THAT LAST ONE AGAIN?
FISH AND CHIPS, AND PERHAPS A CAN OF CREAM SODA EACH?
NO, NO, THE ONE BEFORE THAT.
TAKE OVER HOLLYWOOD?
THAT'S IT. WE'LL MAKE A MOVIE!
WE HAVEN'T BEEN THINKING STRAIGHT, WE NEED TO MASH OUR IDEAS TOGETHER, A STRAIGHT-UP SPORT IS FAR TOO BORING FOR TODAY'S SHORT-ATTENTION-SPAN AUDIENCES, WE NEED TO MIX IT UP, HYBRIDIZE...
A SPORTS-FUSION FILM?
THAT'S THE STUFF!
SPORT AND COWBOYS MUSICALS?
SPORT AND ROMANCE AND HORROR?
SPORT-RUDE?
SPORT AND SCIENCE FICTION AND FANTASY?
YOU'VE NAILED IT, JET GIRL - THAT'S THE ONE! A SPORTS SCI-FI MOVIE!
I CAN ENVISION IT ALREADY. LOAD THE CAMERAS, GET ME MY DIRECTORS CHAIR, IT'S GONNA BE A HUGE HIT, IT'S GONNA BE CALLED...

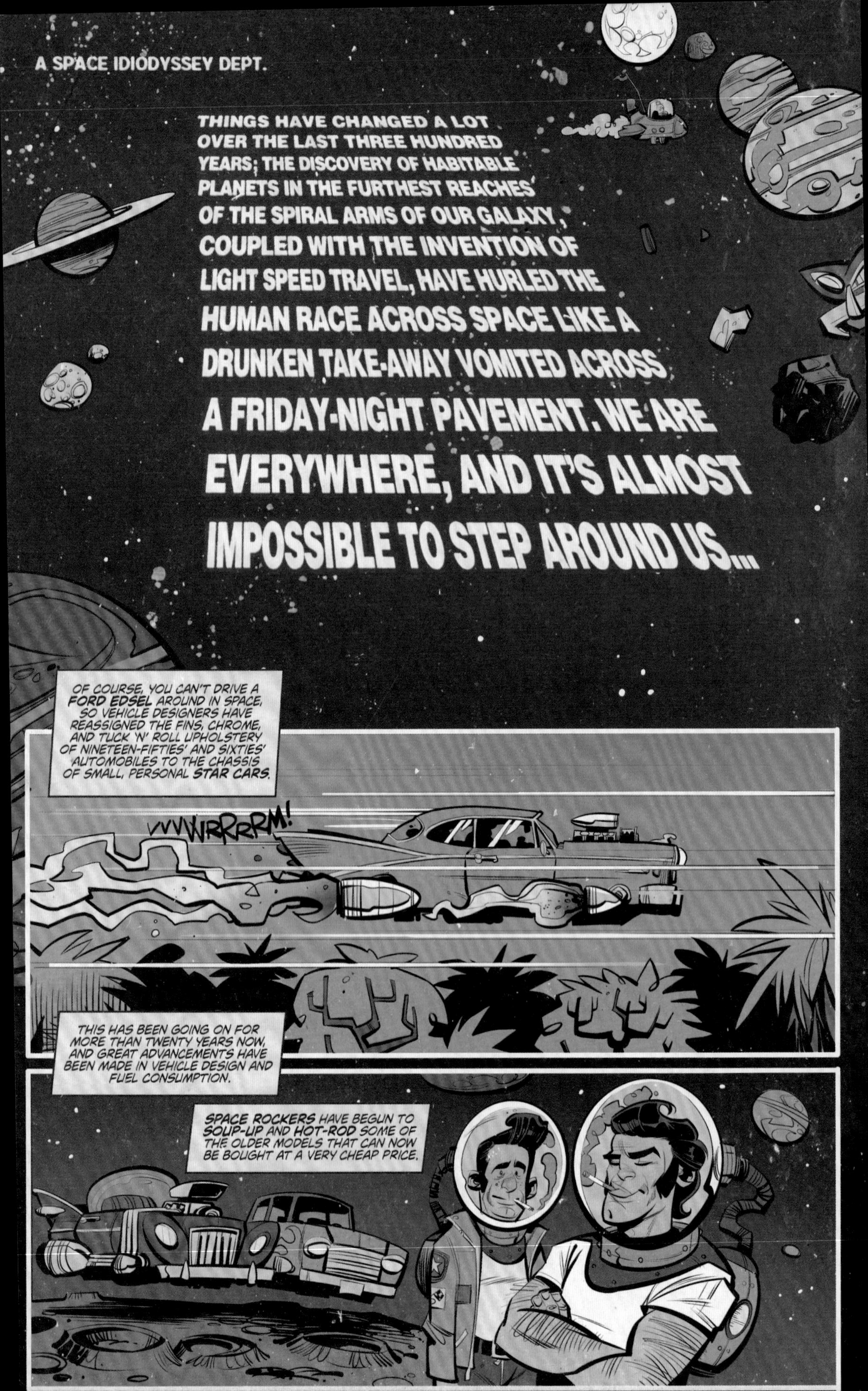
A SPACE IDIODYSSEY DEPT.
THINGS HAVE CHANGED A LOT OVER THE LAST THREE HUNDRED YEARS; THE DISCOVERY OF HABITABLE PLANETS IN THE FURTHEST REACHES OF THE SPIRAL ARMS OF OUR GALAXY, COUPLED WITH THE INVENTION OF LIGHT SPEED TRAVEL, HAVE HURLED THE HUMAN RACE ACROSS SPACE LIKE A DRUNKEN TAKE-AWAY VOMITED ACROSS A FRIDAY-NIGHT PAVEMENT. WE ARE EVERYWHERE, AND IT'S ALMOST IMPOSSIBLE TO STEP AROUND US...
OF COURSE, YOU CAN'T DRIVE A FORD EDSEL AROUND IN SPACE, SO VEHICLE DESIGNERS HAVE REASSIGNED THE FINS, CHROME, AND TUCK 'N' ROLL UPHOLSTERY OF NINETEEN-FIFTIES' AND SIXTIES' AUTOMOBILES TO THE CHASSIS OF SMALL, PERSONAL STAR CARS.
VVVVWRRRRM!
THIS HAS BEEN GOING ON FOR MORE THAN TWENTY YEARS NOW, AND GREAT ADVANCEMENTS HAVE BEEN MADE IN VEHICLE DESIGN AND FUEL CONSUMPTION.
SPACE ROCKERS HAVE BEGUN TO SOUP-UP AND HOT-ROD SOME OF THE OLDER MODELS THAT CAN NOW BE BOUGHT AT A VERY CHEAP PRICE.

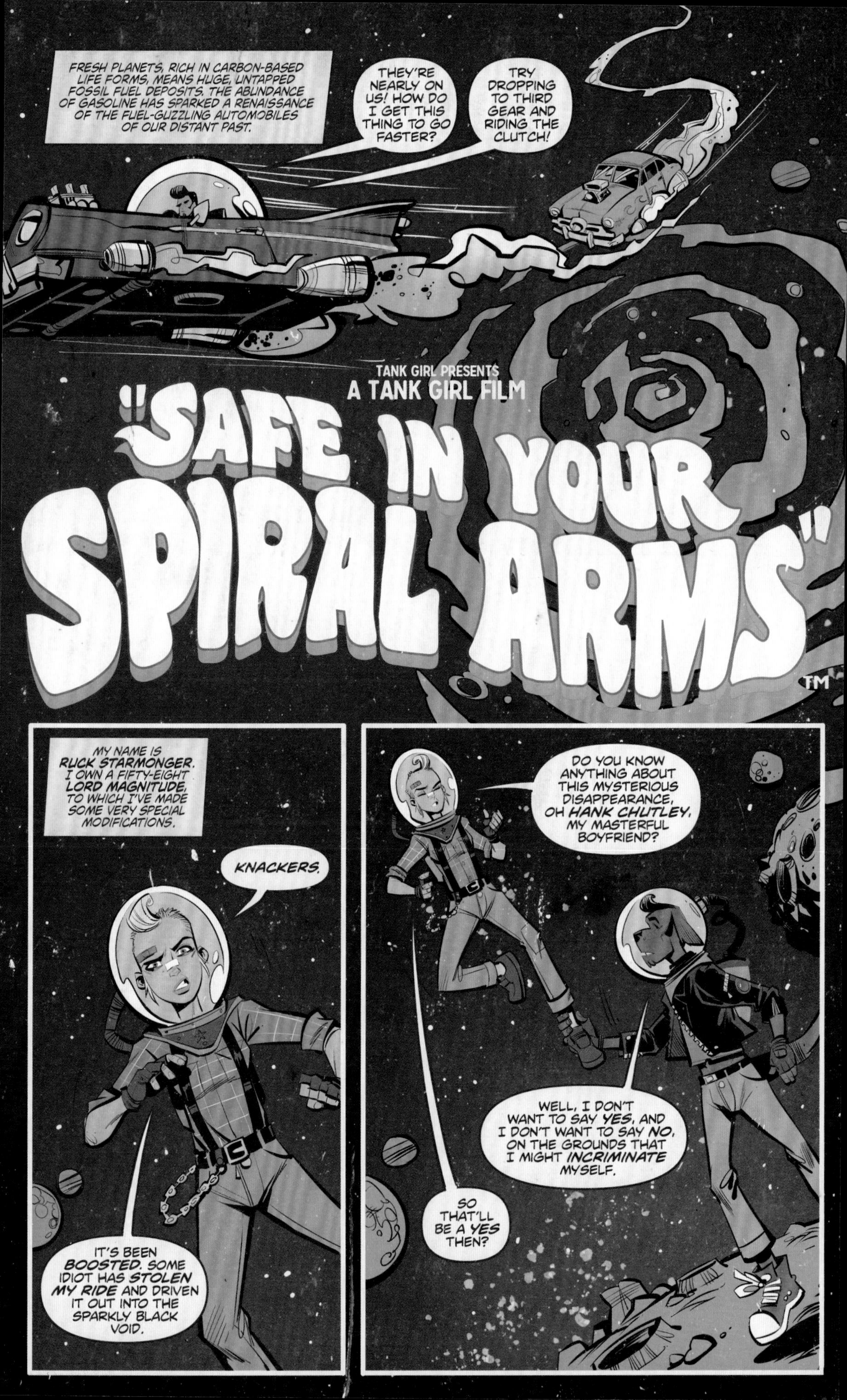
FRESH PLANETS, RICH IN CARBON-BASED LIFE FORMS, MEANS HUGE, UNTAPPED FOSSIL FUEL DEPOSITS. THE ABUNDANCE OF GASOLINE HAS SPARKED A RENAISSANCE OF THE FUEL-GUZZLING AUTOMOBILES OF OUR DISTANT PAST.
THEY'RE NEARLY ON US! HOW DO I GET THIS THING TO GO FASTER?
TRY DROPPING TO THIRD GEAR AND RIDING THE CLUTCH!
TANK GIRL PRESENTS
A TANK GIRL FILM
"SAFE IN YOUR SPIRAL ARMS"™
MY NAME IS RUCK STARMONGER. I OWN A FIFTY-EIGHT LORD MAGNITUDE, TO WHICH I'VE MADE SOME VERY SPECIAL MODIFICATIONS.
KNACKERS.
IT'S BEEN BOOSTED. SOME IDIOT HAS STOLEN MY RIDE AND DRIVEN IT OUT INTO THE SPARKLY BLACK VOID.
DO YOU KNOW ANYTHING ABOUT THIS MYSTERIOUS DISAPPEARANCE, OH HANK CHUTLEY, MY MASTERFUL BOYFRIEND?
WELL, I DON'T WANT TO SAY YES, AND I DON'T WANT TO SAY NO, ON THE GROUNDS THAT I MIGHT INCRIMINATE MYSELF.
SO THAT'LL BE A YES THEN?

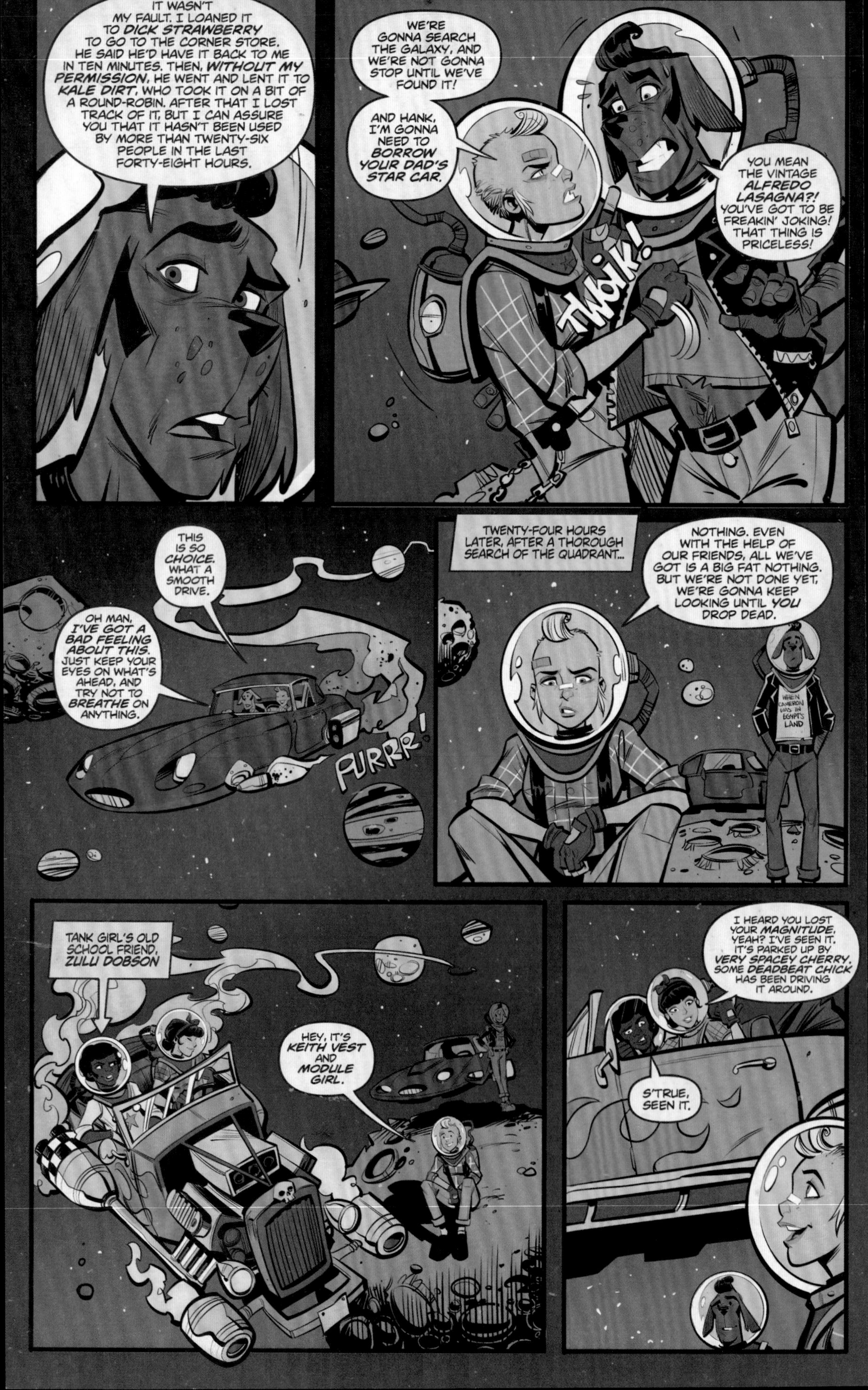

IT WASN'T MY FAULT. I LOANED IT TO DICK STRAWBERRY TO GO TO THE CORNER STORE. HE SAID HE'D HAVE IT BACK TO ME IN TEN MINUTES. THEN, WITHOUT MY PERMISSION, HE WENT AND LENT IT TO KALE DIRT, WHO TOOK IT ON A BIT OF A ROUND-ROBIN. AFTER THAT I LOST TRACK OF IT, BUT I CAN ASSURE YOU THAT IT HASN'T BEEN USED BY MORE THAN TWENTY-SIX PEOPLE IN THE LAST FORTY-EIGHT HOURS.
WE'RE GONNA SEARCH THE GALAXY, AND WE'RE NOT GONNA STOP UNTIL WE'VE FOUND IT!
AND HANK, I'M GONNA NEED TO BORROW YOUR DAD'S STAR CAR.
TWOIK!
YOU MEAN THE VINTAGE ALFREDO LASAGNA?! YOU'VE GOT TO BE FREAKIN' JOKING! THAT THING IS PRICELESS!
THIS IS SO CHOICE. WHAT A SMOOTH DRIVE.
OH MAN, I'VE GOT A BAD FEELING ABOUT THIS. JUST KEEP YOUR EYES ON WHAT'S AHEAD, AND TRY NOT TO BREATHE ON ANYTHING.
PURRR!
TWENTY-FOUR HOURS LATER, AFTER A THOROUGH SEARCH OF THE QUADRANT...
NOTHING. EVEN WITH THE HELP OF OUR FRIENDS, ALL WE'VE GOT IS A BIG FAT NOTHING. BUT WE'RE NOT DONE YET. WE'RE GONNA KEEP LOOKING UNTIL YOU DROP DEAD.
WHEN CAMERON WAS IN EGYPT'S LAND
TANK GIRL'S OLD SCHOOL FRIEND, ZULU DOBSON
HEY, IT'S KEITH VEST AND MODULE GIRL.
I HEARD YOU LOST YOUR MAGNITUDE. YEAH? I'VE SEEN IT. IT'S PARKED UP BY VERY SPACEY CHERRY. SOME DEADBEAT CHICK HAS BEEN DRIVING IT AROUND.
S'TRUE, SEEN IT.

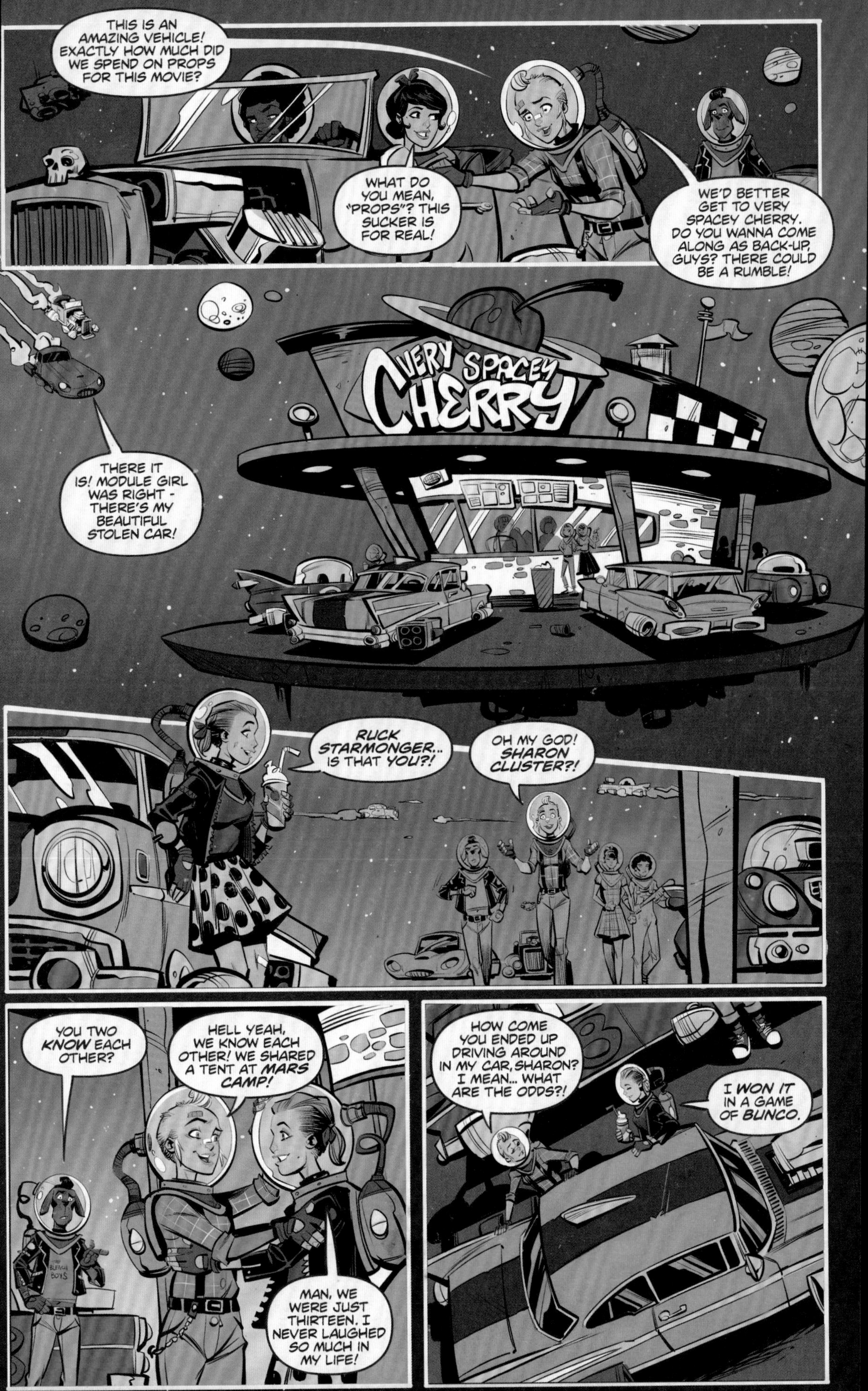

THIS IS AN AMAZING VEHICLE! EXACTLY HOW MUCH DID WE SPEND ON PROPS FOR THIS MOVIE?
WHAT DO YOU MEAN, "PROPS"? THIS SUCKER IS FOR REAL!
WE'D BETTER GET TO VERY SPACEY CHERRY. DO YOU WANNA COME ALONG AS BACK-UP, GUYS? THERE COULD BE A RUMBLE!
VERY SPACEY CHERRY
THERE IT IS! MODULE GIRL WAS RIGHT - THERE'S MY BEAUTIFUL STOLEN CAR!
RUCK STARMONGER... IS THAT YOU?!
OH MY GOD! SHARON CLUSTER?!
YOU TWO KNOW EACH OTHER?
HELL YEAH, WE KNOW EACH OTHER! WE SHARED A TENT AT MARS CAMP!
MAN, WE WERE JUST THIRTEEN. I NEVER LAUGHED SO MUCH IN MY LIFE!
HOW COME YOU ENDED UP DRIVING AROUND IN MY CAR, SHARON? I MEAN... WHAT ARE THE ODDS?!
I WON IT IN A GAME OF BUNCO.

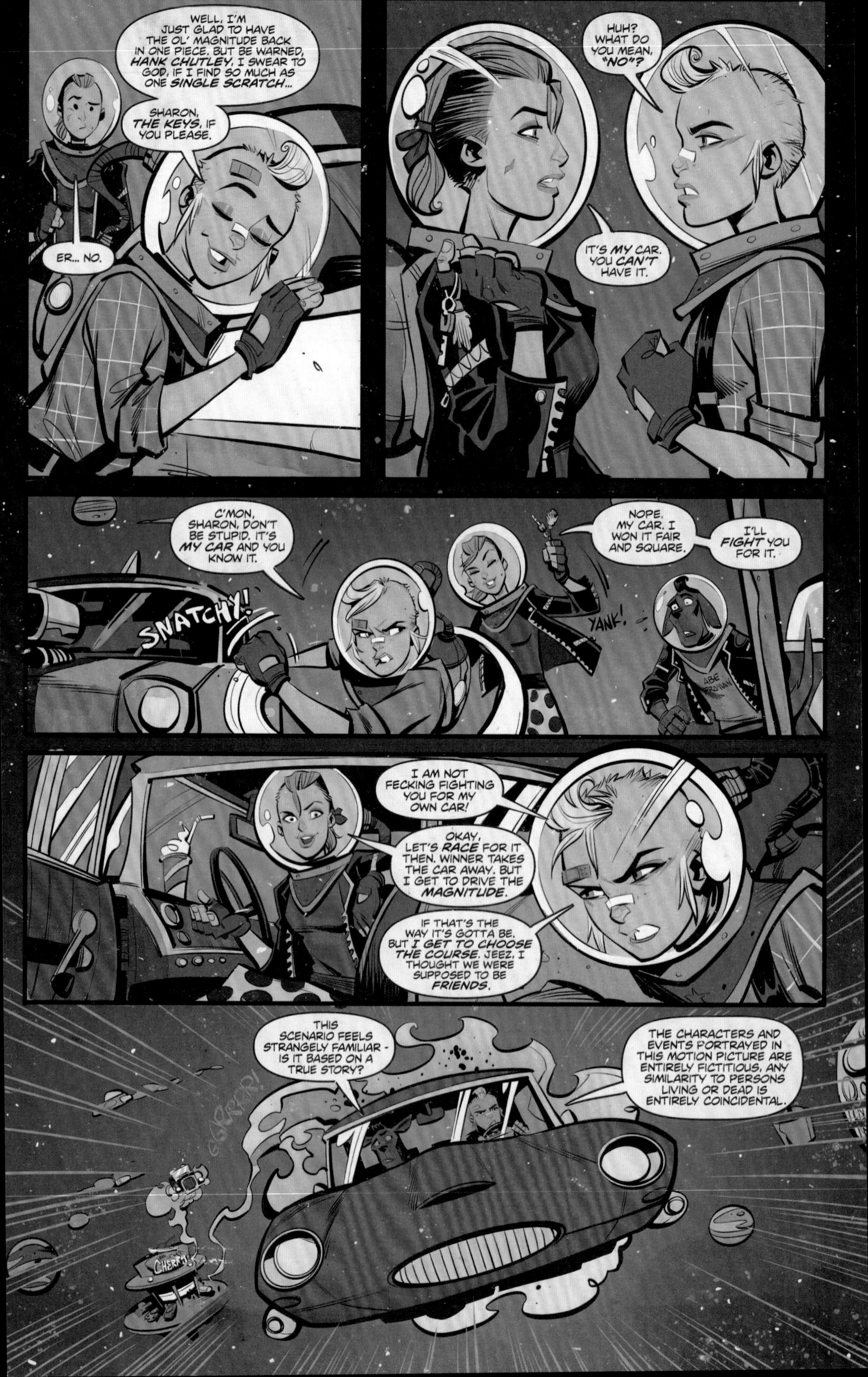

WELL, I'M JUST GLAD TO HAVE THE OL' MAGNITUDE BACK IN ONE PIECE. BUT BE WARNED, HANK CHUTLEY, I SWEAR TO GOD, IF I FIND SO MUCH AS ONE SINGLE SCRATCH...
SHARON, THE KEYS, IF YOU PLEASE.
ER... NO.
HUH? WHAT DO YOU MEAN, "NO"?
IT'S MY CAR. YOU CAN'T HAVE IT.
C'MON, SHARON, DON'T BE STUPID. IT'S MY CAR AND YOU KNOW IT.
SNATCHY!
NOPE, MY CAR. I WON IT FAIR AND SQUARE.
I'LL FIGHT YOU FOR IT.
YANK!
I AM NOT FECKING FIGHTING YOU FOR MY OWN CAR!
OKAY, LET'S RACE FOR IT THEN. WINNER TAKES THE CAR AWAY. BUT I GET TO DRIVE THE MAGNITUDE.
IF THAT'S THE WAY IT'S GOTTA BE. BUT I GET TO CHOOSE THE COURSE. JEEZ, I THOUGHT WE WERE SUPPOSED TO BE FRIENDS.
THIS SCENARIO FEELS STRANGELY FAMILIAR - IS IT BASED ON A TRUE STORY?
THE CHARACTERS AND EVENTS PORTRAYED IN THIS MOTION PICTURE ARE ENTIRELY FICTITIOUS, ANY SIMILARITY TO PERSONS LIVING OR DEAD IS ENTIRELY COINCIDENTAL.
CHERRY!

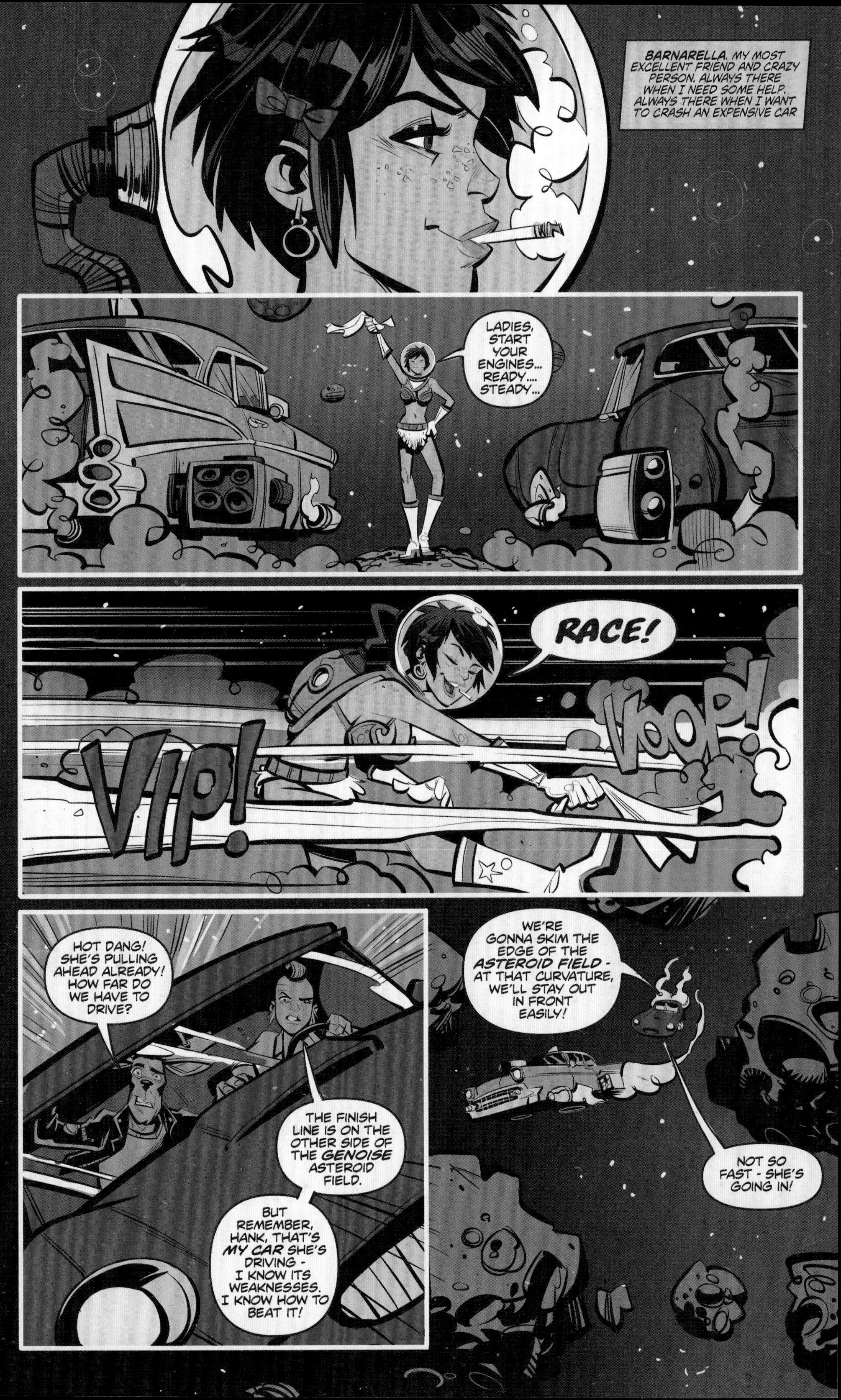
BARNARELLA. MY MOST EXCELLENT FRIEND AND CRAZY PERSON. ALWAYS THERE WHEN I NEED SOME HELP. ALWAYS THERE WHEN I WANT TO CRASH AN EXPENSIVE CAR
LADIES, START YOUR ENGINES... READY.... STEADY...
RACE!
VIP!
VOOP!
HOT DANG! SHE'S PULLING AHEAD ALREADY! HOW FAR DO WE HAVE TO DRIVE?
THE FINISH LINE IS ON THE OTHER SIDE OF THE GENOISE ASTEROID FIELD.
BUT REMEMBER, HANK, THAT'S MY CAR SHE'S DRIVING - I KNOW ITS WEAKNESSES. I KNOW HOW TO BEAT IT!
WE'RE GONNA SKIM THE EDGE OF THE ASTEROID FIELD - AT THAT CURVATURE, WE'LL STAY OUT IN FRONT EASILY!
NOT SO FAST - SHE'S GOING IN!

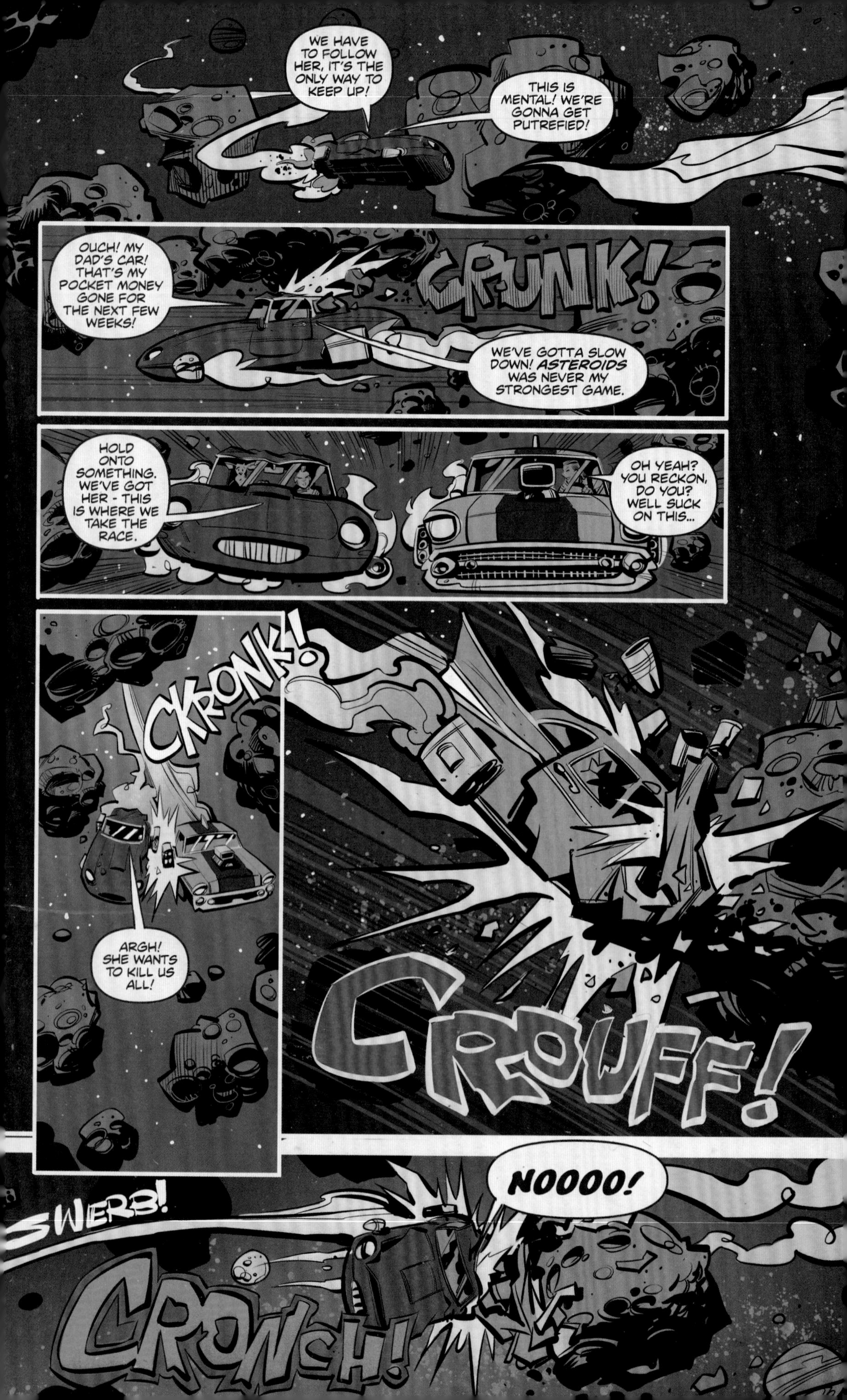
WE HAVE TO FOLLOW HER, IT'S THE ONLY WAY TO KEEP UP!
THIS IS MENTAL! WE'RE GONNA GET PUTREFIED!
OUCH! MY DAD'S CAR! THAT'S MY POCKET MONEY GONE FOR THE NEXT FEW WEEKS!
CRUNK!
WE'VE GOTTA SLOW DOWN! ASTEROIDS WAS NEVER MY STRONGEST GAME.
HOLD ONTO SOMETHING. WE'VE GOT HER - THIS IS WHERE WE TAKE THE RACE.
OH YEAH? YOU RECKON, DO YOU? WELL SUCK ON THIS...
CKRONK!
ARGH! SHE WANTS TO KILL US ALL!
CROUFF!
SWERB!
NOOOO!
CRONCH!

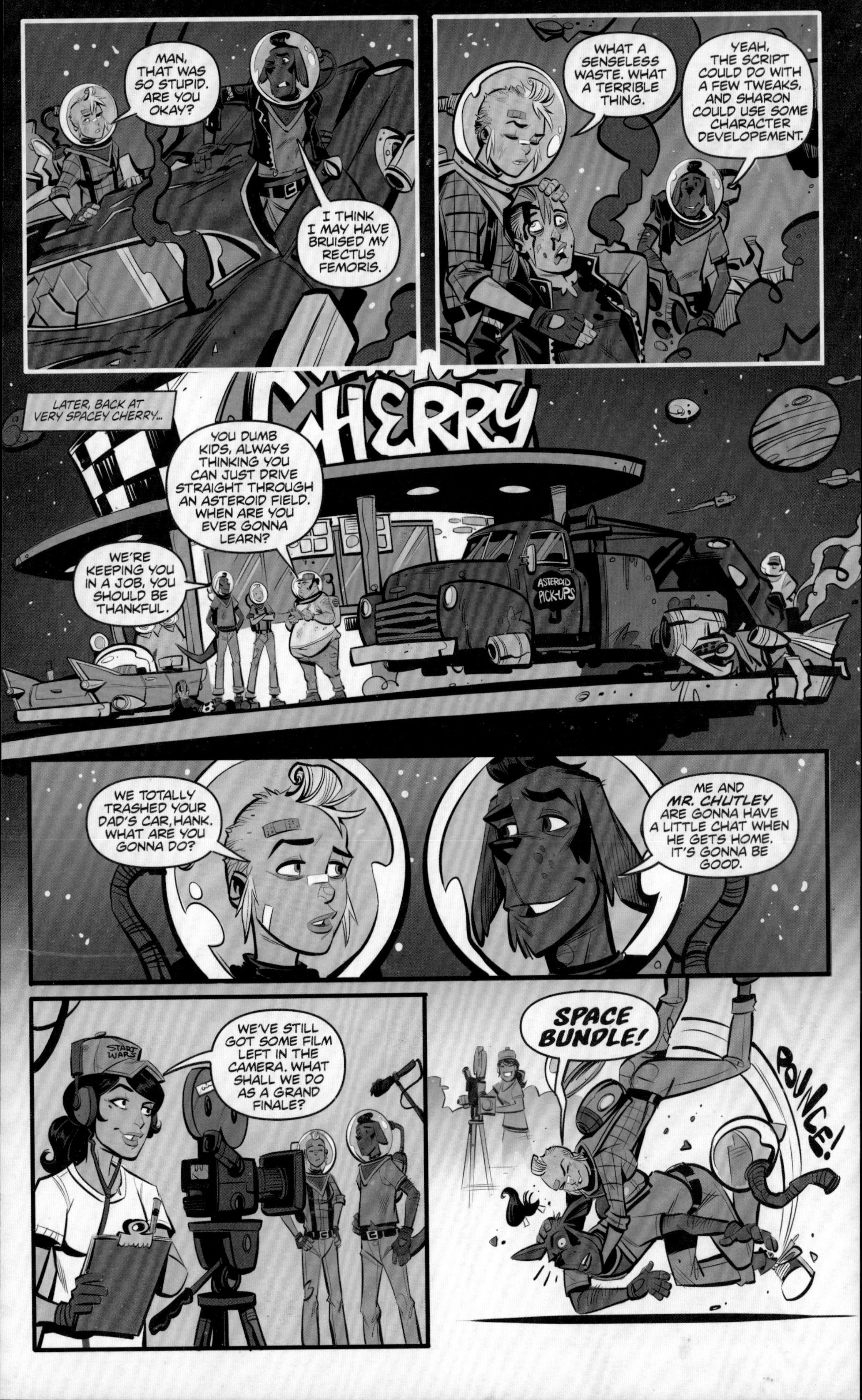
MAN, THAT WAS SO STUPID. ARE YOU OKAY?
I THINK I MAY HAVE BRUISED MY RECTUS FEMORIS.
WHAT A SENSELESS WASTE. WHAT A TERRIBLE THING.
YEAH, THE SCRIPT COULD DO WITH A FEW TWEAKS, AND SHARON COULD USE SOME CHARACTER DEVELOPEMENT.
CHERRY
LATER, BACK AT VERY SPACEY CHERRY...
YOU DUMB KIDS, ALWAYS THINKING YOU CAN JUST DRIVE STRAIGHT THROUGH AN ASTEROID FIELD. WHEN ARE YOU EVER GONNA LEARN?
WE'RE KEEPING YOU IN A JOB, YOU SHOULD BE THANKFUL.
ASTEROID PICK-UPS
WE TOTALLY TRASHED YOUR DAD'S CAR, HANK. WHAT ARE YOU GONNA DO?
ME AND MR. CHUTLEY ARE GONNA HAVE A LITTLE CHAT WHEN HE GETS HOME. IT'S GONNA BE GOOD.
START WARS
WE'VE STILL GOT SOME FILM LEFT IN THE CAMERA. WHAT SHALL WE DO AS A GRAND FINALE?
SPACE BUNDLE!
POUNCE!

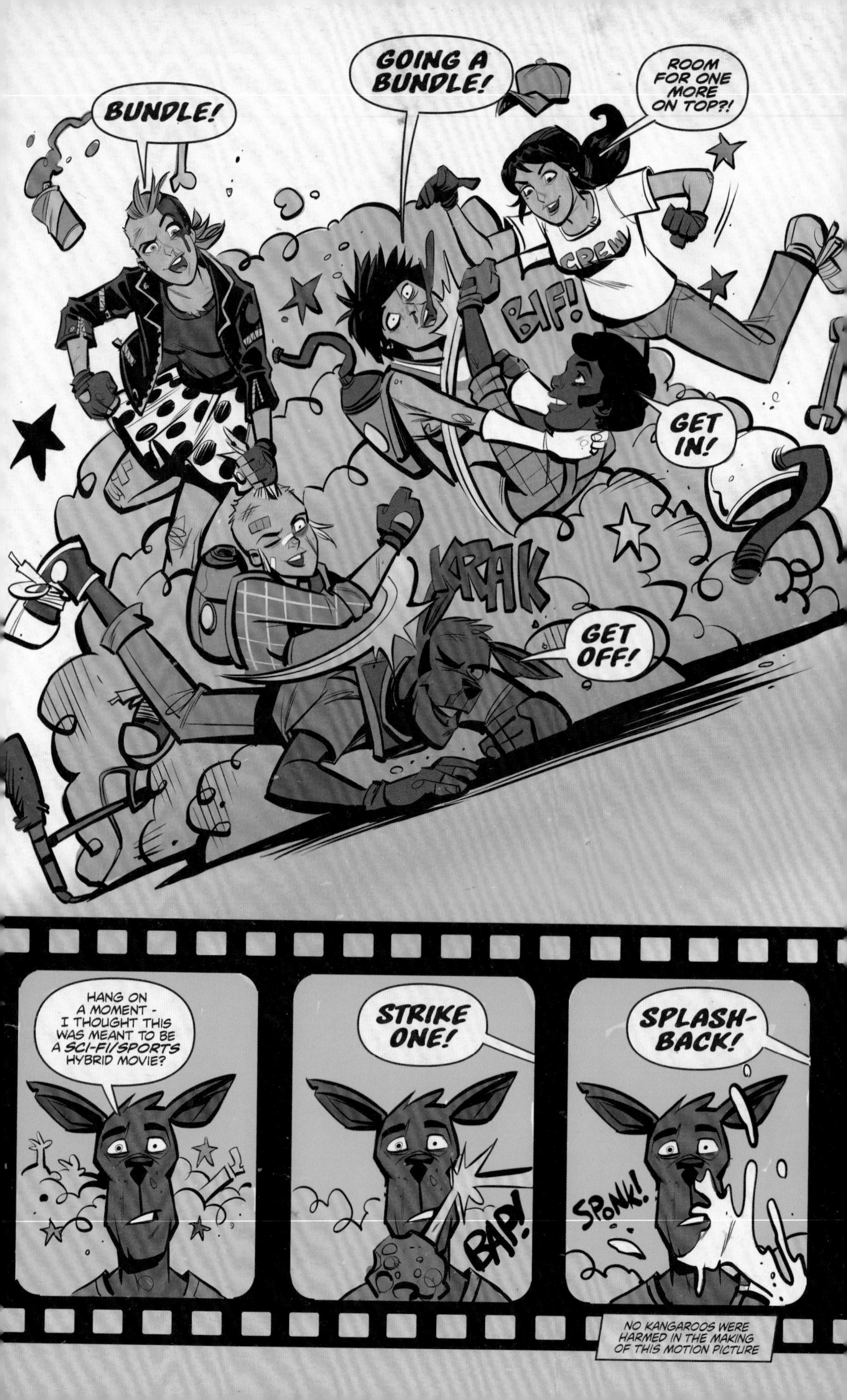

BUNDLE!
GOING A BUNDLE!
ROOM FOR ONE MORE ON TOP?!
CREW
BIF!
GET IN!
KRAK
GET OFF!
HANG ON A MOMENT - I THOUGHT THIS WAS MEANT TO BE A SCI-FI/SPORTS HYBRID MOVIE?
STRIKE ONE!
BAP!
SPLASH-BACK!
SPONK!
NO KANGAROOS WERE HARMED IN THE MAKING OF THIS MOTION PICTURE

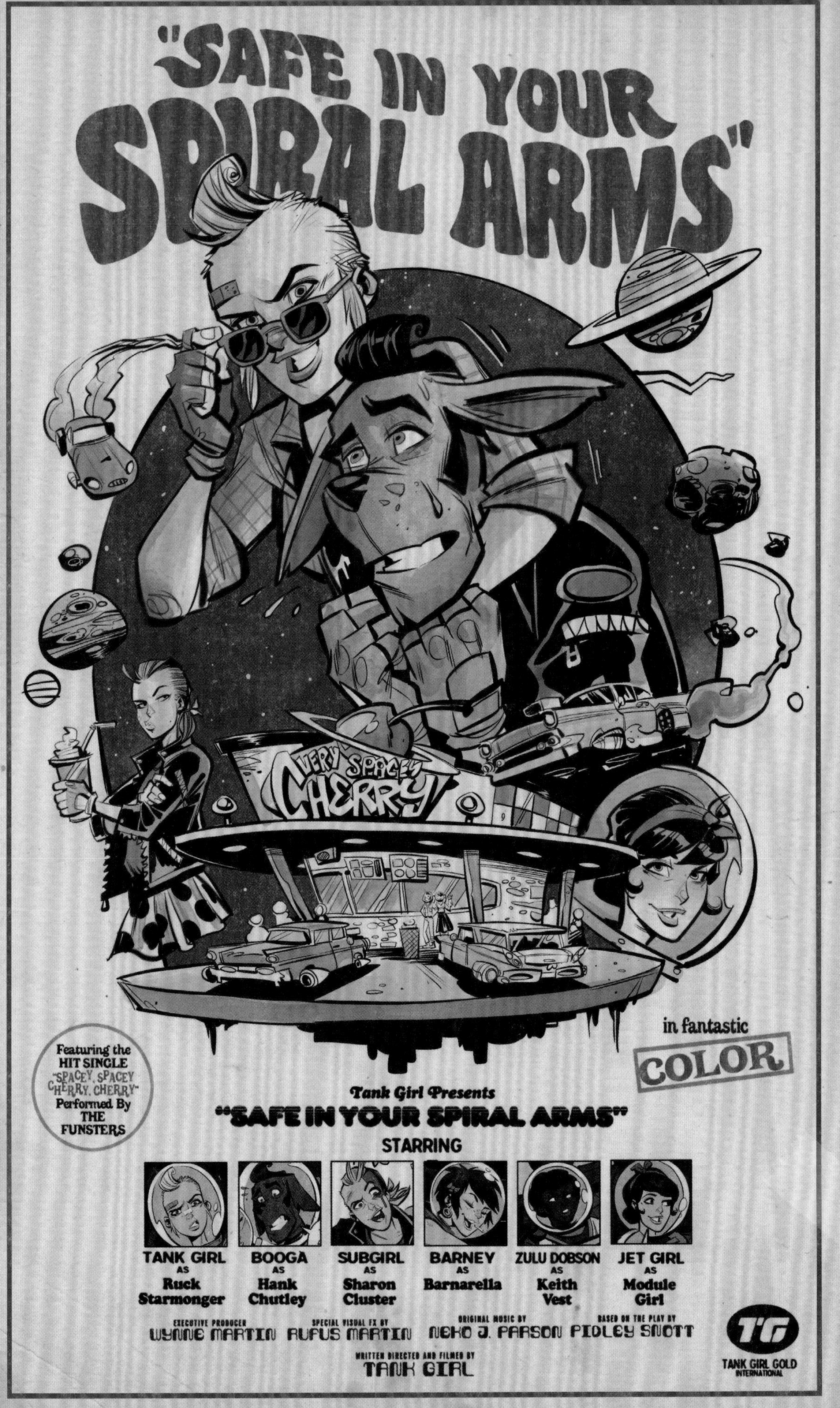

"SAFE IN YOUR SPIRAL ARMS"
VERY SPACEY CHERRY
in fantastic
COLOR
Featuring the HIT SINGLE "SPACEY, SPACEY CHERRY, CHERRY" Performed By THE FUNSTERS
Tank Girl Presents
"SAFE IN YOUR SPIRAL ARMS"
STARRING
TANK GIRL AS Ruck Starmonger
BOOGA AS Hank Chutley
SUBGIRL AS Sharon Cluster
BARNEY AS Barnarella
ZULU DOBSON AS Keith Vest
JET GIRL AS Module Girl
EXECUTIVE PRODUCER WYNNE MARTIN
SPECIAL VISUAL FX BY RUFUS MARTIN
ORIGINAL MUSIC BY NEKO J. PARSON
BASED ON THE PLAY BY PIDLEY SNOTT
WRITTEN DIRECTED AND FILMED BY TANK GIRL
TG
TANK GIRL GOLD INTERNATIONAL

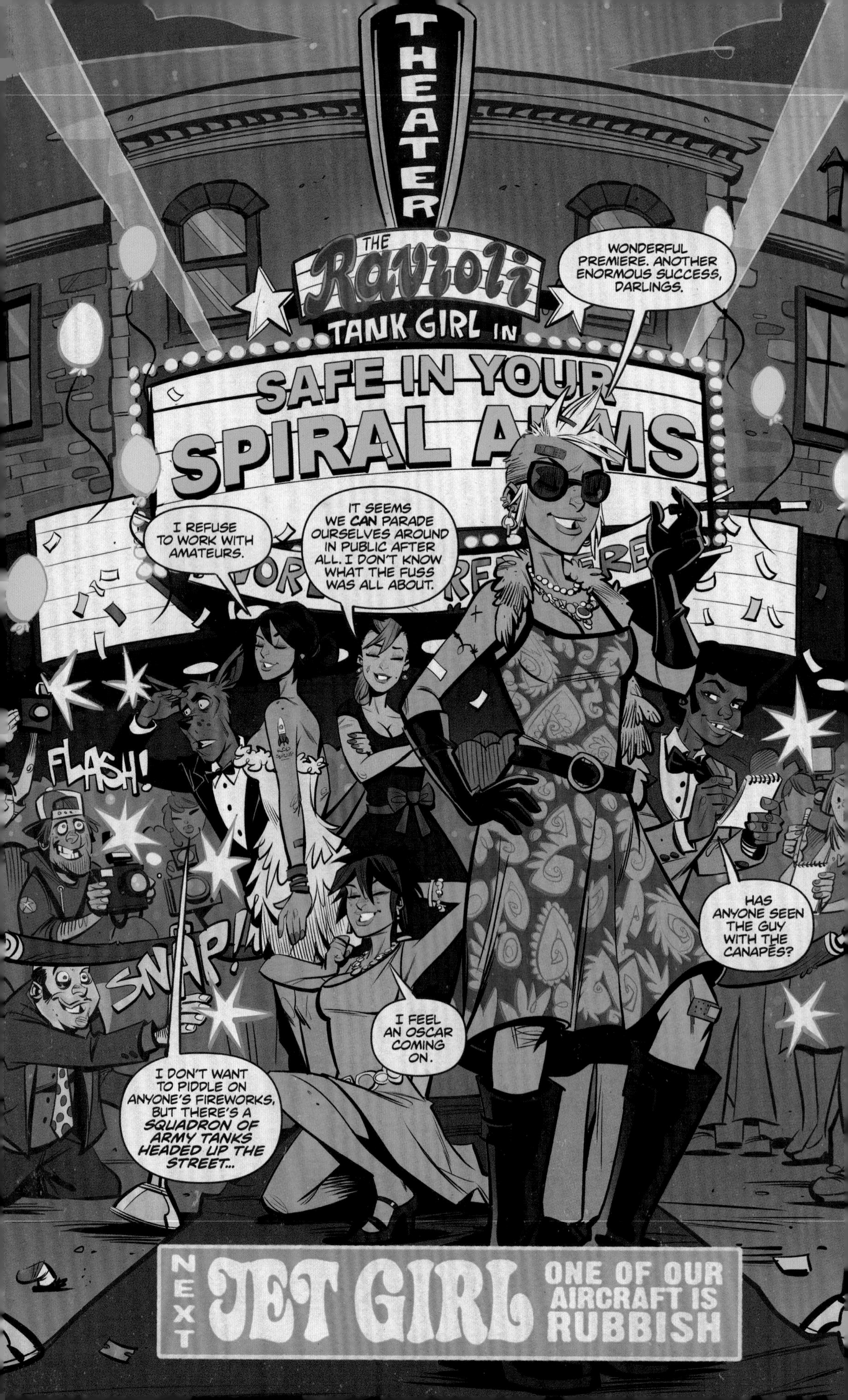
THEATER
THE Ravioli
TANK GIRL IN
SAFE IN YOUR SPIRAL ARMS
WONDERFUL PREMIERE. ANOTHER ENORMOUS SUCCESS, DARLINGS.
I REFUSE TO WORK WITH AMATEURS.
IT SEEMS WE CAN PARADE OURSELVES AROUND IN PUBLIC AFTER ALL. I DON'T KNOW WHAT THE FUSS WAS ALL ABOUT.
FLASH!
HAS ANYONE SEEN THE GUY WITH THE CANAPÉS?
SNAP!
I FEEL AN OSCAR COMING ON.
I DON'T WANT TO PIDDLE ON ANYONE'S FIREWORKS, BUT THERE'S A SQUADRON OF ARMY TANKS HEADED UP THE STREET...
NEXT JET GIRL ONE OF OUR AIRCRAFT IS RUBBISH

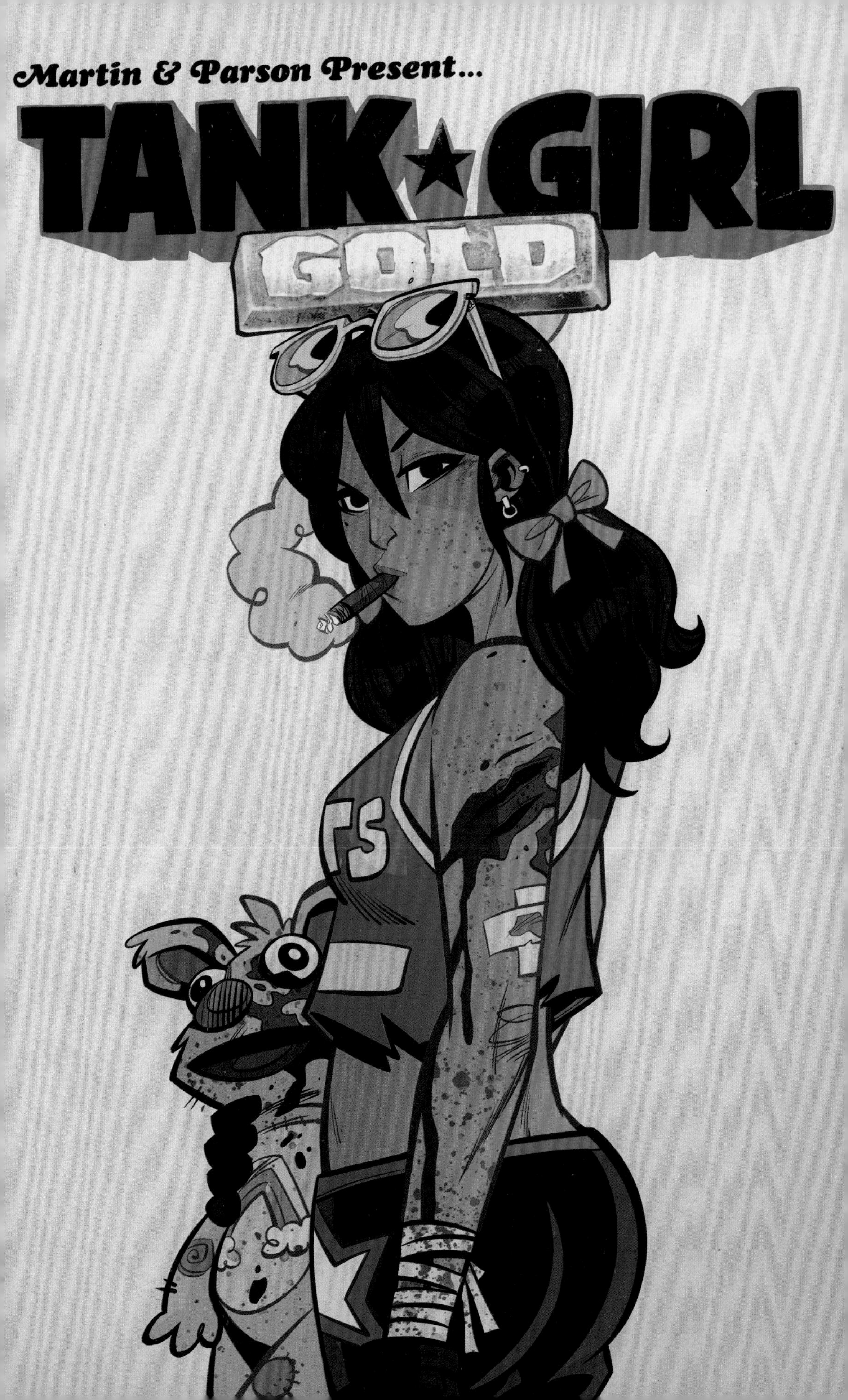
Martin & Parson Present...
TANK GIRL
GOLD

Hippie Destroyed by Flowers

You think that
the world owes
you something?
That it'll wipe
your arse for you
for the rest of
your life?
That you don't
have to do
anything, yet
you deserve
everything?

You are sorely
mistaken
my friend

Pick up your
shitty mess

Be kind

Be humble

Be happy

Or get
the fuck
off of my
planet

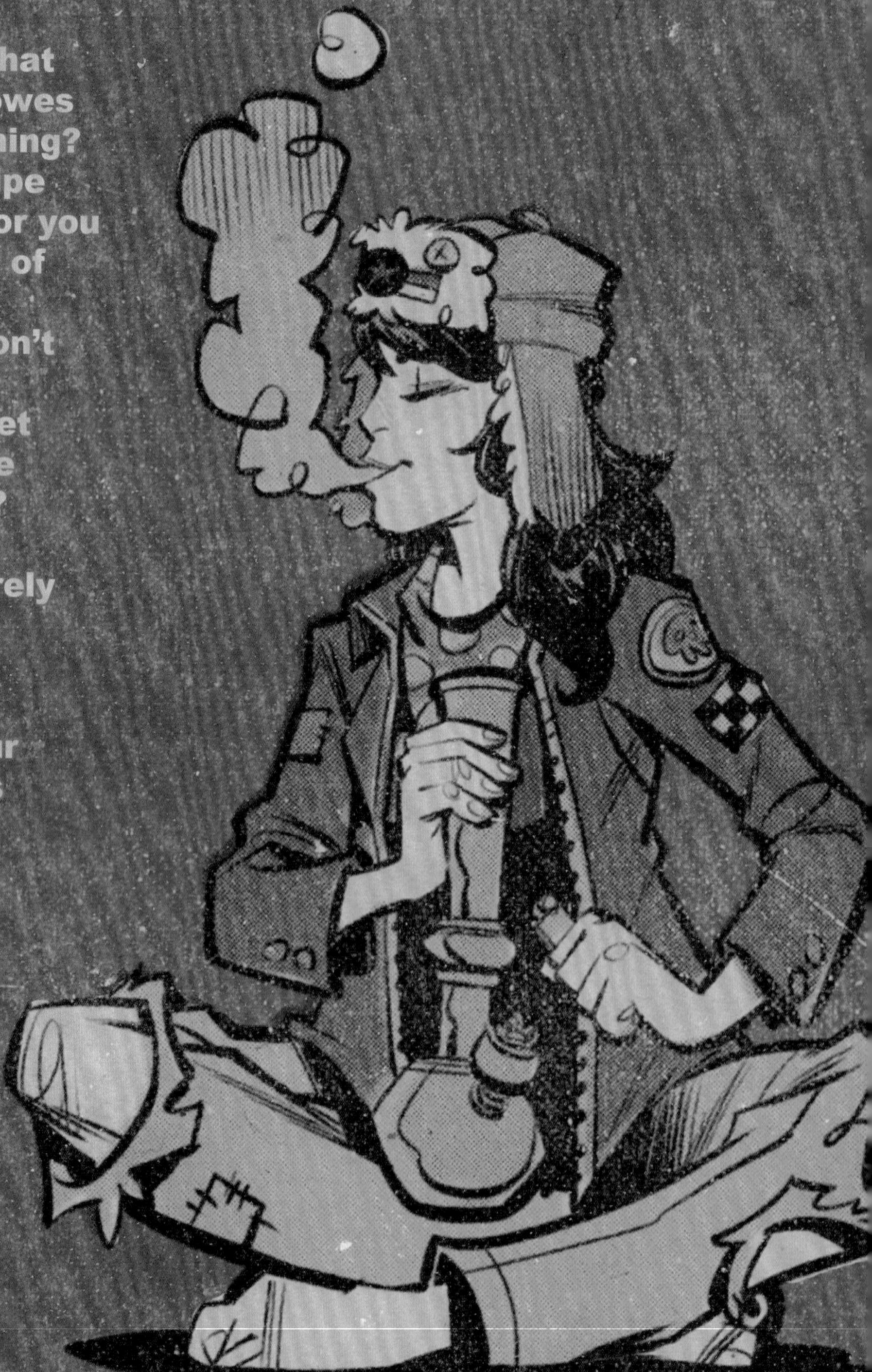

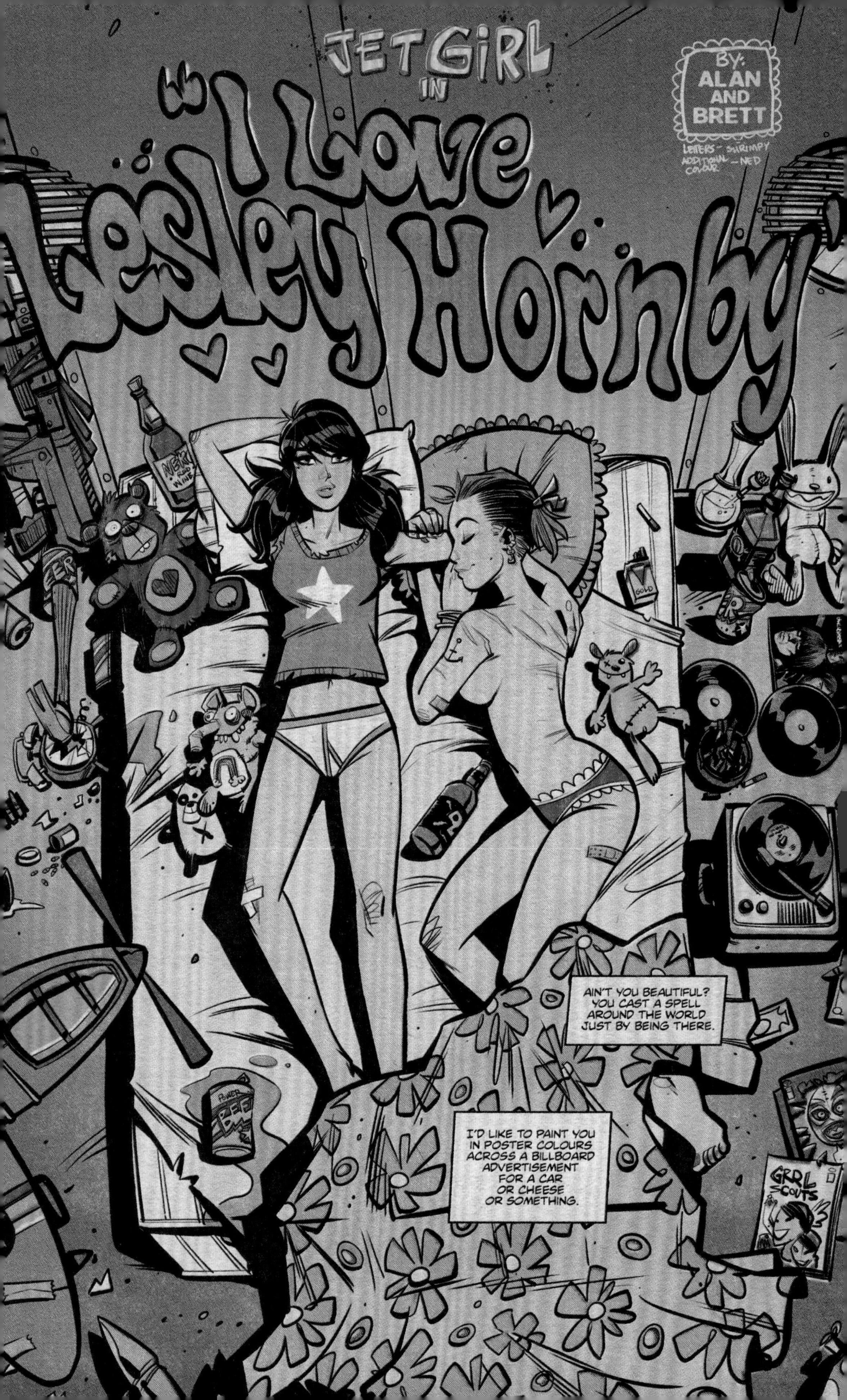

JET GIRL IN
"I Love Lesley Hornby"
By: ALAN AND BRETT
LETTERS - SHRIMPY
ADDITIONAL COLOUR - NED
AIN'T YOU BEAUTIFUL? YOU CAST A SPELL AROUND THE WORLD JUST BY BEING THERE.
I'D LIKE TO PAINT YOU IN POSTER COLOURS ACROSS A BILLBOARD ADVERTISEMENT FOR A CAR OR CHEESE OR SOMETHING.
GRRL SCOUTS

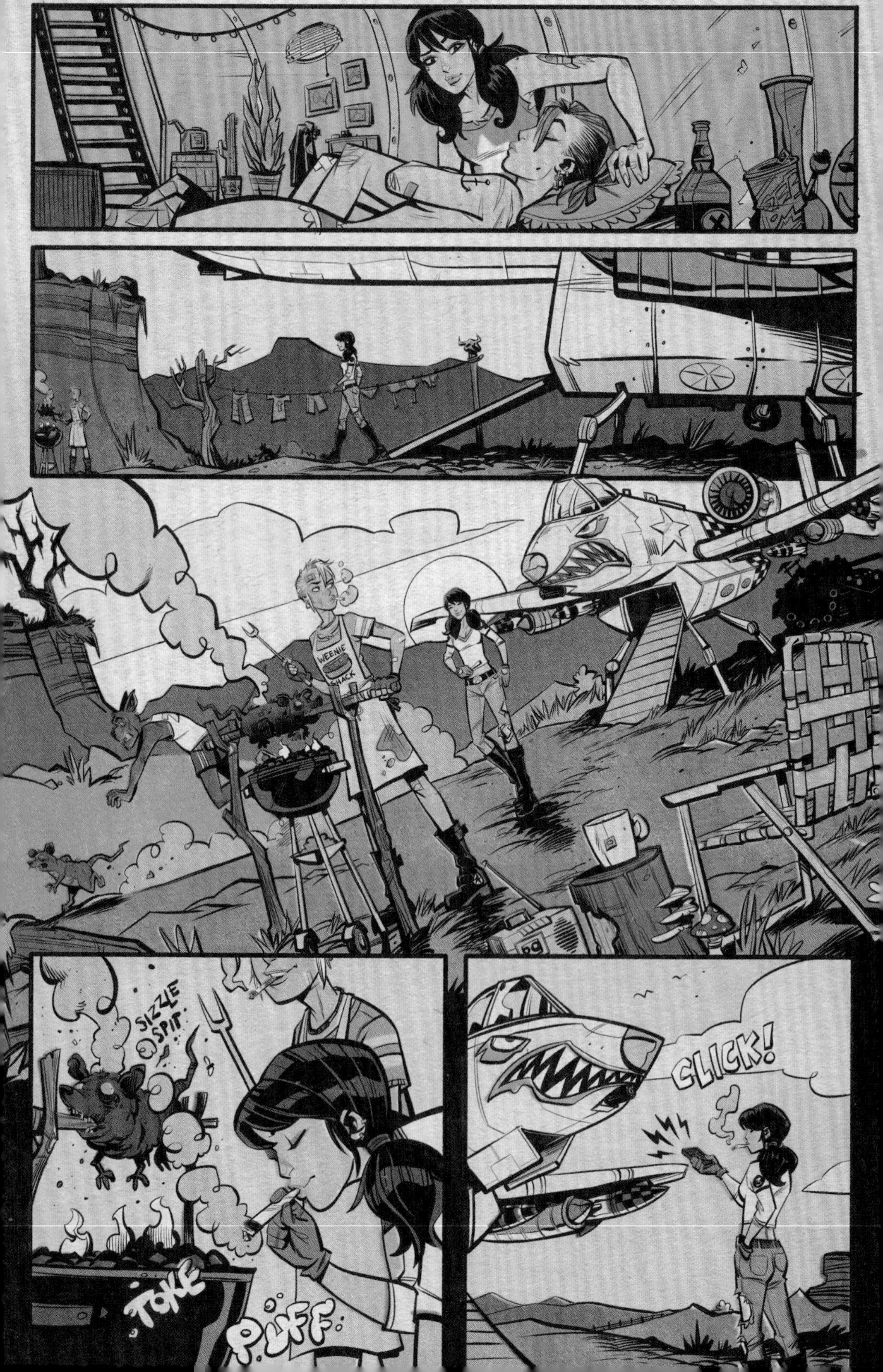
WEENIE SHACK
SIZZLE
SPIT
TOKE
PUFF
CLICK!

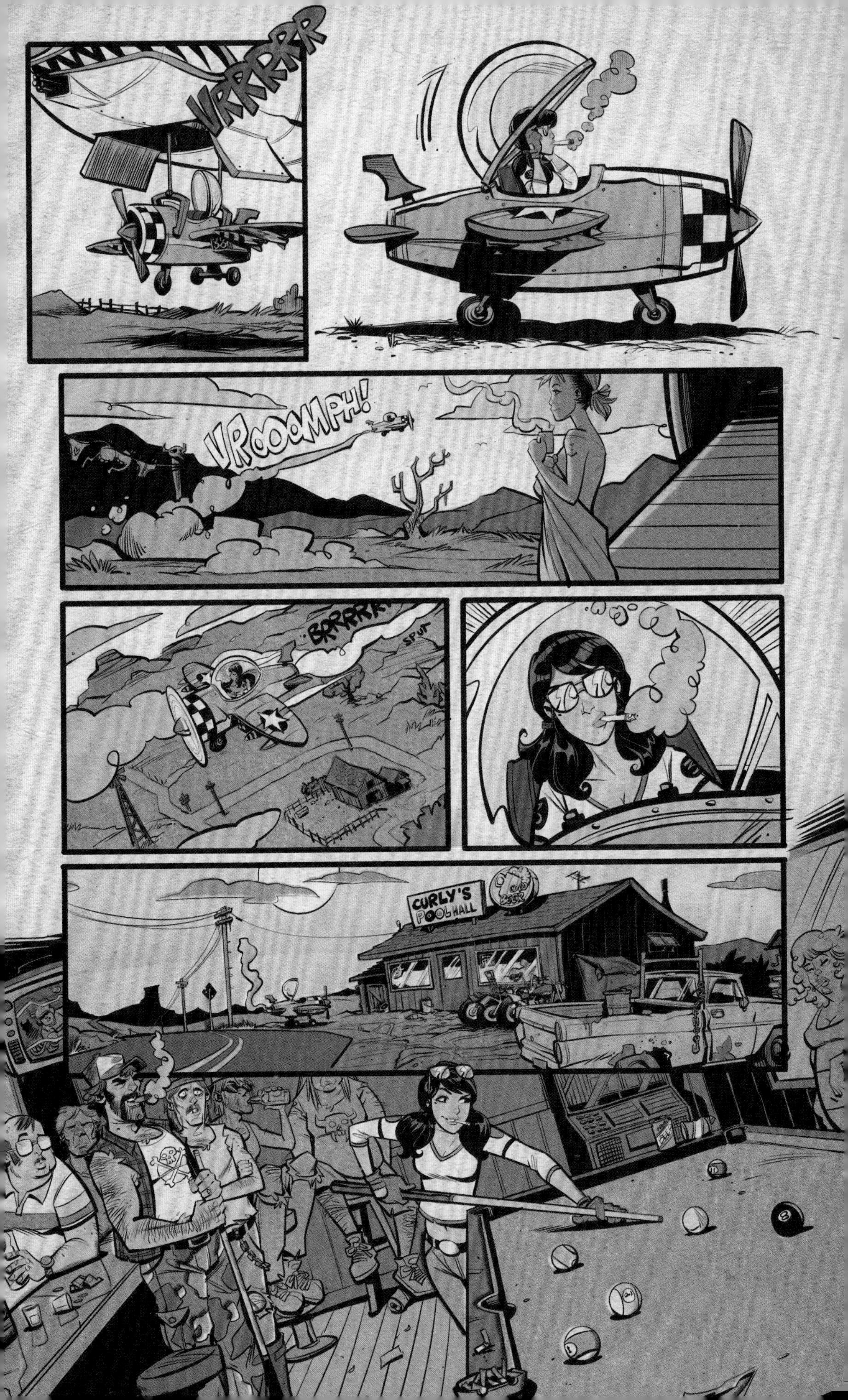
VRRRRR
VROOOMPH!
BRRRRR
SPUT
CURLY'S POOL HALL
COLD BEER

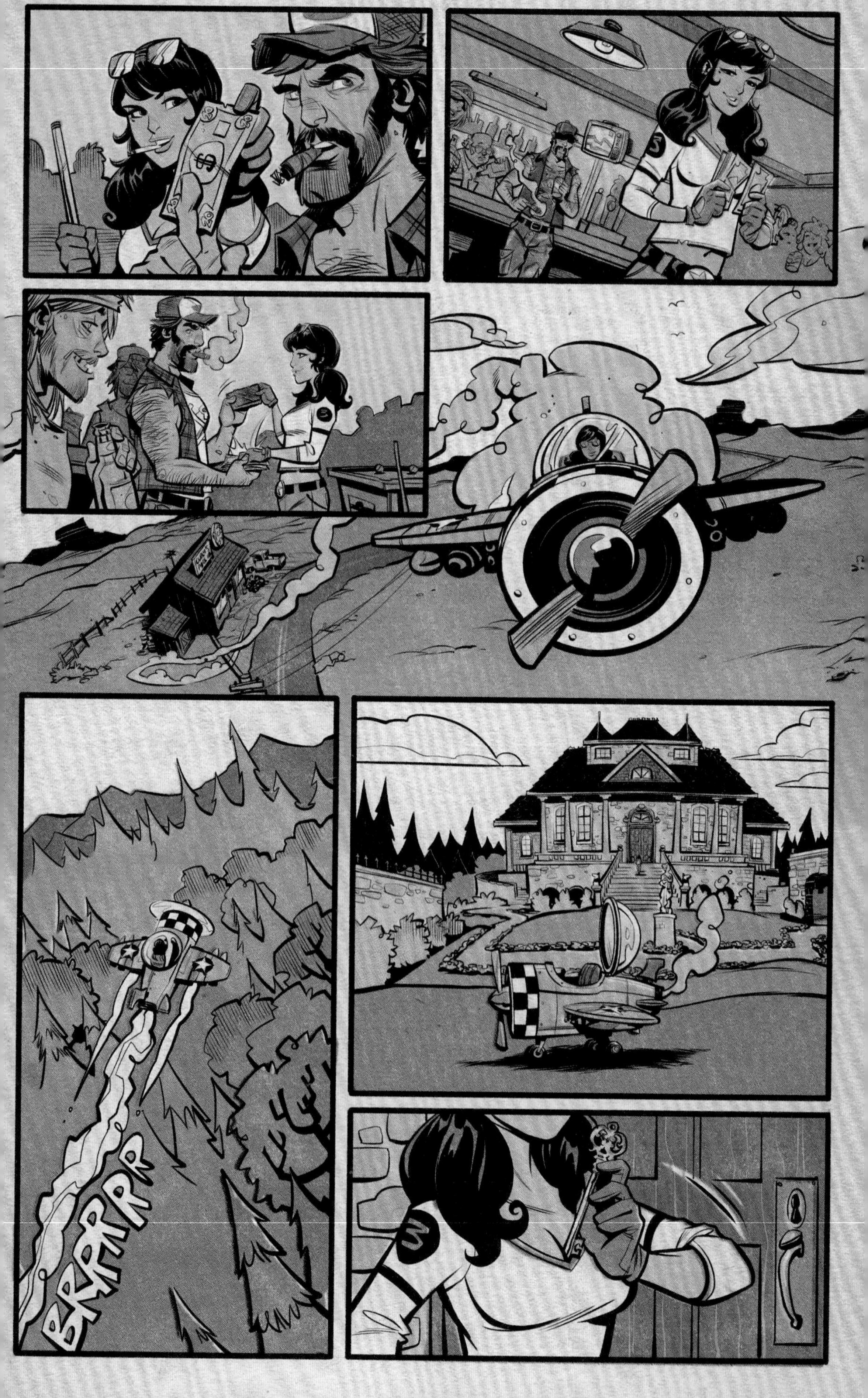
BRRRRR

CLUNK-
CREAK

CHUNK!

POP TARTS

MUNCHY!

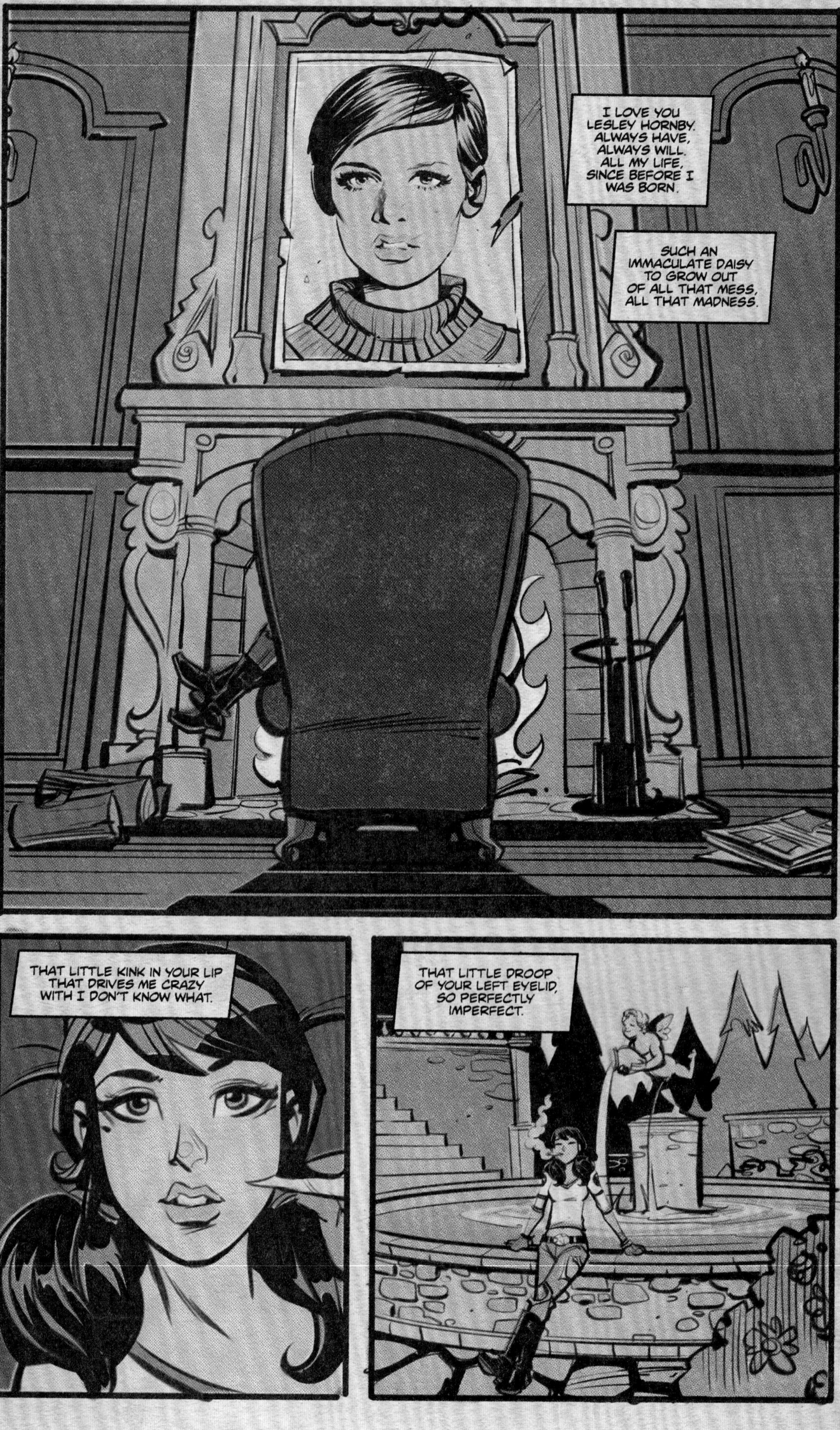
I LOVE YOU LESLEY HORNBY. ALWAYS HAVE, ALWAYS WILL. ALL MY LIFE, SINCE BEFORE I WAS BORN.
SUCH AN IMMACULATE DAISY TO GROW OUT OF ALL THAT MESS, ALL THAT MADNESS.
THAT LITTLE KINK IN YOUR LIP THAT DRIVES ME CRAZY WITH I DON'T KNOW WHAT.
THAT LITTLE DROOP OF YOUR LEFT EYELID, SO PERFECTLY IMPERFECT.

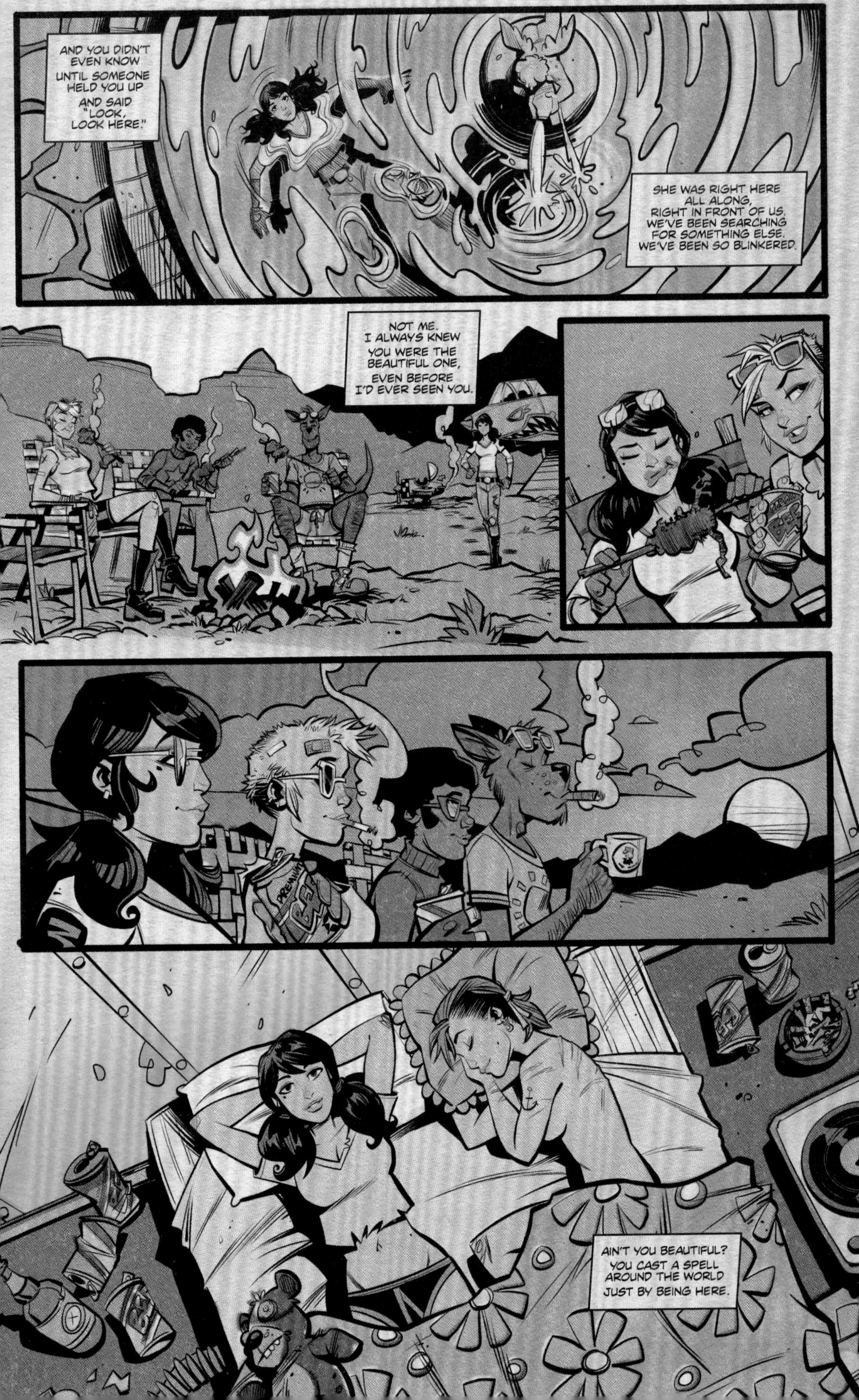
AND YOU DIDN'T EVEN KNOW UNTIL SOMEONE HELD YOU UP AND SAID "LOOK. LOOK HERE."
SHE WAS RIGHT HERE ALL ALONG, RIGHT IN FRONT OF US. WE'VE BEEN SEARCHING FOR SOMETHING ELSE. WE'VE BEEN SO BLINKERED.
NOT ME. I ALWAYS KNEW YOU WERE THE BEAUTIFUL ONE, EVEN BEFORE I'D EVER SEEN YOU.
AIN'T YOU BEAUTIFUL? YOU CAST A SPELL AROUND THE WORLD JUST BY BEING HERE.

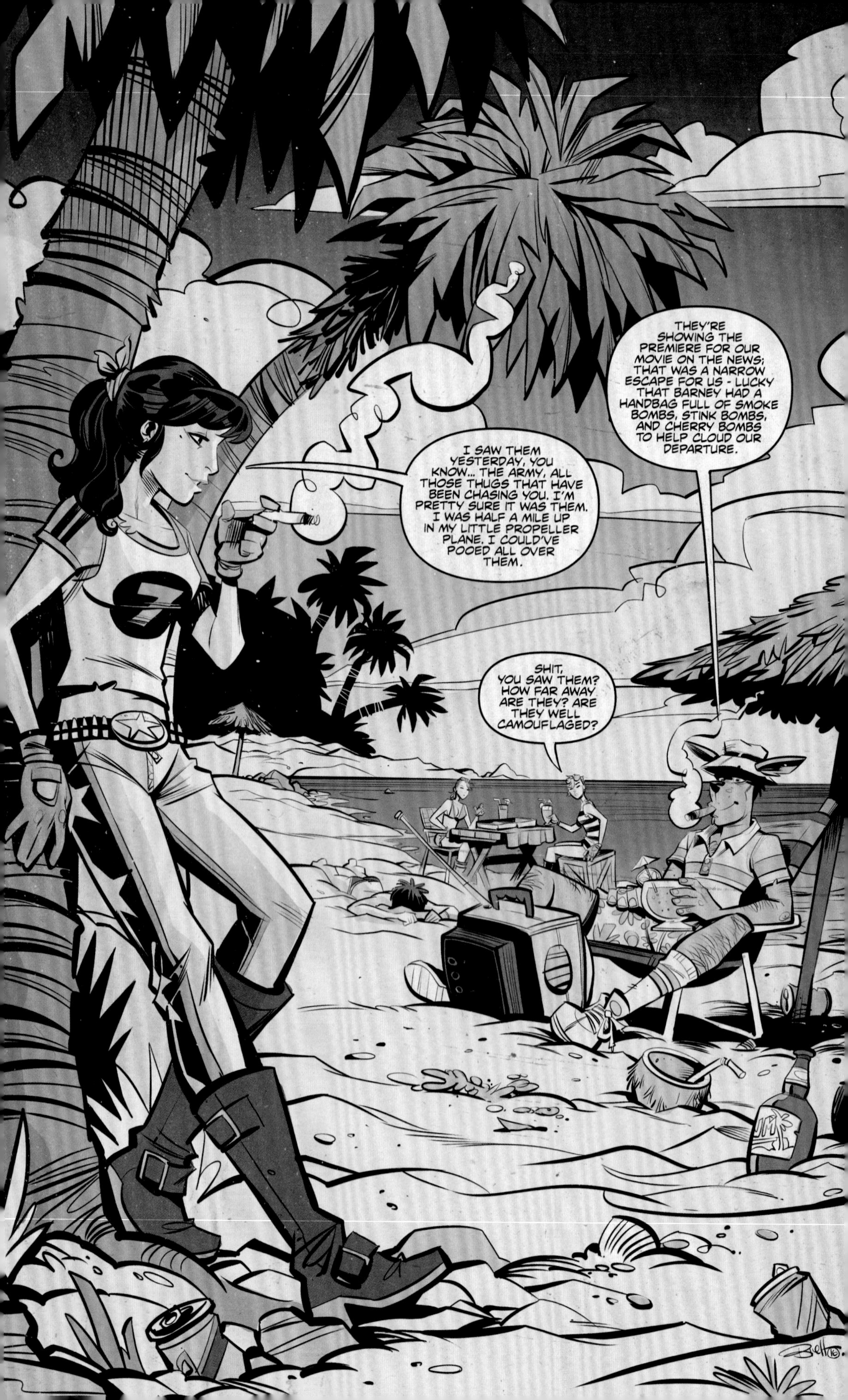

THEY'RE SHOWING THE PREMIERE FOR OUR MOVIE ON THE NEWS; THAT WAS A NARROW ESCAPE FOR US - LUCKY THAT BARNEY HAD A HANDBAG FULL OF SMOKE BOMBS, STINK BOMBS, AND CHERRY BOMBS TO HELP CLOUD OUR DEPARTURE.
I SAW THEM YESTERDAY, YOU KNOW... THE ARMY, ALL THOSE THUGS THAT HAVE BEEN CHASING YOU. I'M PRETTY SURE IT WAS THEM. I WAS HALF A MILE UP IN MY LITTLE PROPELLER PLANE. I COULD'VE POOED ALL OVER THEM.
SHIT, YOU SAW THEM? HOW FAR AWAY ARE THEY? ARE THEY WELL CAMOUFLAGED?

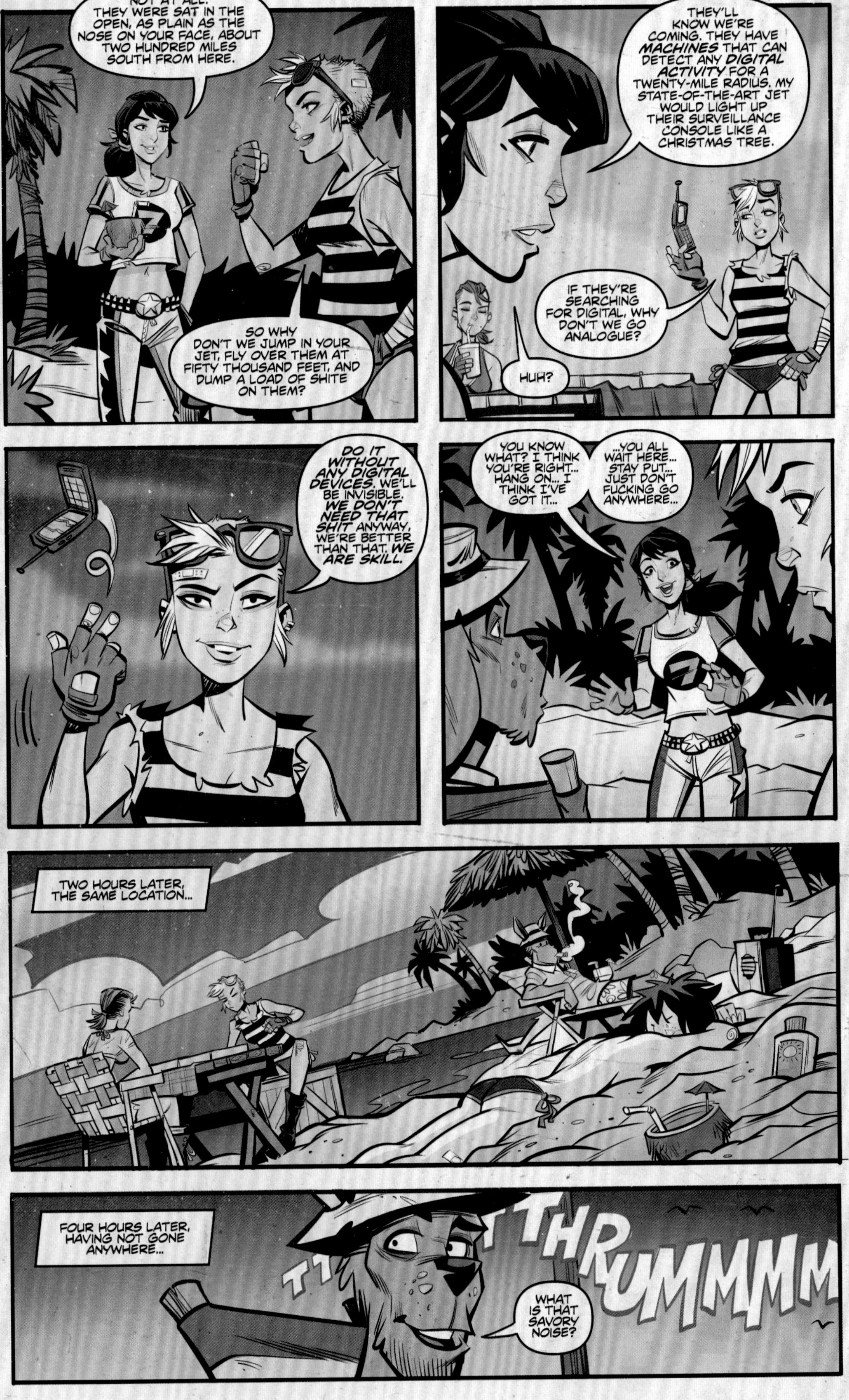
NOT AT ALL. THEY WERE SAT IN THE OPEN, AS PLAIN AS THE NOSE ON YOUR FACE, ABOUT TWO HUNDRED MILES SOUTH FROM HERE.
SO WHY DON'T WE JUMP IN YOUR JET, FLY OVER THEM AT FIFTY THOUSAND FEET, AND DUMP A LOAD OF SHITE ON THEM?
THEY'LL KNOW WE'RE COMING. THEY HAVE MACHINES THAT CAN DETECT ANY DIGITAL ACTIVITY FOR A TWENTY-MILE RADIUS. MY STATE-OF-THE-ART JET WOULD LIGHT UP THEIR SURVEILLANCE CONSOLE LIKE A CHRISTMAS TREE.
IF THEY'RE SEARCHING FOR DIGITAL, WHY DON'T WE GO ANALOGUE?
HUH?
DO IT WITHOUT ANY DIGITAL DEVICES. WE'LL BE INVISIBLE. WE DON'T NEED THAT SHIT ANYWAY, WE'RE BETTER THAN THAT. WE ARE SKILL.
YOU KNOW WHAT? I THINK YOU'RE RIGHT... HANG ON... I THINK I'VE GOT IT...
...YOU ALL WAIT HERE... STAY PUT... JUST DON'T FUCKING GO ANYWHERE...
TWO HOURS LATER, THE SAME LOCATION...
FOUR HOURS LATER, HAVING NOT GONE ANYWHERE...
TTTTHRUMMMMM
WHAT IS THAT SAVORY NOISE?

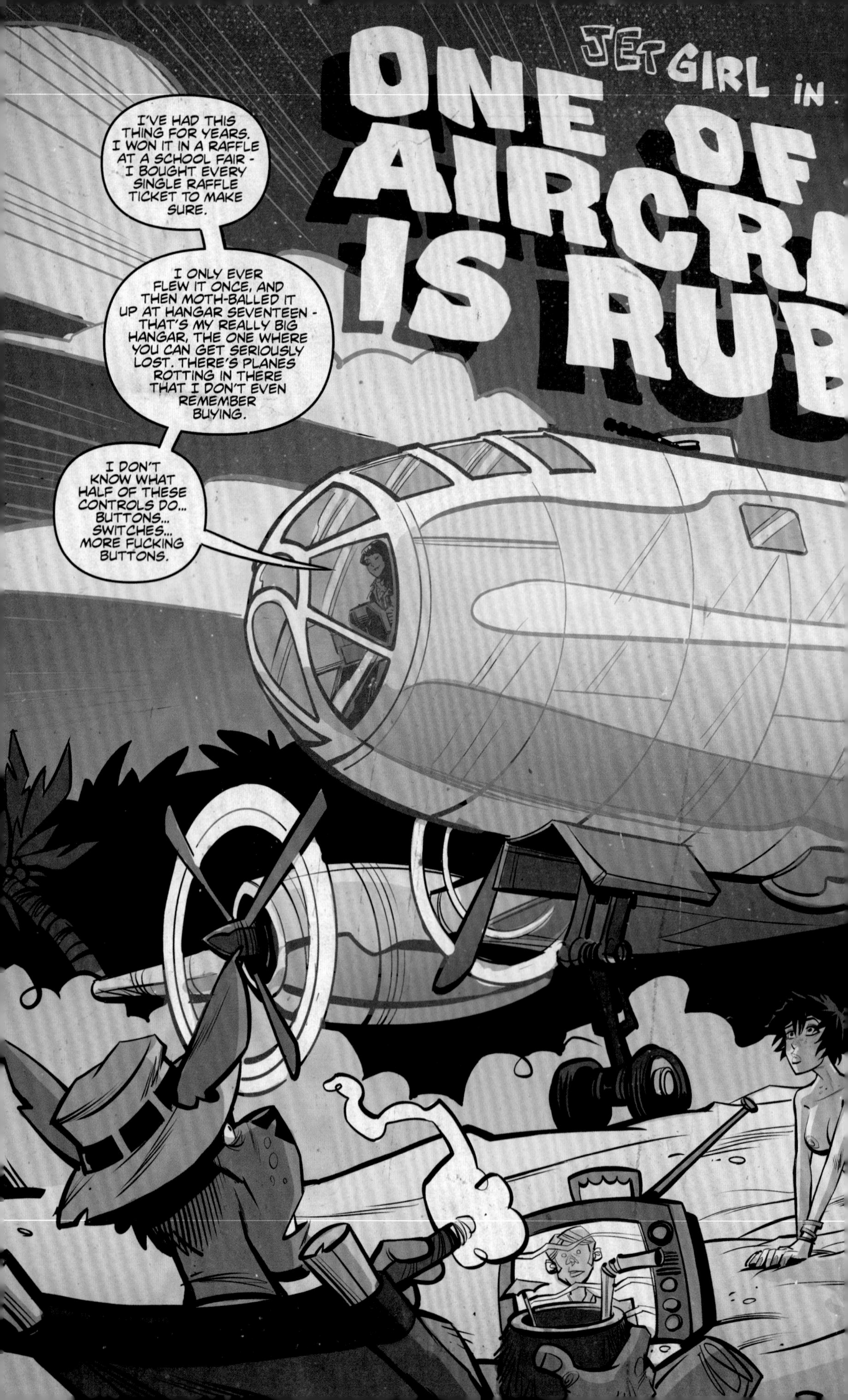
JET GIRL IN
ONE OF AIRCR IS RUB
I'VE HAD THIS THING FOR YEARS. I WON IT IN A RAFFLE AT A SCHOOL FAIR - I BOUGHT EVERY SINGLE RAFFLE TICKET TO MAKE SURE.
I ONLY EVER FLEW IT ONCE, AND THEN MOTH-BALLED IT UP AT HANGAR SEVENTEEN - THAT'S MY REALLY BIG HANGAR, THE ONE WHERE YOU CAN GET SERIOUSLY LOST. THERE'S PLANES ROTTING IN THERE THAT I DON'T EVEN REMEMBER BUYING.
I DON'T KNOW WHAT HALF OF THESE CONTROLS DO... BUTTONS... SWITCHES... MORE FUCKING BUTTONS.

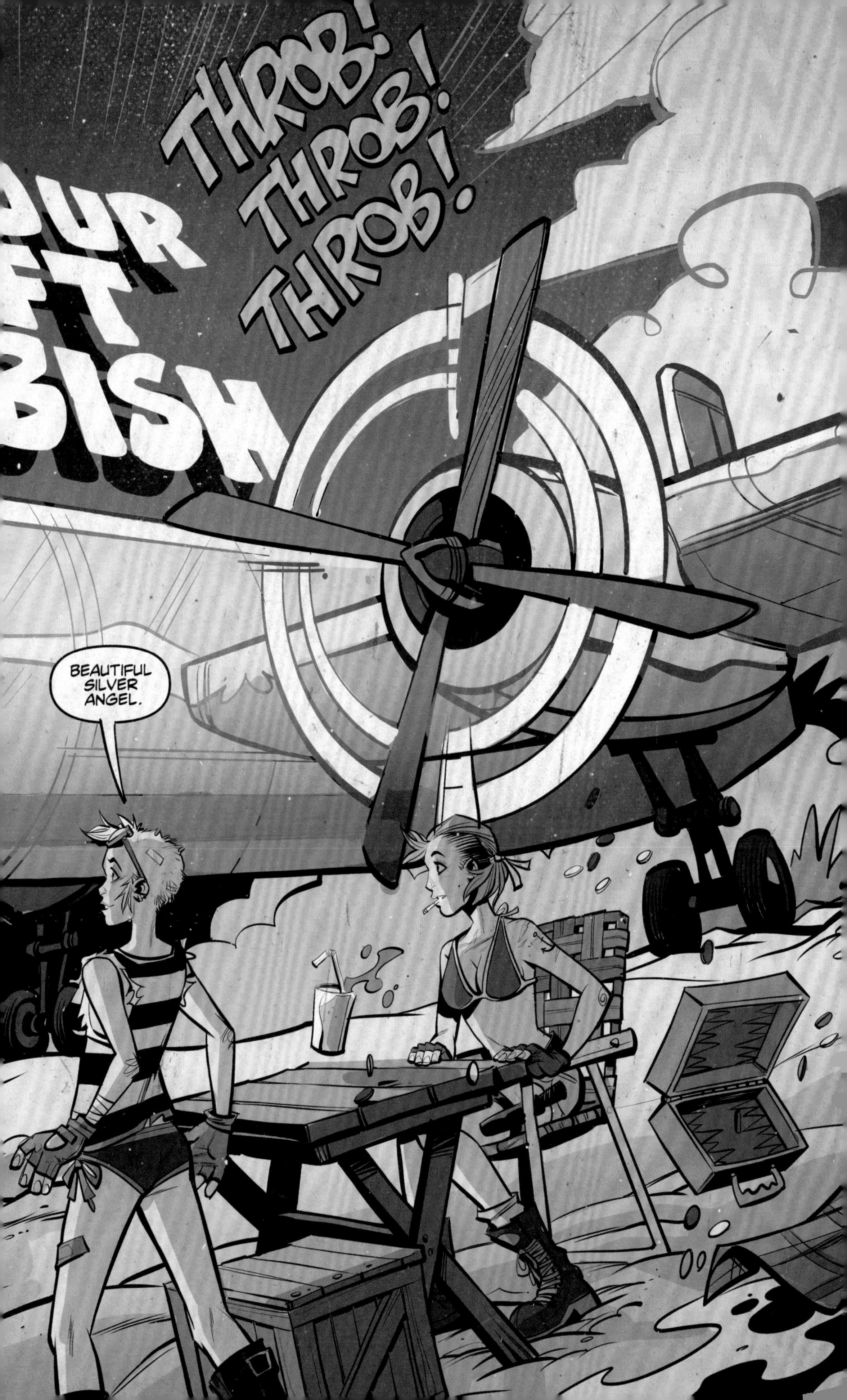
THROB! THROB! THROB!
BEAUTIFUL SILVER ANGEL.

THIS IS IT. THIS IS MY *BIG PLAN*. THE *BOEING B-29 SUPERFORTRESS*. THE MOST GLORIOUS, HIGH ALTITUDE STRATEGIC BOMBER OF THE TWENTIETH CENTURY. IT HAS A PRESSURIZED CABIN, FOUR REMOTELY CONTROLLED GUN TURRETS, AND IS PACKED WITH NINTEEN-FORTY-FOUR-CUTTING-EDGE-NON-DIGITAL TECHNOLOGY.

IT WAS ONE OF THESE THAT DROPPED THE ATOMIC BOMB - ENOLA GAY, "YOU SHOULD'VE STAYED AT HOME YESTERDAY". IS THAT WHAT YOU'VE GOT IN MIND NOW?

I WAS GONNA STUFF THE NOSE OF THIS CRAPPY LITTLE *JAPANESE SUICIDE* JET WITH PENTAERYTHRITOL TETRANITRATE PLASTIC, LAUNCH IT FROM THE SUPERFORTRESS VIA RADIO CONTROL, AND *SAIL IT STRAIGHT INTO THE MIDDLE OF THE FUCKERS*.

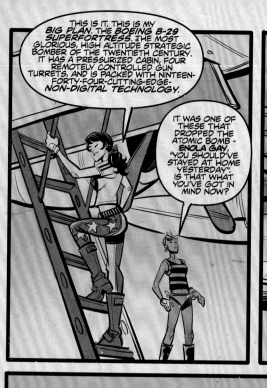

THAT'S A GREAT *BIG PLAN*. YOU TAKE SUB GIRL IN THE BOMBER TO HELP YOU DROP YOUR LOAD. THEN I'LL BRING ON THE GROUND ASSAULT WITH BOOGA AND BARNEY, FINISH THEM OFF WITH SOME SMALL NUKES AND DIRTY BOMBS.

ROGER, SPLODGER.

READY, BABY, LET HER RIP!

THROAR!

BUGGERING BOMBERS.

WHAT A MONSTER MACHINE! THIS IS GONNA BE BRILLIANTLY MESSY!

NURSE!

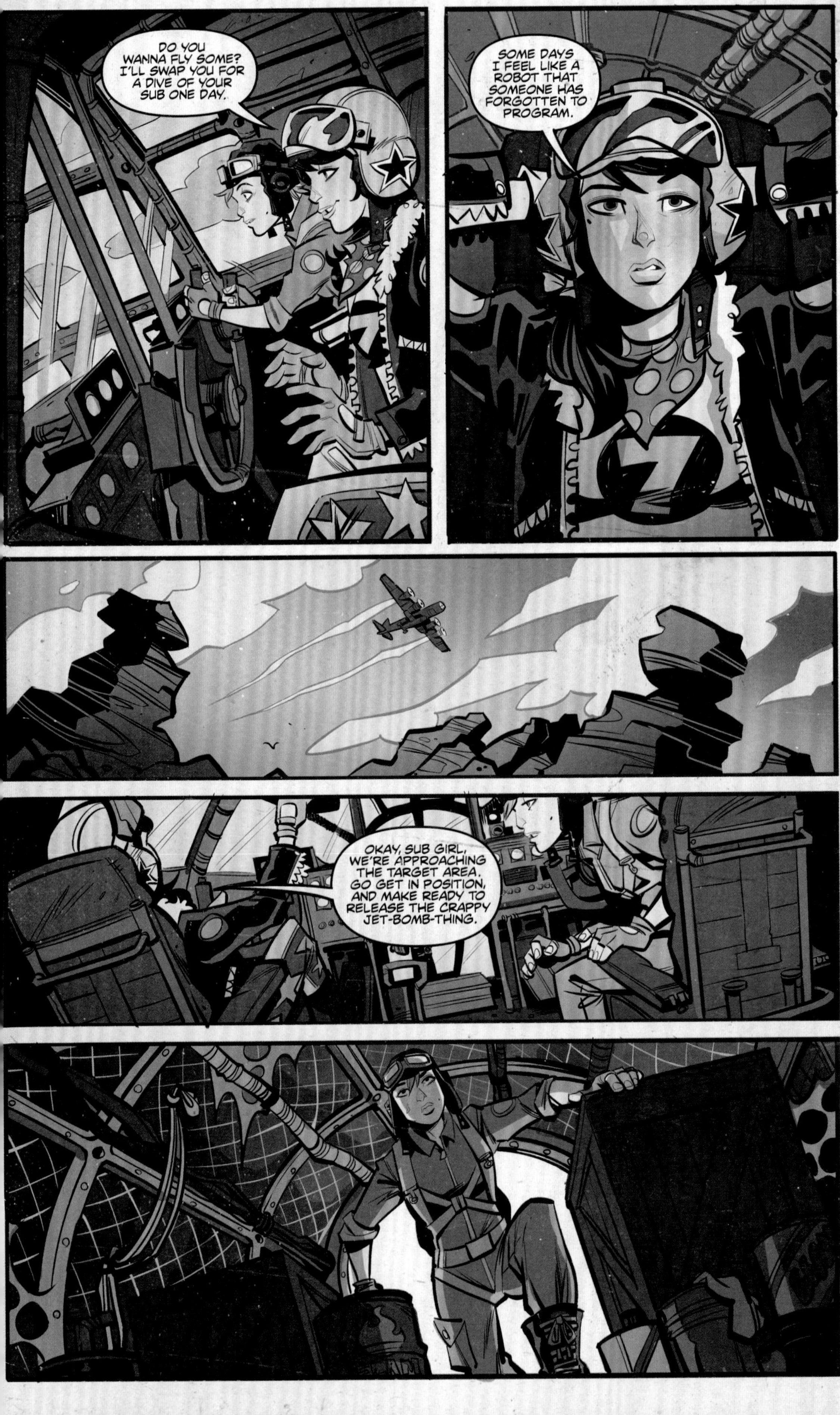
DO YOU WANNA FLY SOME? I'LL SWAP YOU FOR A DIVE OF YOUR SUB ONE DAY.
SOME DAYS I FEEL LIKE A ROBOT THAT SOMEONE HAS FORGOTTEN TO PROGRAM.
OKAY, SUB GIRL, WE'RE APPROACHING THE TARGET AREA. GO GET IN POSITION, AND MAKE READY TO RELEASE THE CRAPPY JET-BOMB-THING.

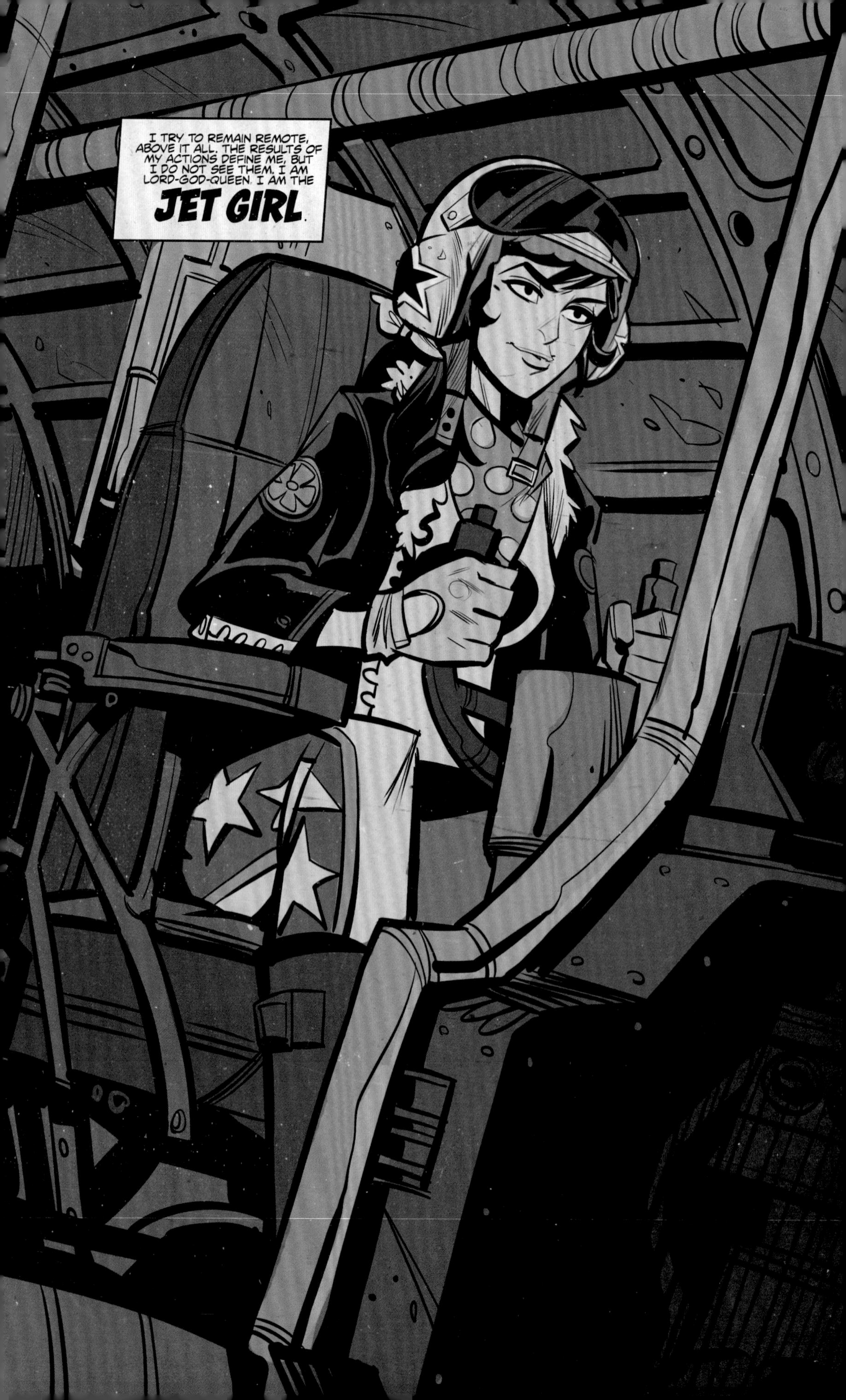
I TRY TO REMAIN REMOTE, ABOVE IT ALL. THE RESULTS OF MY ACTIONS DEFINE ME, BUT I DO NOT SEE THEM. I AM LORD-GOD-QUEEN. I AM THE
JET GIRL.

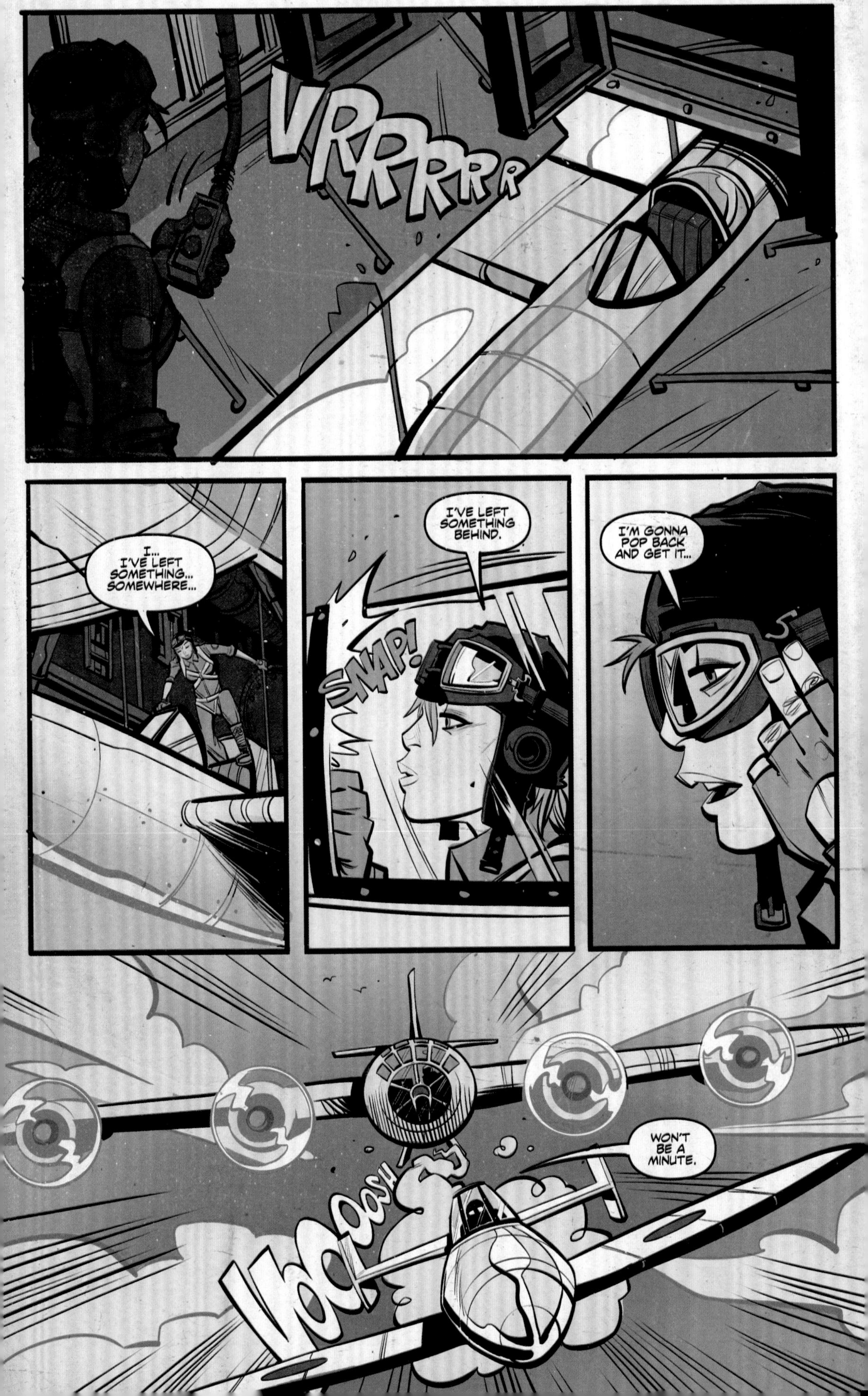
VRRRRRR
I... I'VE LEFT SOMETHING... SOMEWHERE...
I'VE LEFT SOMETHING BEHIND.
SNAP!
I'M GONNA POP BACK AND GET IT...
WON'T BE A MINUTE.
WOOOOSH

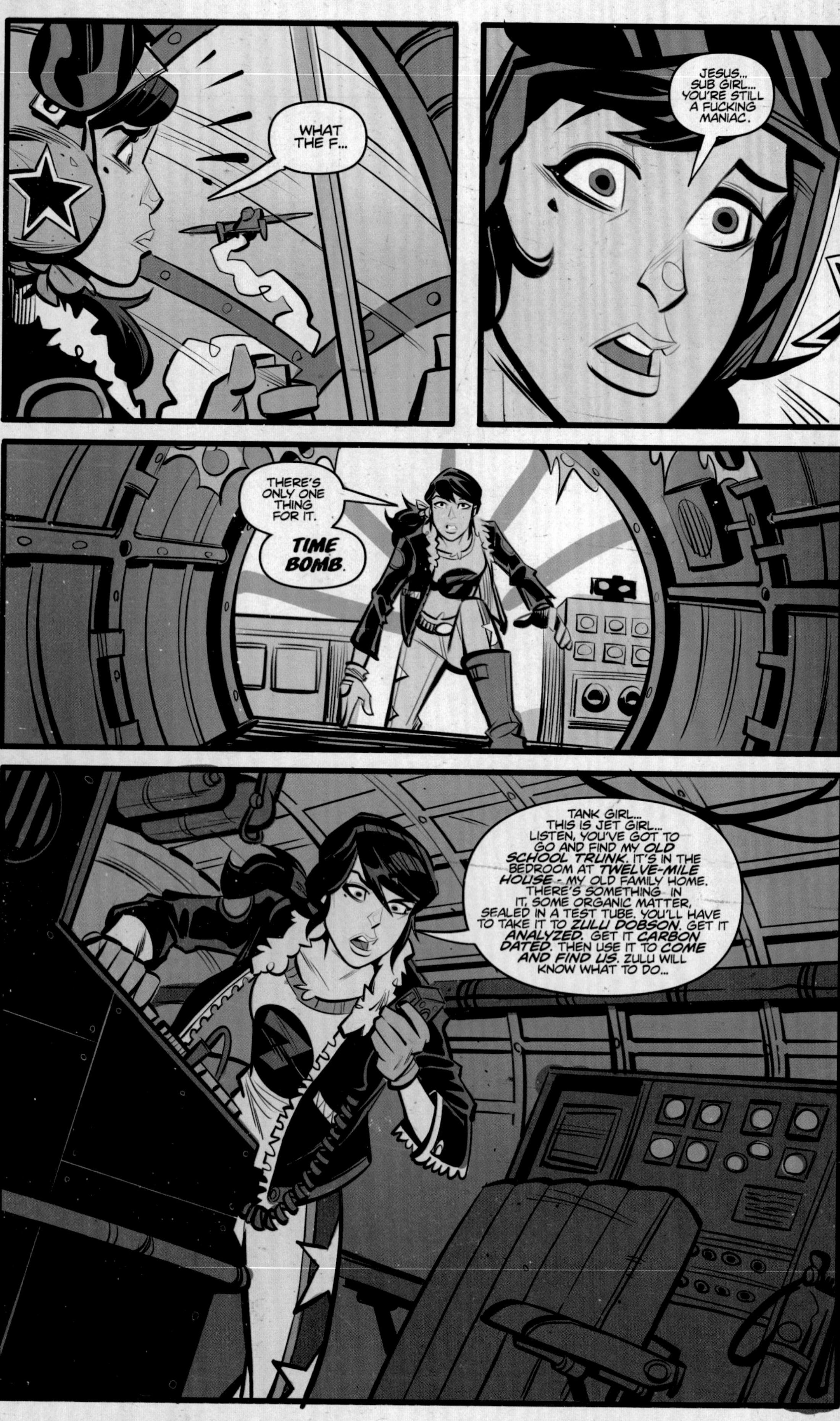
WHAT THE F...
JESUS... SUB GIRL... YOU'RE STILL A FUCKING MANIAC.
THERE'S ONLY ONE THING FOR IT.
TIME BOMB.
TANK GIRL... THIS IS JET GIRL... LISTEN, YOU'VE GOT TO GO AND FIND MY OLD SCHOOL TRUNK. IT'S IN THE BEDROOM AT TWELVE-MILE HOUSE - MY OLD FAMILY HOME. THERE'S SOMETHING IN IT, SOME ORGANIC MATTER, SEALED IN A TEST TUBE. YOU'LL HAVE TO TAKE IT TO ZULU DOBSON. GET IT ANALYZED. GET IT CARBON DATED. THEN USE IT TO COME AND FIND US. ZULU WILL KNOW WHAT TO DO...

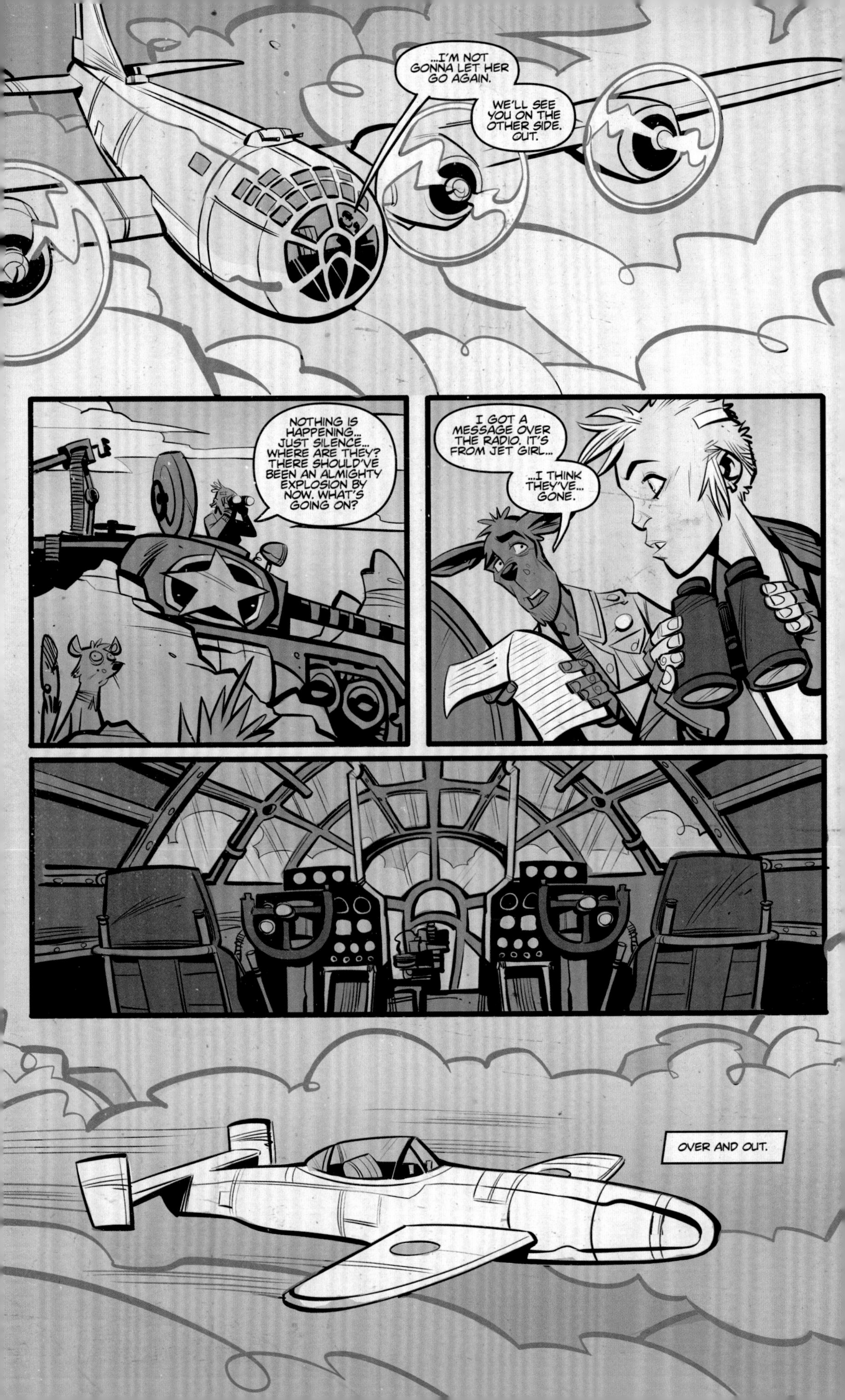
...I'M NOT GONNA LET HER GO AGAIN.
WE'LL SEE YOU ON THE OTHER SIDE. OUT.
NOTHING IS HAPPENING... JUST SILENCE... WHERE ARE THEY? THERE SHOULD'VE BEEN AN ALMIGHTY EXPLOSION BY NOW. WHAT'S GOING ON?
I GOT A MESSAGE OVER THE RADIO. IT'S FROM JET GIRL...
...I THINK THEY'VE... GONE.
OVER AND OUT.

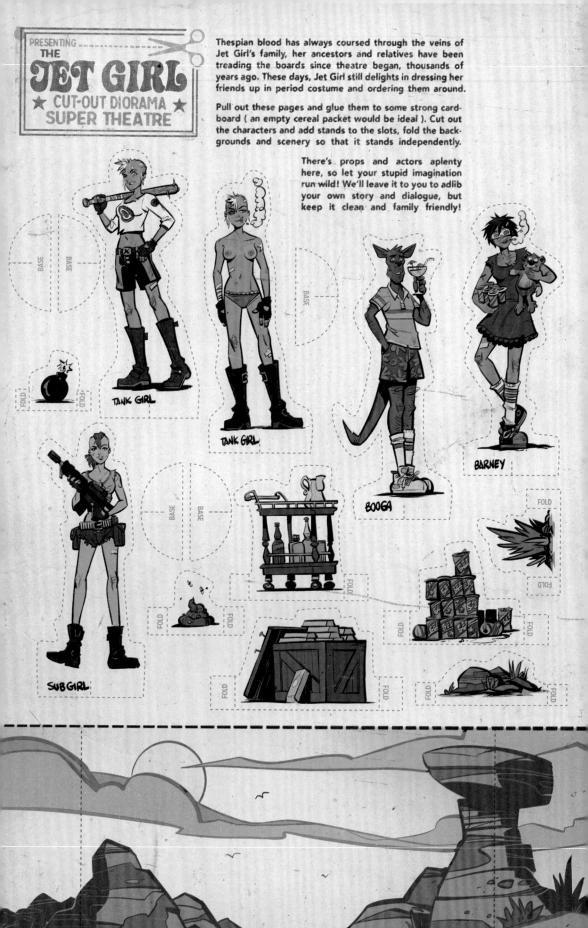

PRESENTING
THE JET GIRL
★ CUT-OUT DIORAMA ★ SUPER THEATRE

Thespian blood has always coursed through the veins of Jet Girl's family, her ancestors and relatives have been treading the boards since theatre began, thousands of years ago. These days, Jet Girl still delights in dressing her friends up in period costume and ordering them around.

Pull out these pages and glue them to some strong cardboard (an empty cereal packet would be ideal). Cut out the characters and add stands to the slots, fold the backgrounds and scenery so that it stands independently.

There's props and actors aplenty here, so let your stupid imagination run wild! We'll leave it to you to adlib your own story and dialogue, but keep it clean and family friendly!

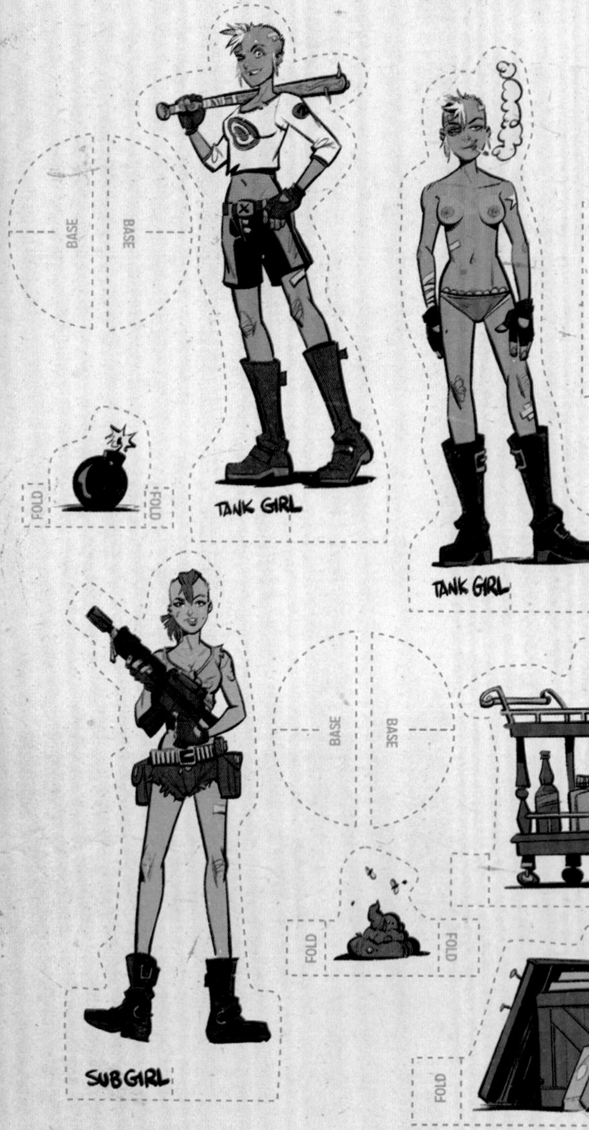
BASE
BASE
FOLD
FOLD
TANK GIRL
TANK GIRL
BASE
BASE
BASE
FOLD
FOLD
FOLD
FOLD
SUBGIRL

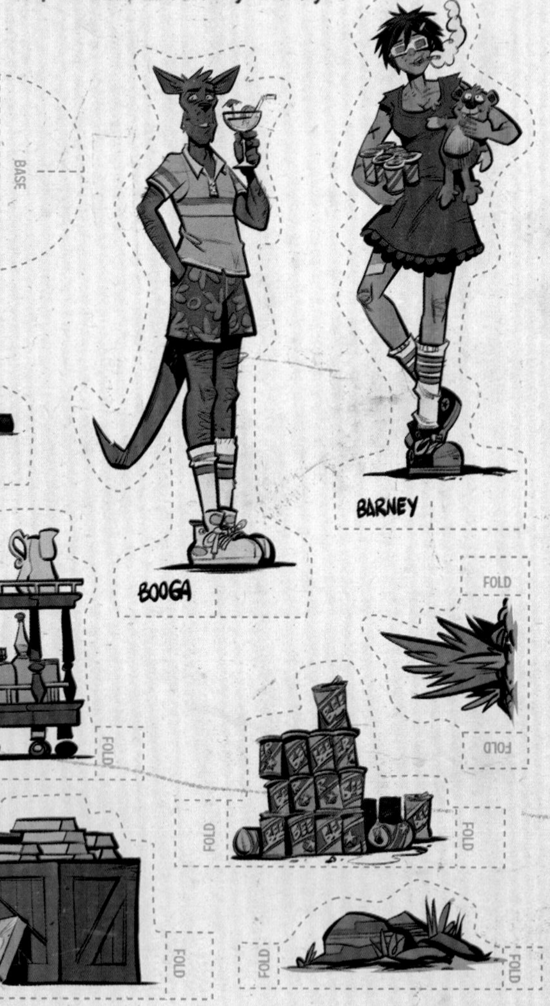
BOOGA
BARNEY
FOLD
FOLD
FOLD
FOLD
FOLD
FOLD
FOLD

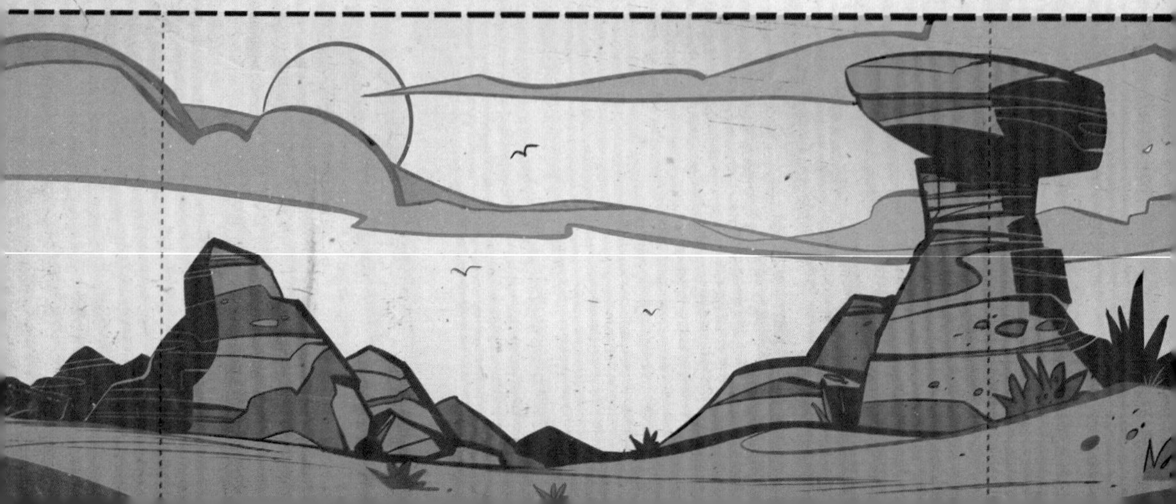

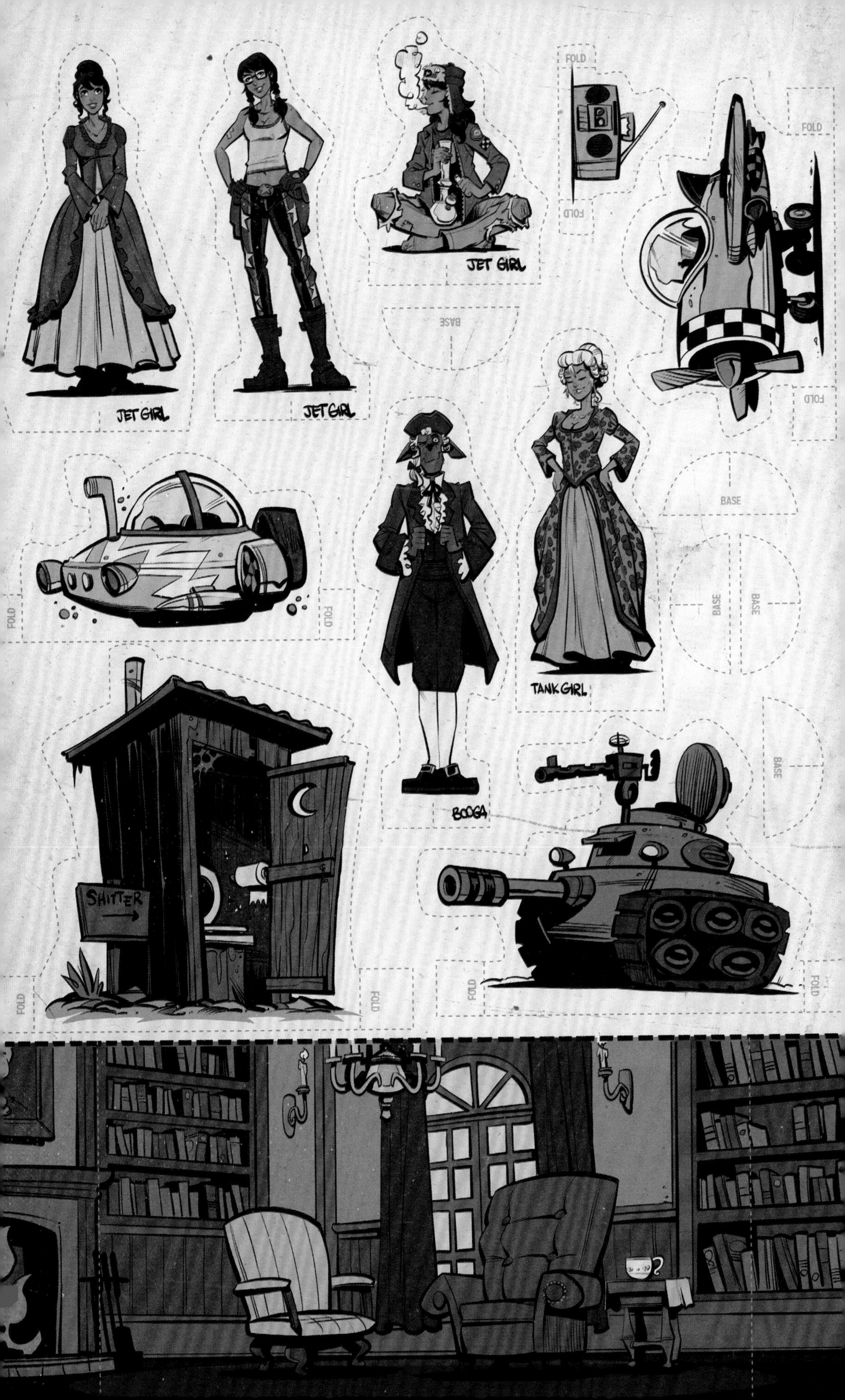
FOLD
FOLD
FOLD
JET GIRL
BASE
JET GIRL
JET GIRL
FOLD
FOLD
FOLD
BASE
BASE
BASE
TANK GIRL
BOOGA
BASE
SHITTER
FOLD
FOLD
FOLD
FOLD

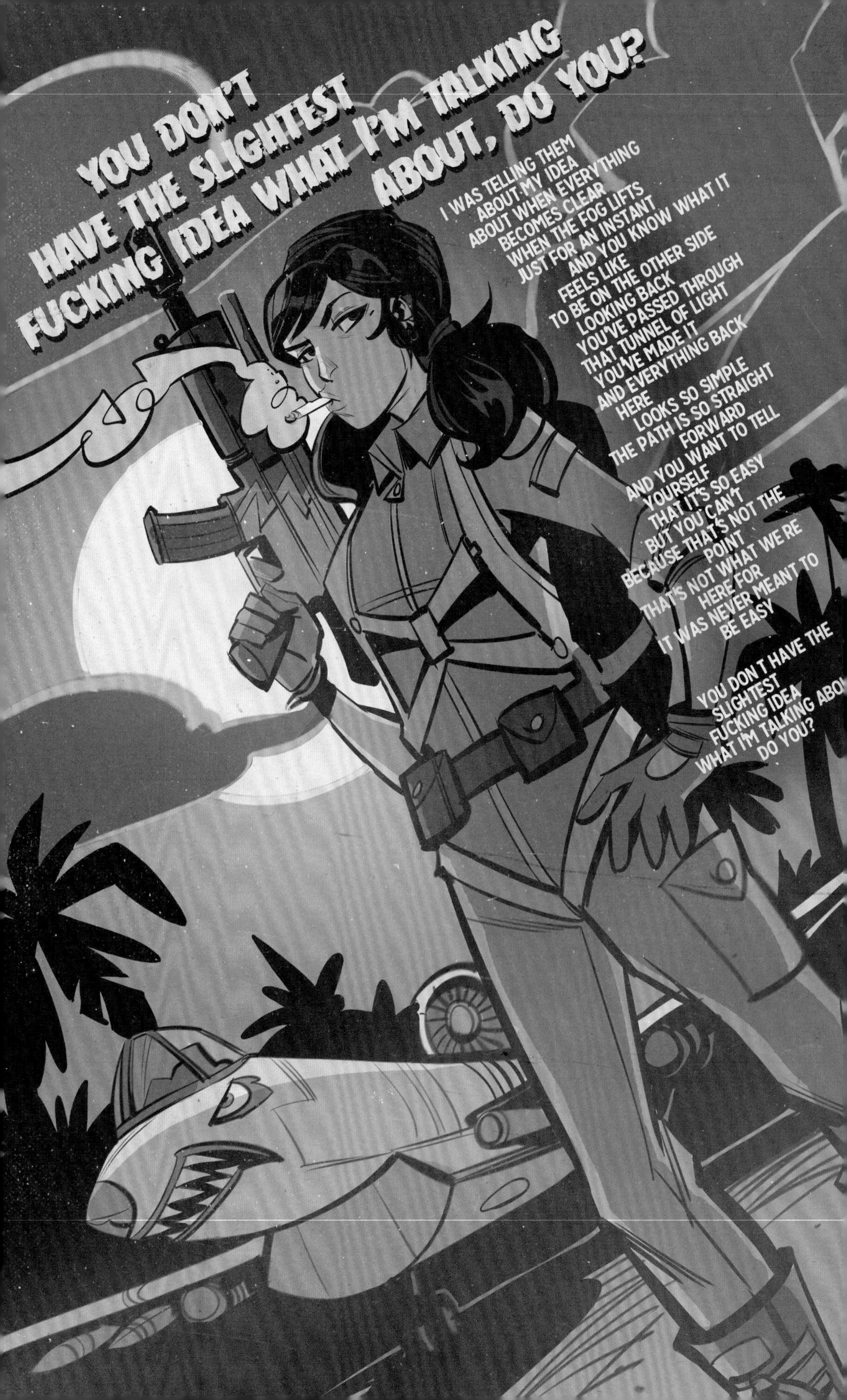
YOU DON'T HAVE THE SLIGHTEST FUCKING IDEA WHAT I'M TALKING ABOUT, DO YOU?
I WAS TELLING THEM
ABOUT MY IDEA
ABOUT WHEN EVERYTHING
BECOMES CLEAR
WHEN THE FOG LIFTS
JUST FOR AN INSTANT
AND YOU KNOW WHAT IT
FEELS LIKE
TO BE ON THE OTHER SIDE
LOOKING BACK
YOU'VE PASSED THROUGH
THAT TUNNEL OF LIGHT
YOU'VE MADE IT
AND EVERYTHING BACK
HERE
LOOKS SO SIMPLE
THE PATH IS SO STRAIGHT
FORWARD
AND YOU WANT TO TELL
YOURSELF
THAT IT'S SO EASY
BUT YOU CAN'T
BECAUSE THAT'S NOT THE
POINT
THAT'S NOT WHAT WE RE
HERE FOR
IT WAS NEVER MEANT TO
BE EASY
YOU DON T HAVE THE
SLIGHTEST
FUCKING IDEA
WHAT I'M TALKING ABO
DO YOU?

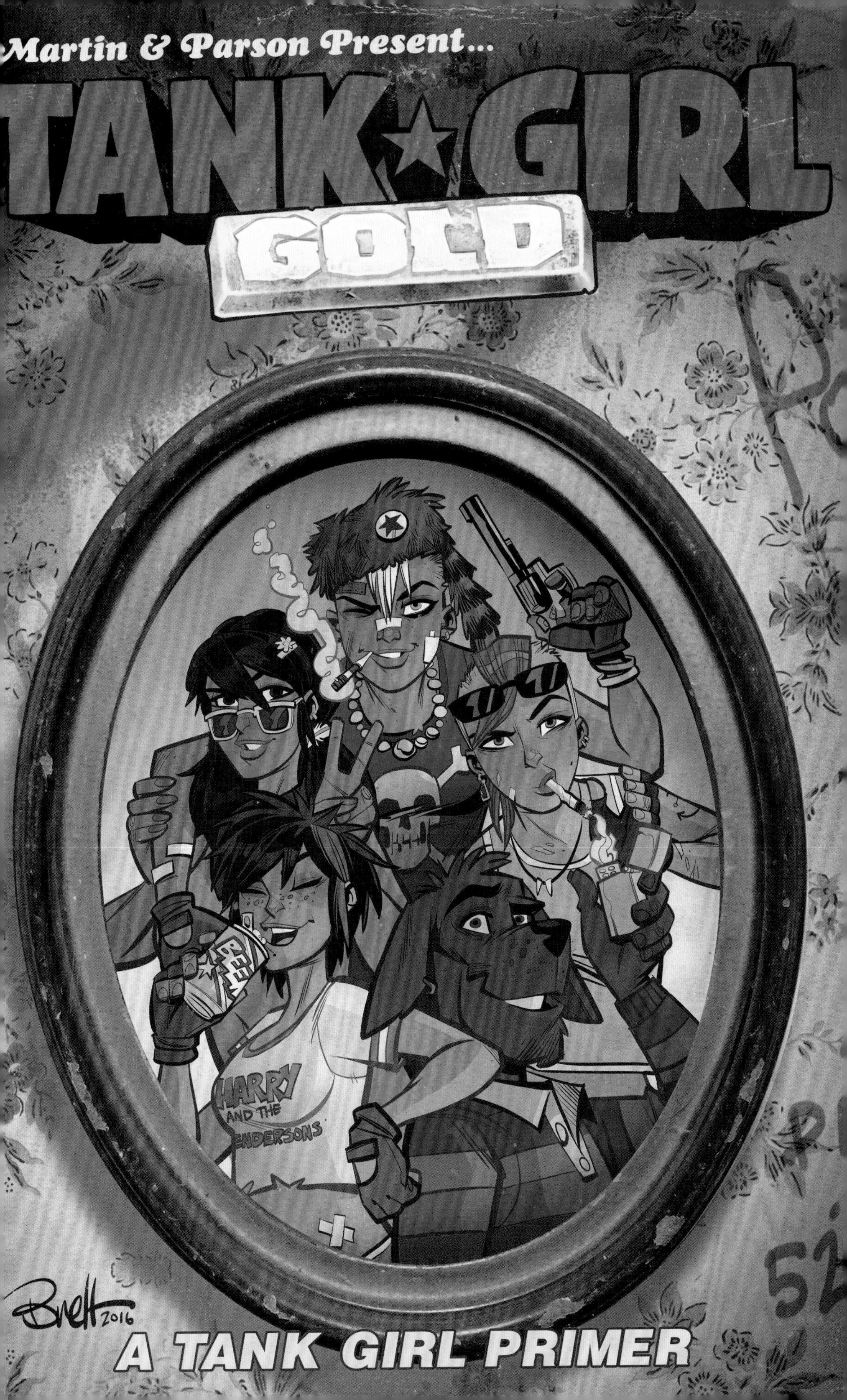
Martin & Parson Present...
TANK GIRL
GOLD
HARRY
AND THE
ENDERSONS
Brett 2016
A TANK GIRL PRIMER

ANGRY INTERVIEWS

Q: What don't you like, Tankie?

T.G.: I don't like being called "Tankie", that's not my fuckin' name. I'm Tank Girl, that's it. That's all I want to be called. Tankie. Tankie. Sounds fuckin' wankie.

Q: Are you surprised that people now refer to a t-shirt showing the red, white, and blue RAF roundel a "Tank Girl t-shirt"?

TG: Christ, I wore that t-shirt once. ONCE. In tribute to Keith Moon's birthday. And now, if I step out without it on, everyone's like "Hey, Tank Girl, where's your fuckin' target t-shirt?". Please, think of me as wearing something - ANYTHING - else. What do you think? That I've been wearing the same t-shirt for thirty years? It's not my fucking costume. It's not Superman's vest, y'know.

Q: What do you think of the current political situation?

TG: Fuck off.

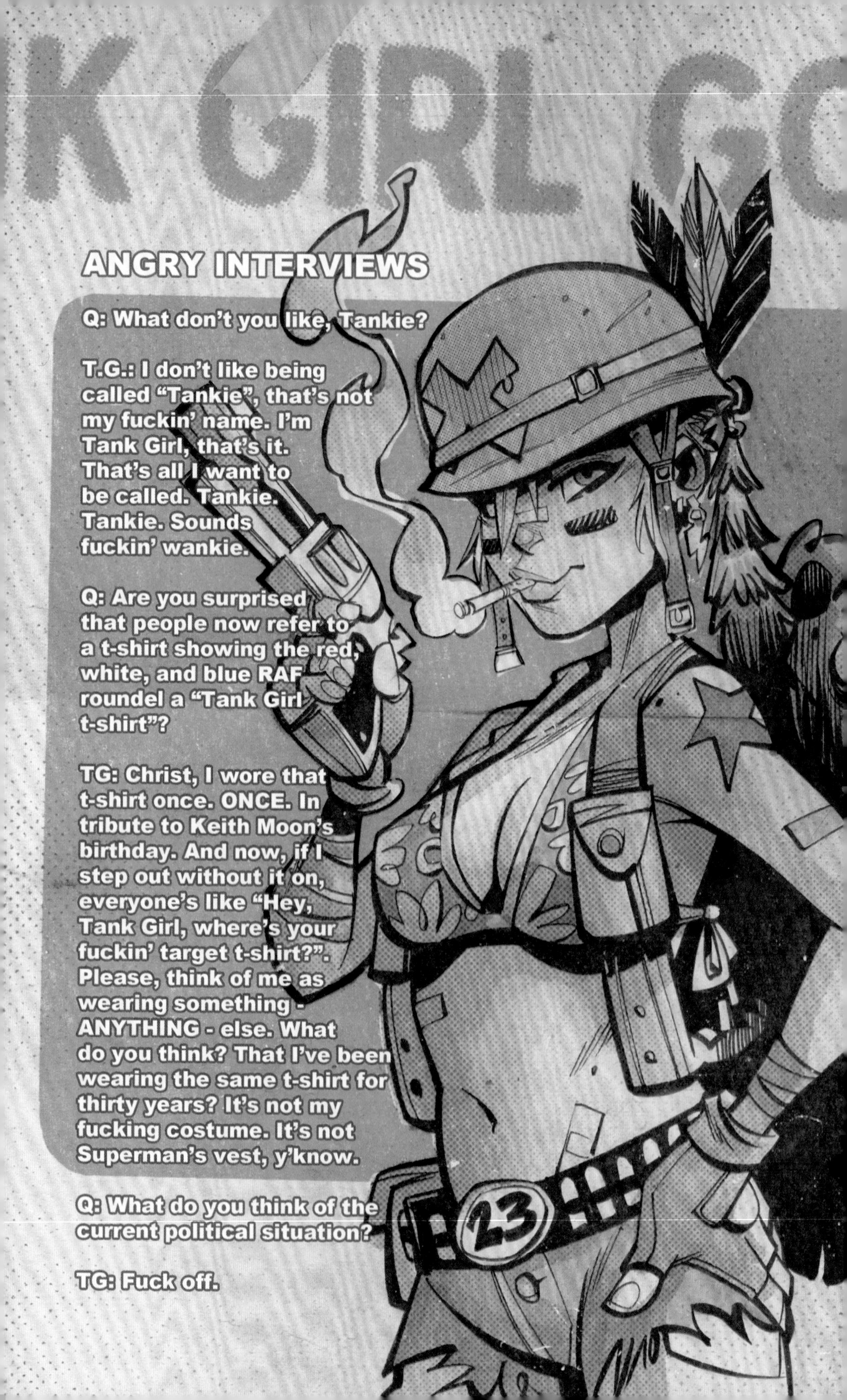

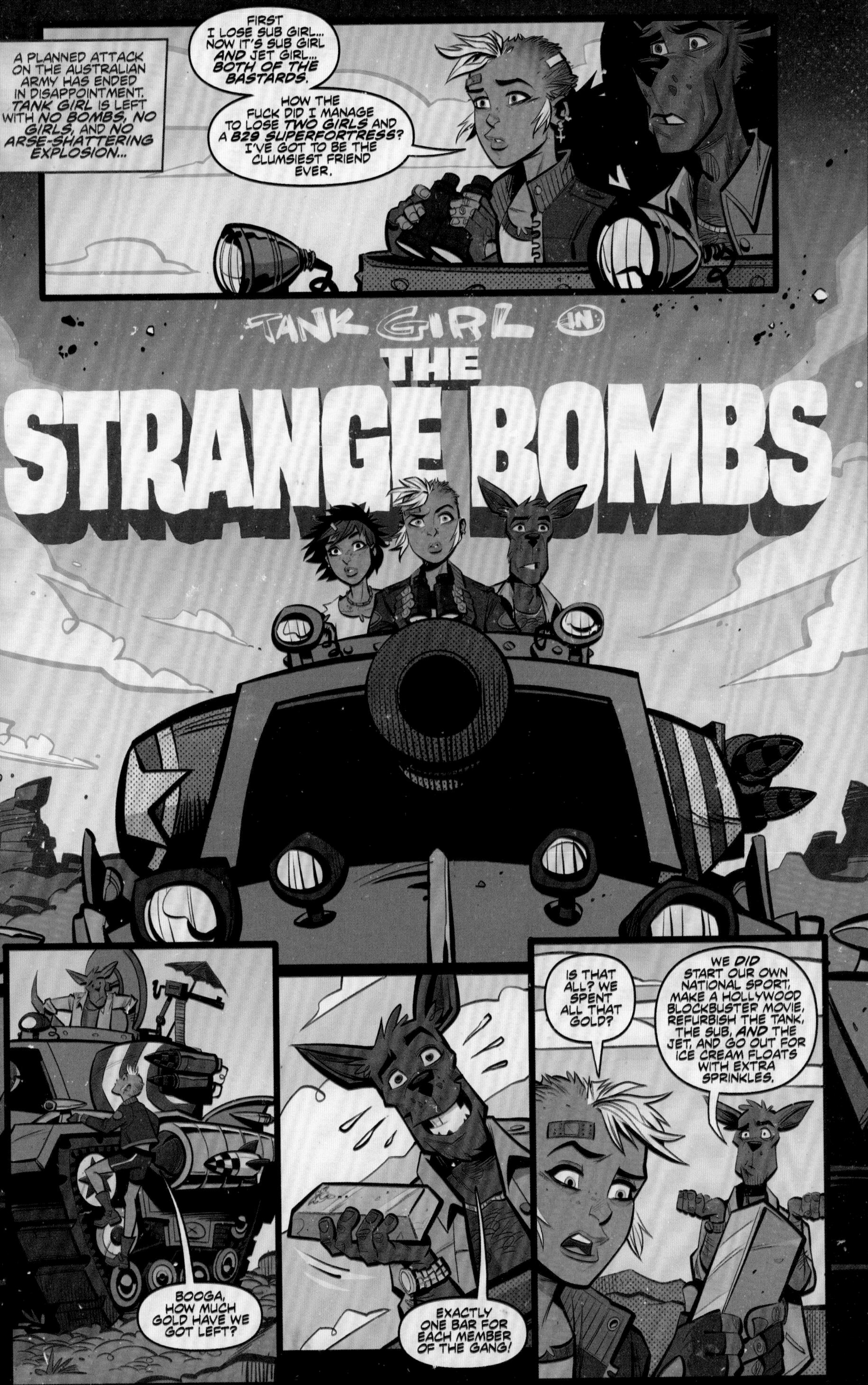
A PLANNED ATTACK ON THE AUSTRALIAN ARMY HAS ENDED IN DISAPPOINTMENT. TANK GIRL IS LEFT WITH NO BOMBS, NO GIRLS, AND NO ARSE-SHATTERING EXPLOSION...
FIRST I LOSE SUB GIRL... NOW IT'S SUB GIRL AND JET GIRL... BOTH OF THE BASTARDS.
HOW THE FUCK DID I MANAGE TO LOSE TWO GIRLS AND A B29 SUPERFORTRESS? I'VE GOT TO BE THE CLUMSIEST FRIEND EVER.
TANK GIRL IN
THE STRANGE BOMBS
BOOGA, HOW MUCH GOLD HAVE WE GOT LEFT?
EXACTLY ONE BAR FOR EACH MEMBER OF THE GANG!
IS THAT ALL? WE SPENT ALL THAT GOLD?
WE DID START OUR OWN NATIONAL SPORT, MAKE A HOLLYWOOD BLOCKBUSTER MOVIE, REFURBISH THE TANK, THE SUB, AND THE JET, AND GO OUT FOR ICE CREAM FLOATS WITH EXTRA SPRINKLES.

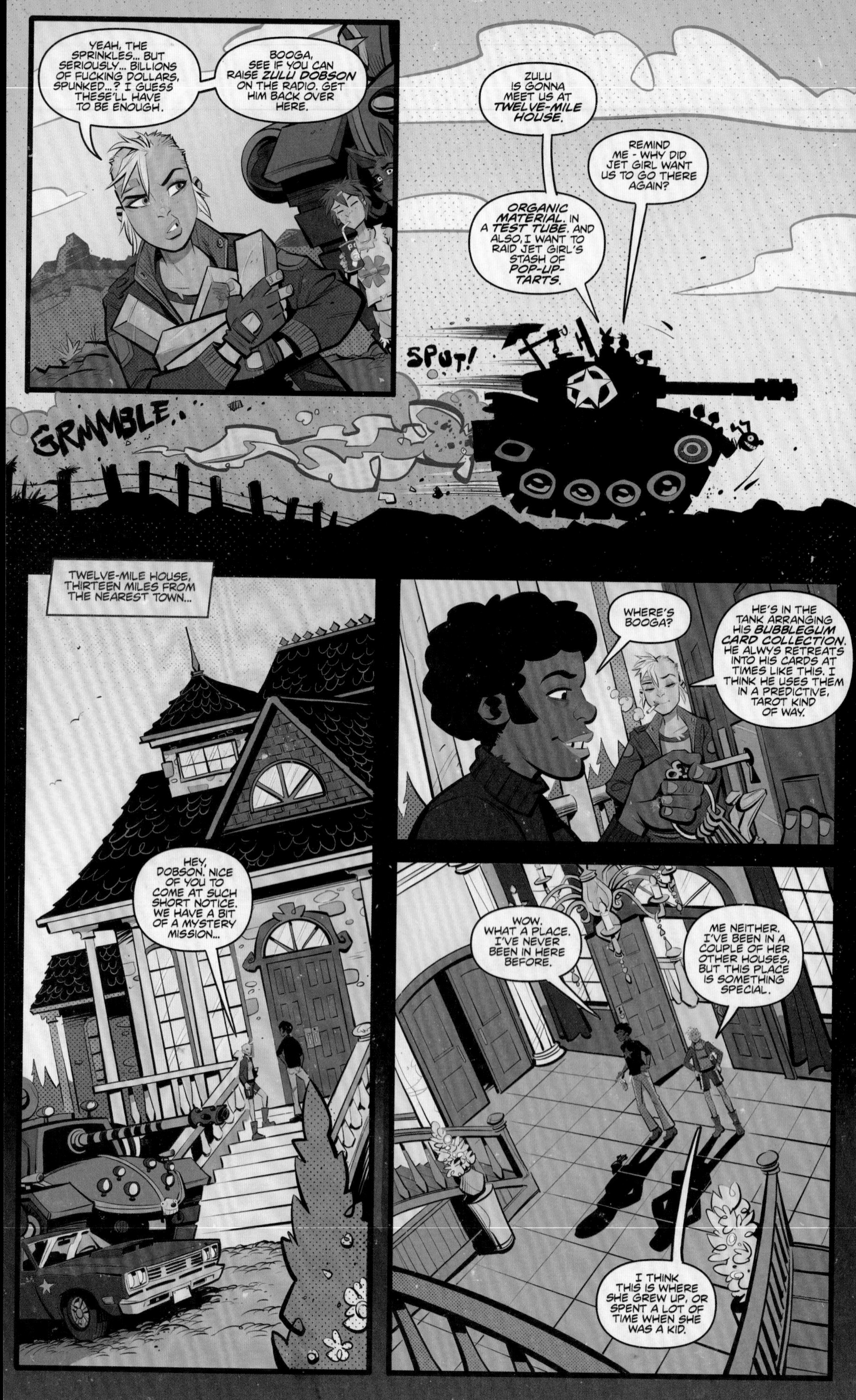
YEAH, THE SPRINKLES... BUT SERIOUSLY... BILLIONS OF FUCKING DOLLARS, SPUNKED...? I GUESS THESE'LL HAVE TO BE ENOUGH.
BOOGA, SEE IF YOU CAN RAISE ZULU DOBSON ON THE RADIO. GET HIM BACK OVER HERE.
ZULU IS GONNA MEET US AT TWELVE-MILE HOUSE.
REMIND ME - WHY DID JET GIRL WANT US TO GO THERE AGAIN?
ORGANIC MATERIAL. IN A TEST TUBE. AND ALSO, I WANT TO RAID JET GIRL'S STASH OF POP-UP-TARTS.
SPUT!
GRMMBLE.
TWELVE-MILE HOUSE, THIRTEEN MILES FROM THE NEAREST TOWN...
HEY, DOBSON. NICE OF YOU TO COME AT SUCH SHORT NOTICE. WE HAVE A BIT OF A MYSTERY MISSION...
WHERE'S BOOGA?
HE'S IN THE TANK ARRANGING HIS BUBBLEGUM CARD COLLECTION. HE ALWYS RETREATS INTO HIS CARDS AT TIMES LIKE THIS. I THINK HE USES THEM IN A PREDICTIVE, TAROT KIND OF WAY.
WOW. WHAT A PLACE. I'VE NEVER BEEN IN HERE BEFORE.
ME NEITHER. I'VE BEEN IN A COUPLE OF HER OTHER HOUSES, BUT THIS PLACE IS SOMETHING SPECIAL.
I THINK THIS IS WHERE SHE GREW UP, OR SPENT A LOT OF TIME WHEN SHE WAS A KID.

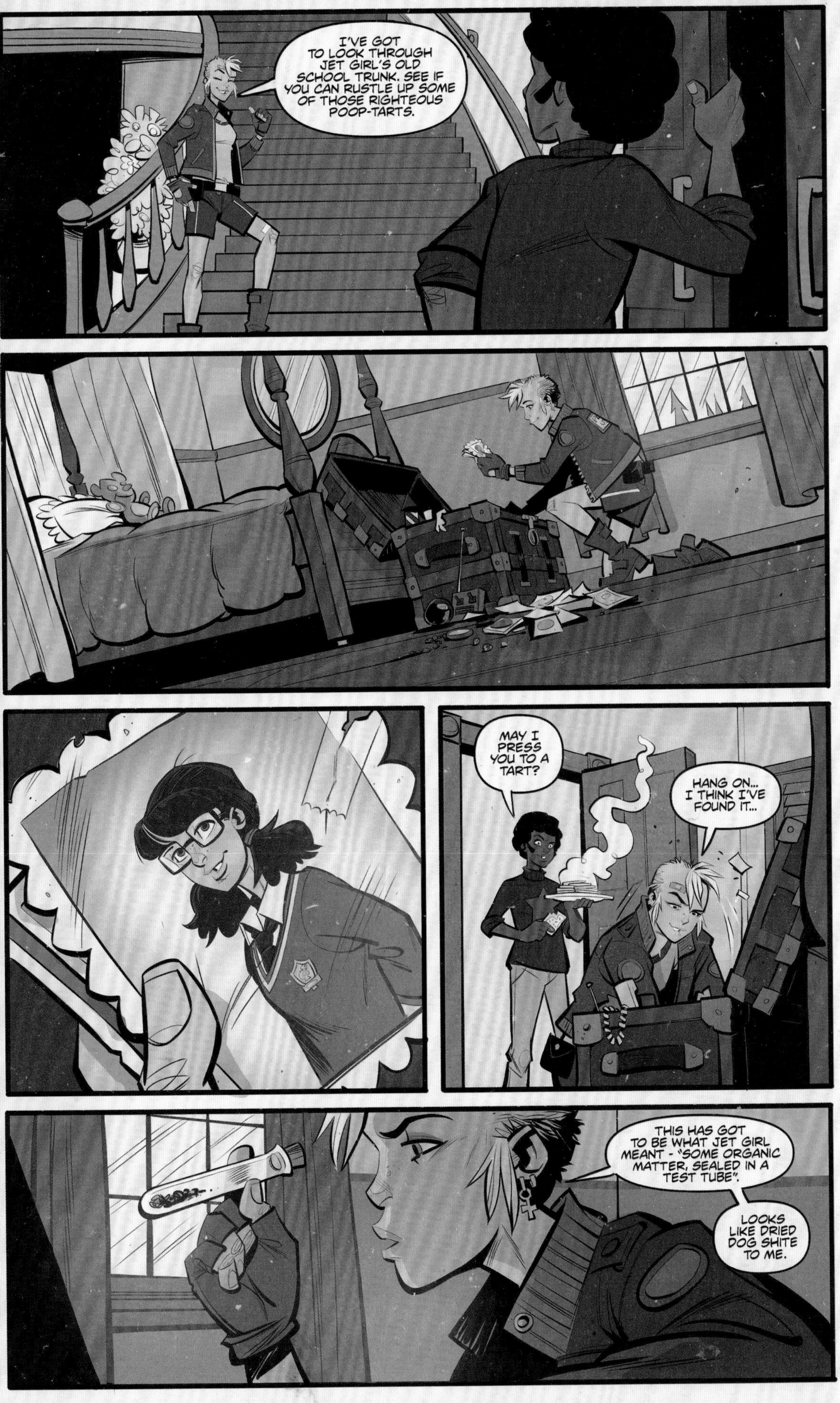
I'VE GOT TO LOOK THROUGH JET GIRL'S OLD SCHOOL TRUNK. SEE IF YOU CAN RUSTLE UP SOME OF THOSE RIGHTEOUS POOP-TARTS.
MAY I PRESS YOU TO A TART?
HANG ON... I THINK I'VE FOUND IT...
THIS HAS GOT TO BE WHAT JET GIRL MEANT - "SOME ORGANIC MATTER, SEALED IN A TEST TUBE".
LOOKS LIKE DRIED DOG SHITE TO ME.

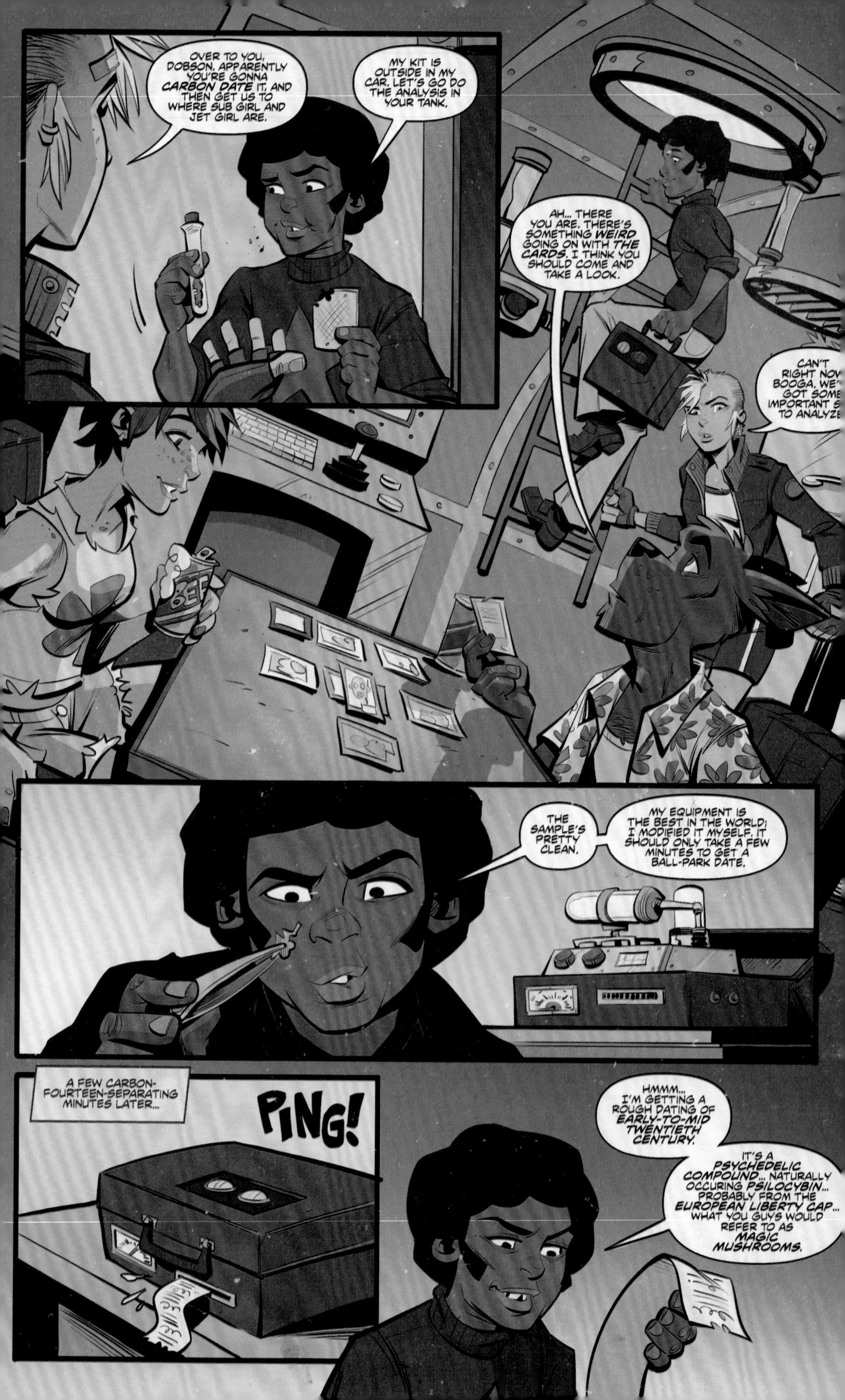
OVER TO YOU, DOBSON. APPARENTLY YOU'RE GONNA CARBON DATE IT, AND THEN GET US TO WHERE SUB GIRL AND JET GIRL ARE.
MY KIT IS OUTSIDE IN MY CAR. LET'S GO DO THE ANALYSIS IN YOUR TANK.
AH... THERE YOU ARE. THERE'S SOMETHING WEIRD GOING ON WITH THE CARDS. I THINK YOU SHOULD COME AND TAKE A LOOK.
THE SAMPLE'S PRETTY CLEAN.
MY EQUIPMENT IS THE BEST IN THE WORLD; I MODIFIED IT MYSELF. IT SHOULD ONLY TAKE A FEW MINUTES TO GET A BALL-PARK DATE.
A FEW CARBON-FOURTEEN-SEPARATING MINUTES LATER...
PING!
HMMM... I'M GETTING A ROUGH DATING OF EARLY-TO-MID TWENTIETH CENTURY.
IT'S A PSYCHEDELIC COMPOUND... NATURALLY OCCURING PSILOCYBIN... PROBABLY FROM THE EUROPEAN LIBERTY CAP... WHAT YOU GUYS WOULD REFER TO AS MAGIC MUSHROOMS.

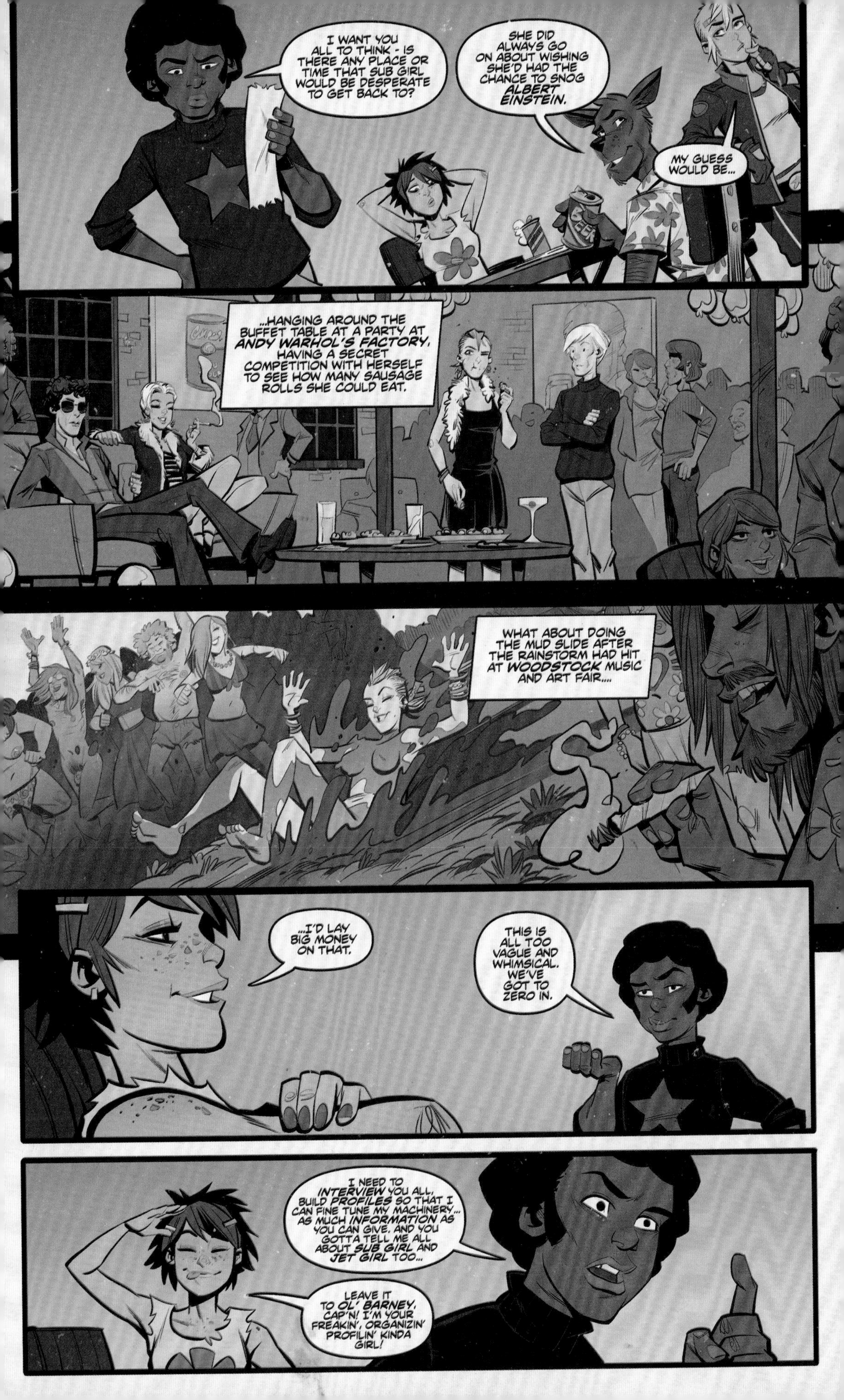
I WANT YOU ALL TO THINK - IS THERE ANY PLACE OR TIME THAT SUB GIRL WOULD BE DESPERATE TO GET BACK TO?
SHE DID ALWAYS GO ON ABOUT WISHING SHE'D HAD THE CHANCE TO SNOG ALBERT EINSTEIN.
MY GUESS WOULD BE...
BEER
...HANGING AROUND THE BUFFET TABLE AT A PARTY AT ANDY WARHOL'S FACTORY, HAVING A SECRET COMPETITION WITH HERSELF TO SEE HOW MANY SAUSAGE ROLLS SHE COULD EAT.
WHAT ABOUT DOING THE MUD SLIDE AFTER THE RAINSTORM HAD HIT AT WOODSTOCK MUSIC AND ART FAIR....
...I'D LAY BIG MONEY ON THAT.
THIS IS ALL TOO VAGUE AND WHIMSICAL. WE'VE GOT TO ZERO IN.
I NEED TO INTERVIEW YOU ALL, BUILD PROFILES SO THAT I CAN FINE TUNE MY MACHINERY... AS MUCH INFORMATION AS YOU CAN GIVE. AND YOU GOTTA TELL ME ALL ABOUT SUB GIRL AND JET GIRL TOO...
LEAVE IT TO OL' BARNEY, CAP'N! I'M YOUR FREAKIN', ORGANIZIN' PROFILIN' KINDA GIRL!

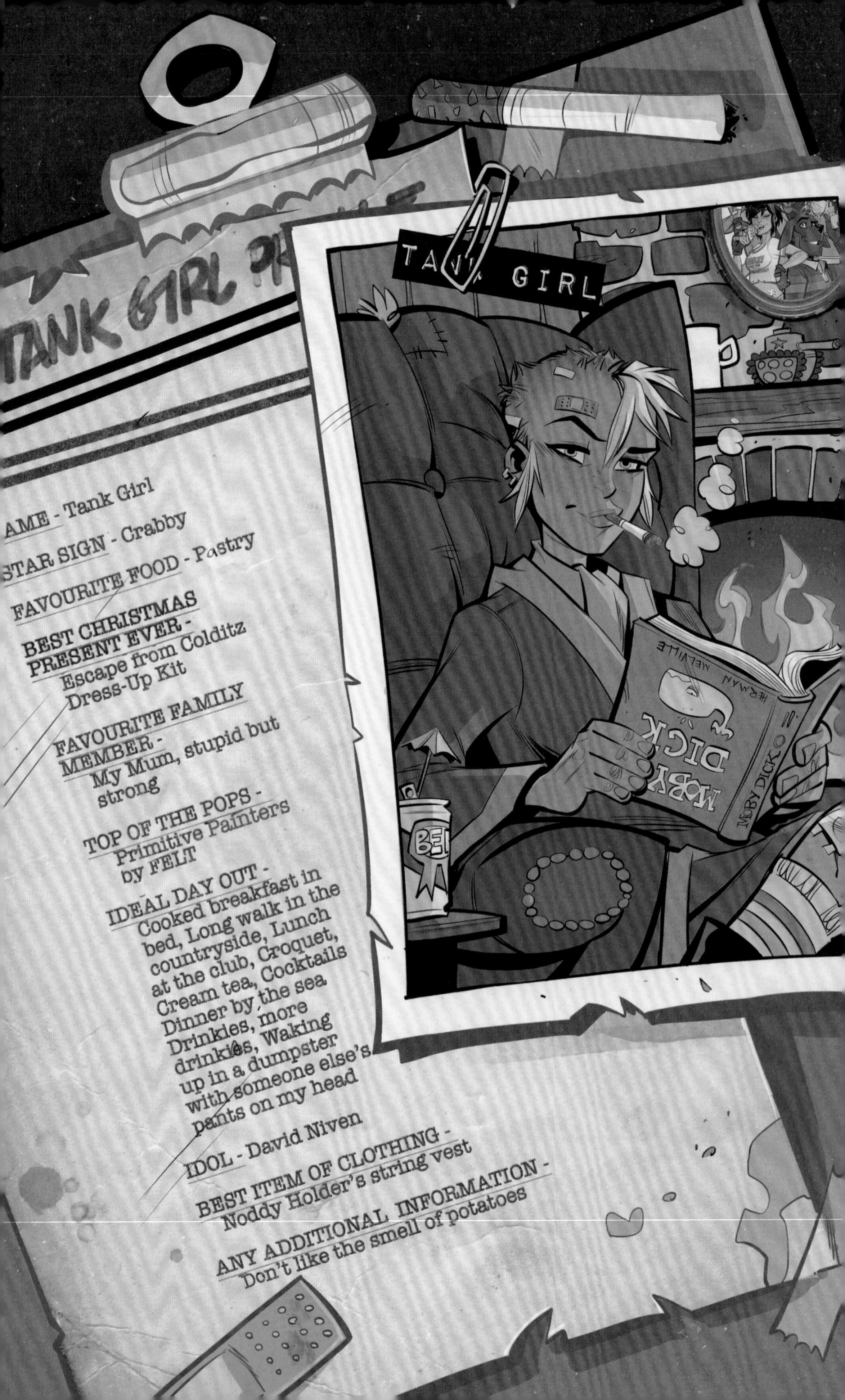

TANK GIRL PR
AME - Tank Girl
STAR SIGN - Crabby
FAVOURITE FOOD - Pastry
BEST CHRISTMAS PRESENT EVER - Escape from Colditz Dress-Up Kit
FAVOURITE FAMILY MEMBER - My Mum, stupid but strong
TOP OF THE POPS - Primitive Painters by FELT
IDEAL DAY OUT - Cooked breakfast in bed, Long walk in the countryside, Lunch at the club, Croquet, Cream tea, Cocktails Dinner by the sea Drinkies, more drinkies, Waking up in a dumpster with someone else's pants on my head
IDOL - David Niven
BEST ITEM OF CLOTHING - Noddy Holder's string vest
ANY ADDITIONAL INFORMATION - Don't like the smell of potatoes
TANK GIRL
MOBY DICK
HERMAN MELVILLE
MOBY DICK

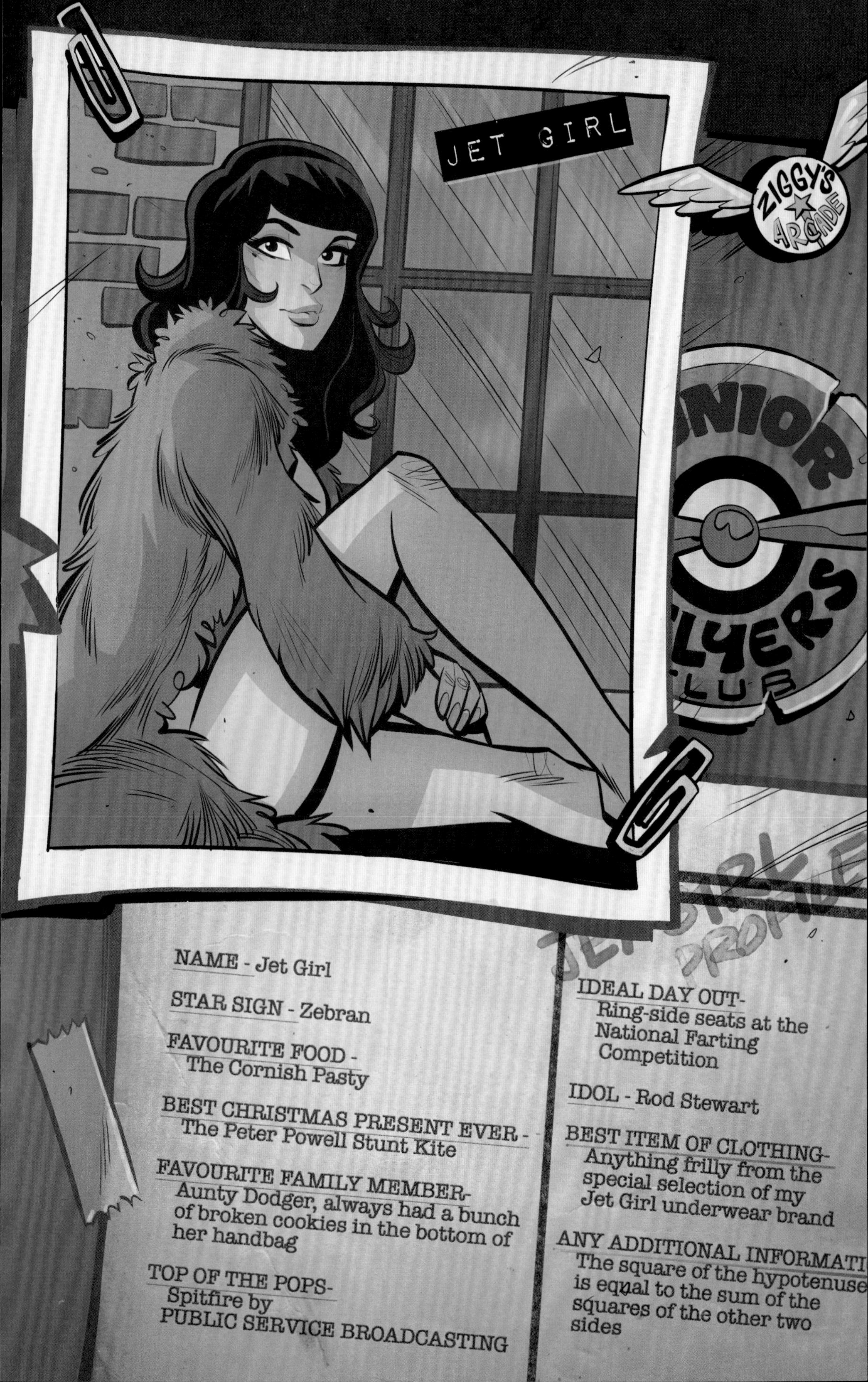
JET GIRL
ZIGGY'S ARCADE
NAME - Jet Girl
STAR SIGN - Zebran
FAVOURITE FOOD - The Cornish Pasty
BEST CHRISTMAS PRESENT EVER - The Peter Powell Stunt Kite
FAVOURITE FAMILY MEMBER- Aunty Dodger, always had a bunch of broken cookies in the bottom of her handbag
TOP OF THE POPS- Spitfire by PUBLIC SERVICE BROADCASTING
IDEAL DAY OUT- Ring-side seats at the National Farting Competition
IDOL - Rod Stewart
BEST ITEM OF CLOTHING- Anything frilly from the special selection of my Jet Girl underwear brand
ANY ADDITIONAL INFORMATI
The square of the hypotenuse is equal to the sum of the squares of the other two sides

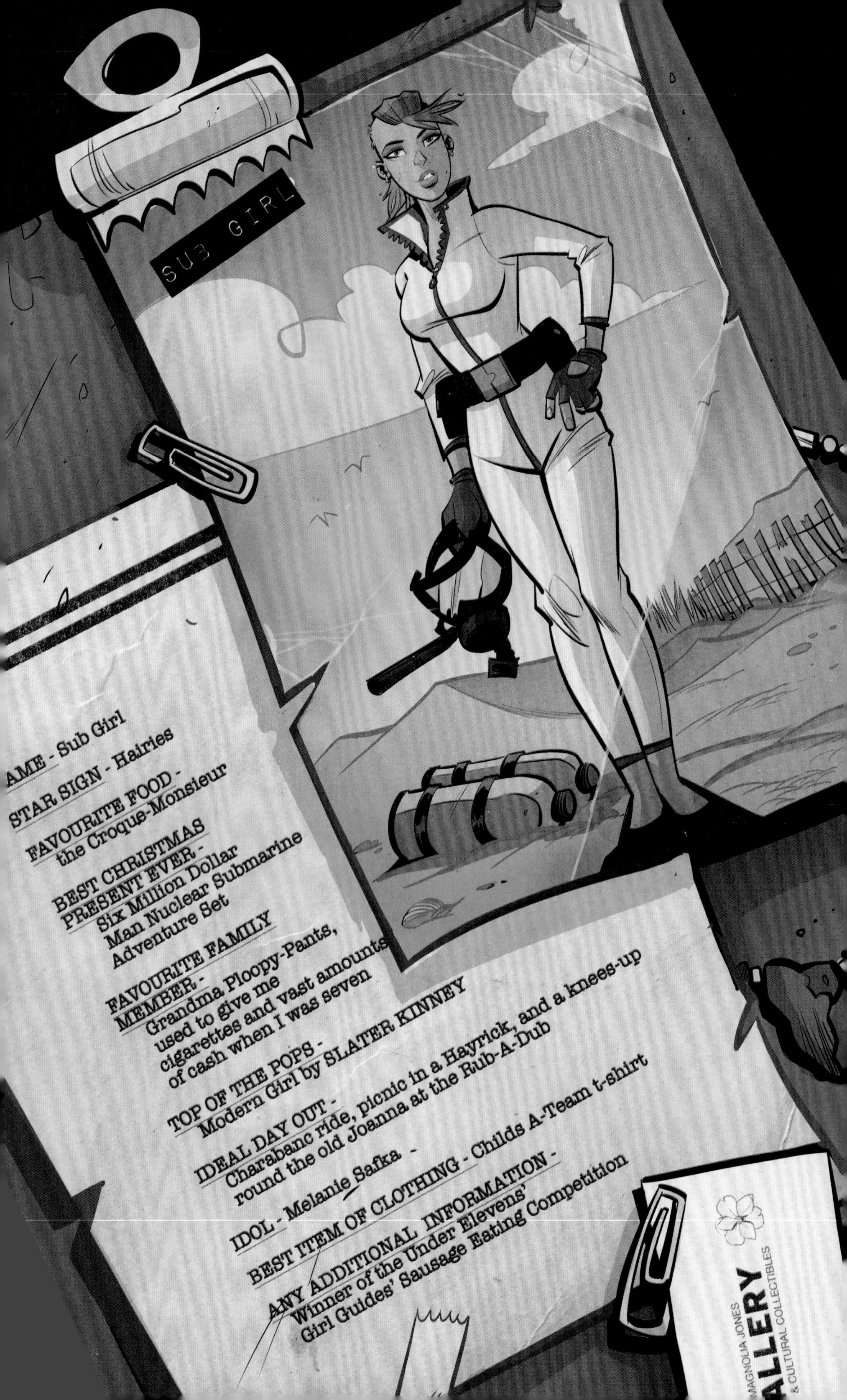
SUB GIRL
AME - Sub Girl
STAR SIGN - Hairies
FAVOURITE FOOD - the Croque-Monsieur
BEST CHRISTMAS PRESENT EVER - Six Million Dollar Man Nuclear Submarine Adventure Set
FAVOURITE FAMILY MEMBER - Grandma Ploopy-Pants, used to give me cigarettes and vast amounts of cash when I was seven
TOP OF THE POPS - Modern Girl by SLATER KINNEY
IDEAL DAY OUT - Charabanc ride, picnic in a Hayrick, and a knees-up round the old Joanna at the Rub-A-Dub
IDOL - Melanie Safka -
BEST ITEM OF CLOTHING - Childs A-Team t-shirt
ANY ADDITIONAL INFORMATION - Winner of the Under Elevens' Girl Guides' Sausage Eating Competition
MAGNOLIA JONES
ALLERY
& CULTURAL COLLECTIBLES

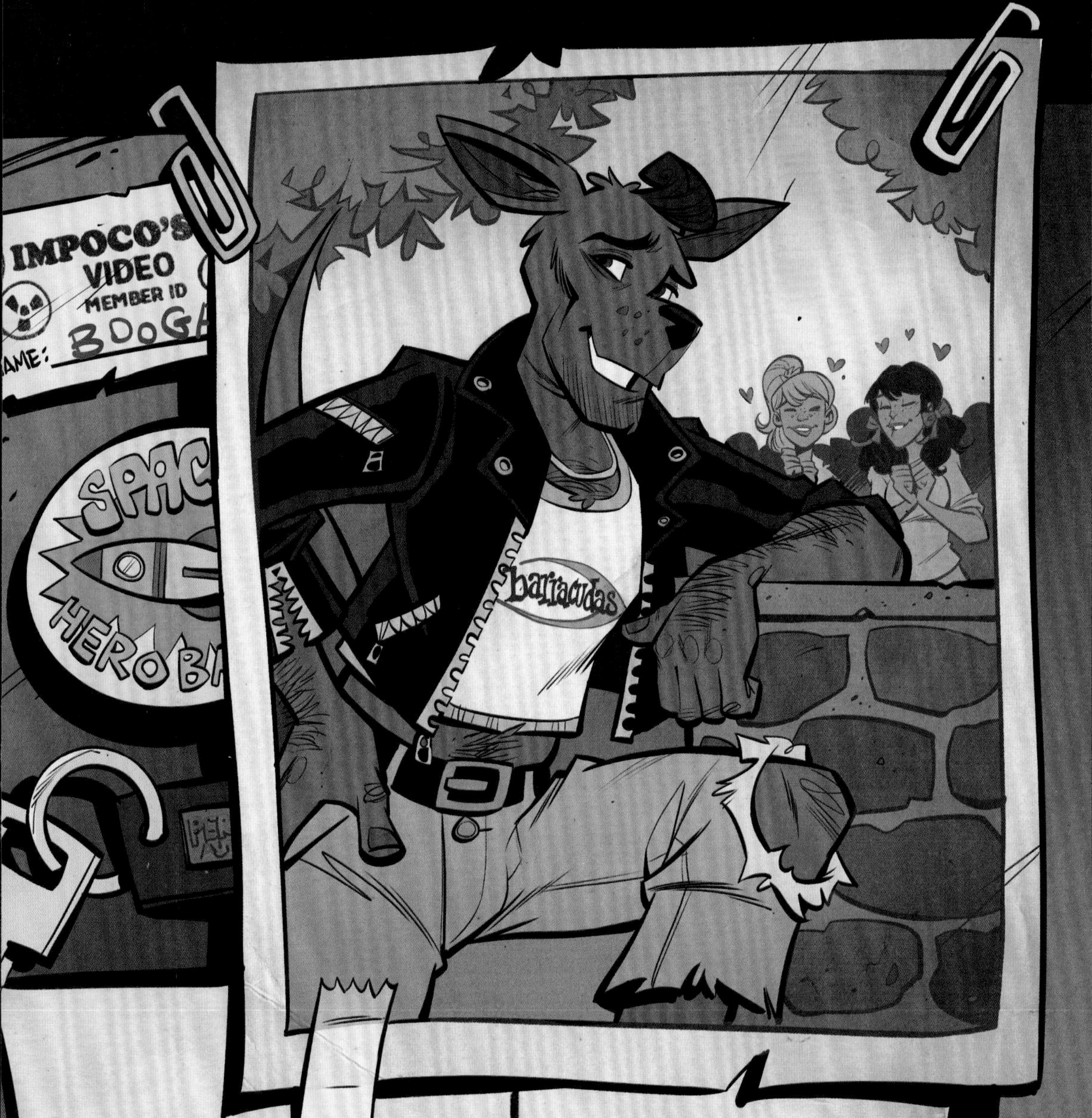
IMPOCO'S
VIDEO
MEMBER ID
AME: BOOGA
barracudas

NAME - Booga

STAR SIGN - I'm a Zodiac

FAVOURITE FOOD -
Lunch

BEST CHRISTMAS PRESENT EVER -
the Evel Knievel Grand Canyon Drag Rocket Super Twat Stunt Cycle Chopper

FAVOURITE FAMILY MEMBER-
My little brother Nobbler. - Our kid, Great to have on your side in a fight, but never learnt to wipe his own arse

TOP OF THE POPS-
Something in the Air by THUNDERCLAP NEWMAN

IDEAL DAY OUT-
Disney Land on acid

IDOL - Freddy Laker

BEST ITEM OF CLOTHING-
Leather jacket gifted to me by Marky Ramone

ANY ADDITIONAL INFORMATION-
I owe you a twenty

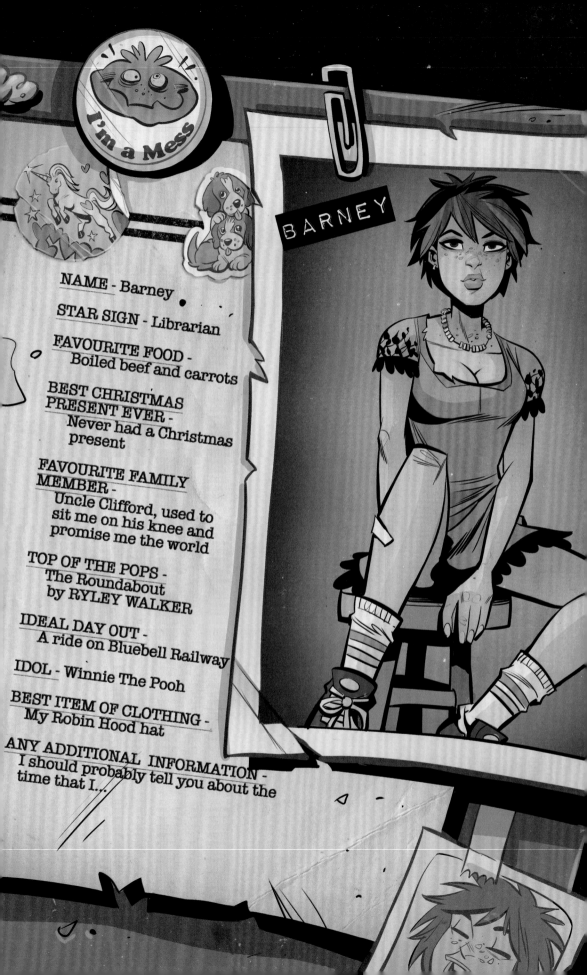

I'm a Mess

BARNEY

NAME - Barney

STAR SIGN - Librarian

FAVOURITE FOOD - Boiled beef and carrots

BEST CHRISTMAS PRESENT EVER - Never had a Christmas present

FAVOURITE FAMILY MEMBER - Uncle Clifford, used to sit me on his knee and promise me the world

TOP OF THE POPS - The Roundabout by RYLEY WALKER

IDEAL DAY OUT - A ride on Bluebell Railway

IDOL - Winnie The Pooh

BEST ITEM OF CLOTHING - My Robin Hood hat

ANY ADDITIONAL INFORMATION - I should probably tell you about the time that I...

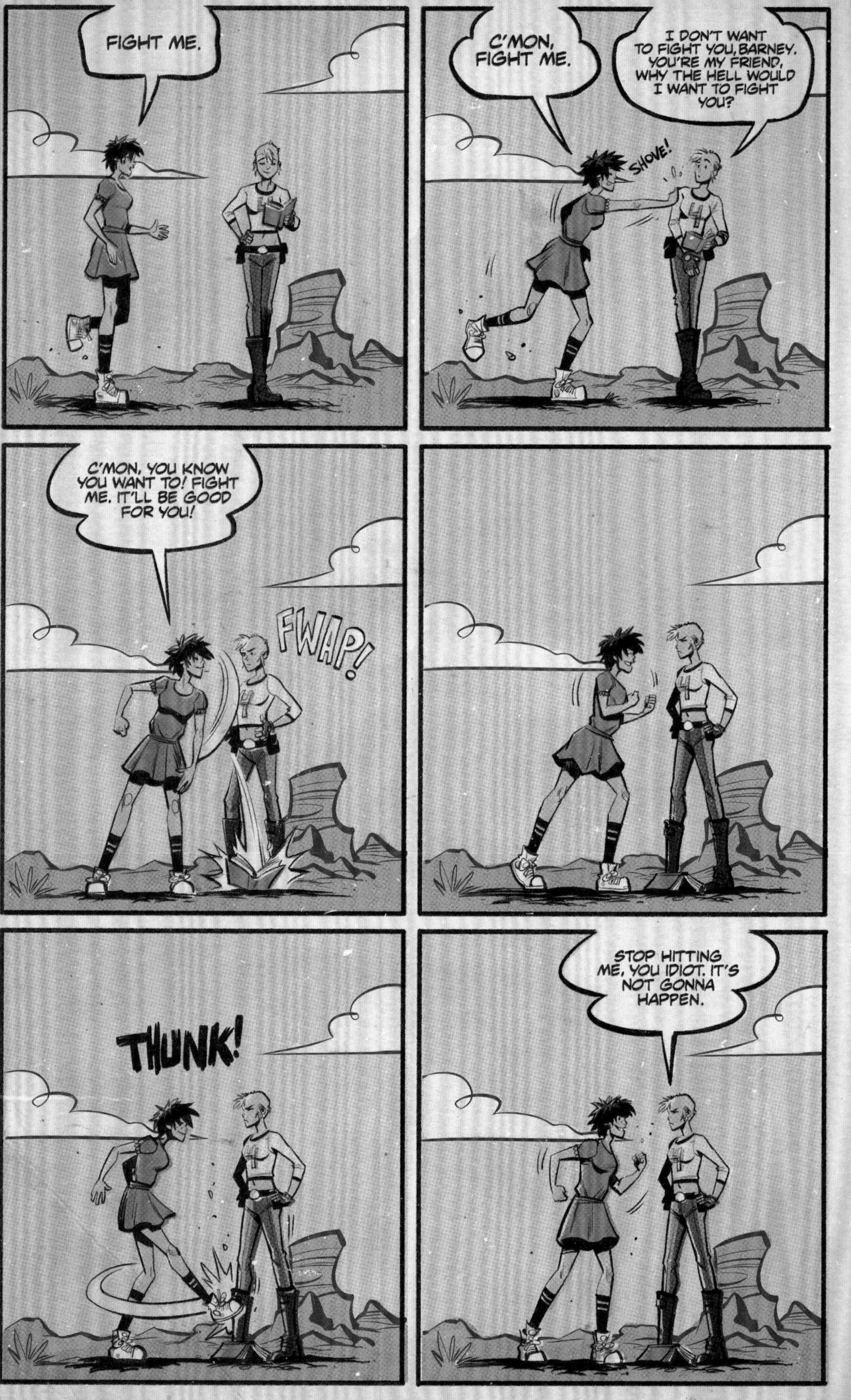
FIGHT ME.
C'MON, FIGHT ME.
I DON'T WANT TO FIGHT YOU, BARNEY. YOU'RE MY FRIEND, WHY THE HELL WOULD I WANT TO FIGHT YOU?
SHOVE!
C'MON, YOU KNOW YOU WANT TO! FIGHT ME. IT'LL BE GOOD FOR YOU!
FWAP!
THUNK!
STOP HITTING ME, YOU IDIOT. IT'S NOT GONNA HAPPEN.

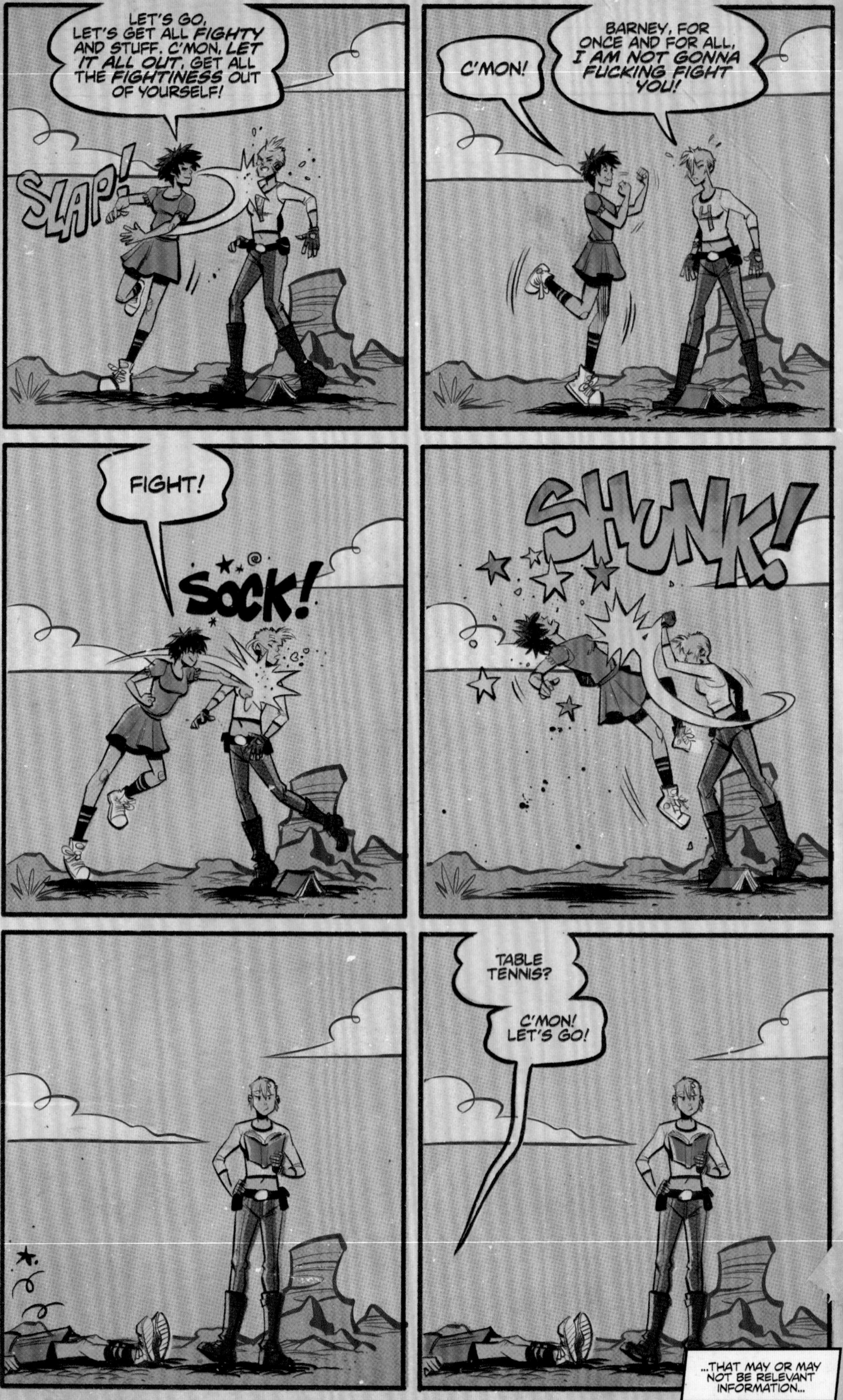

LET'S GO, LET'S GET ALL FIGHTY AND STUFF. C'MON, LET IT ALL OUT, GET ALL THE FIGHTINESS OUT OF YOURSELF!
SLAP!
C'MON!
BARNEY, FOR ONCE AND FOR ALL, I AM NOT GONNA FUCKING FIGHT YOU!
FIGHT!
SOCK!
SHUNK!
TABLE TENNIS?
C'MON! LET'S GO!
...THAT MAY OR MAY NOT BE RELEVANT INFORMATION...

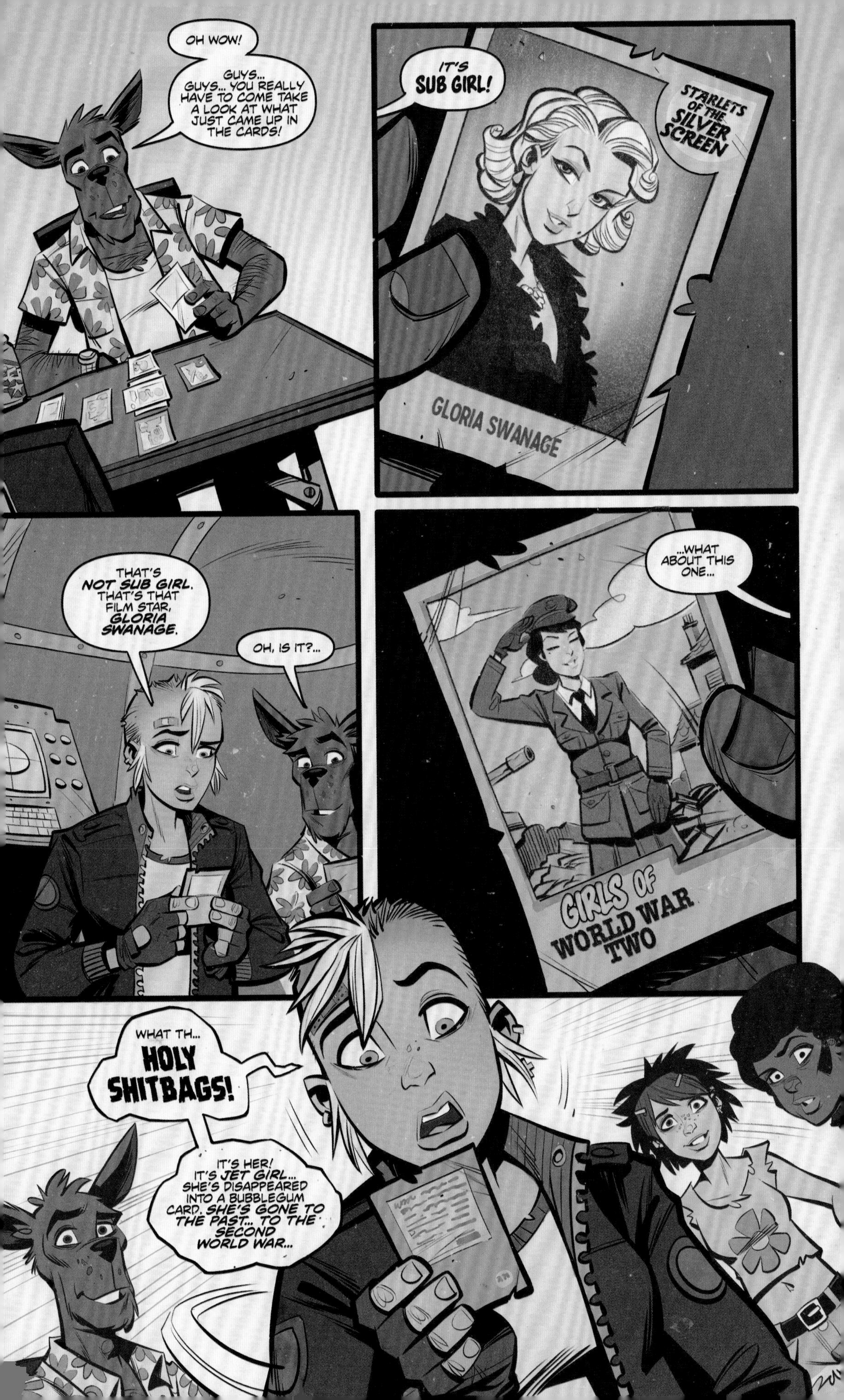

OH WOW!
GUYS... GUYS... YOU REALLY HAVE TO COME TAKE A LOOK AT WHAT JUST CAME UP IN THE CARDS!
IT'S SUB GIRL!
STARLETS OF THE SILVER SCREEN
GLORIA SWANAGE
THAT'S NOT SUB GIRL. THAT'S THAT FILM STAR, GLORIA SWANAGE.
OH, IS IT?...
...WHAT ABOUT THIS ONE...
GIRLS OF WORLD WAR TWO
WHAT TH... HOLY SHITBAGS!
IT'S HER! IT'S JET GIRL... SHE'S DISAPPEARED INTO A BUBBLEGUM CARD. SHE'S GONE TO THE PAST... TO THE SECOND WORLD WAR...

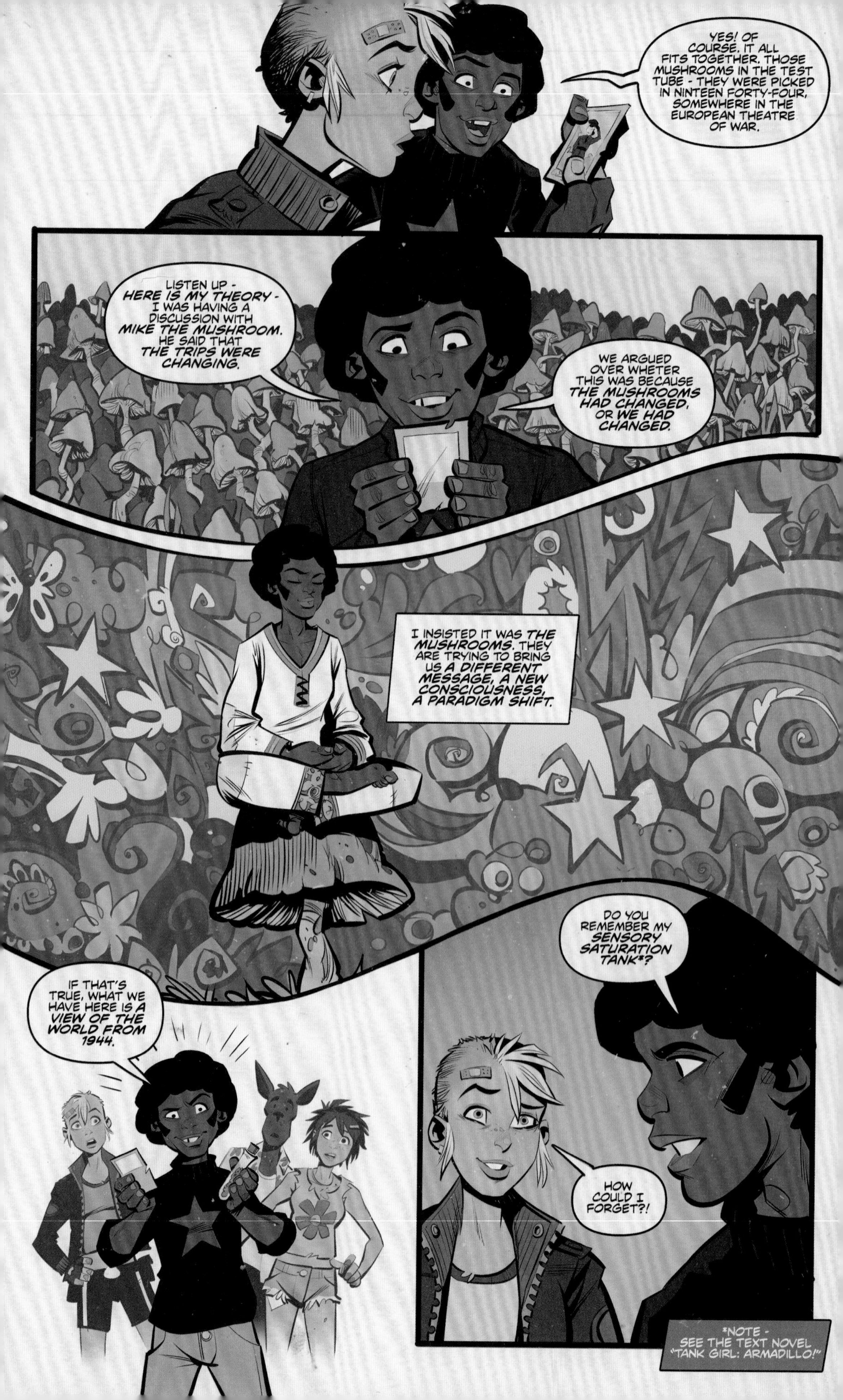
YES! OF COURSE. IT ALL FITS TOGETHER. THOSE MUSHROOMS IN THE TEST TUBE - THEY WERE PICKED IN NINTEEN FORTY-FOUR, SOMEWHERE IN THE EUROPEAN THEATRE OF WAR.
LISTEN UP - HERE IS MY THEORY - I WAS HAVING A DISCUSSION WITH MIKE THE MUSHROOM. HE SAID THAT THE TRIPS WERE CHANGING.
WE ARGUED OVER WHETER THIS WAS BECAUSE THE MUSHROOMS HAD CHANGED, OR WE HAD CHANGED.
I INSISTED IT WAS THE MUSHROOMS. THEY ARE TRYING TO BRING US A DIFFERENT MESSAGE, A NEW CONSCIOUSNESS, A PARADIGM SHIFT.
IF THAT'S TRUE, WHAT WE HAVE HERE IS A VIEW OF THE WORLD FROM 1944.
DO YOU REMEMBER MY SENSORY SATURATION TANK*?
HOW COULD I FORGET?!
*NOTE - SEE THE TEXT NOVEL "TANK GIRL: ARMADILLO!"

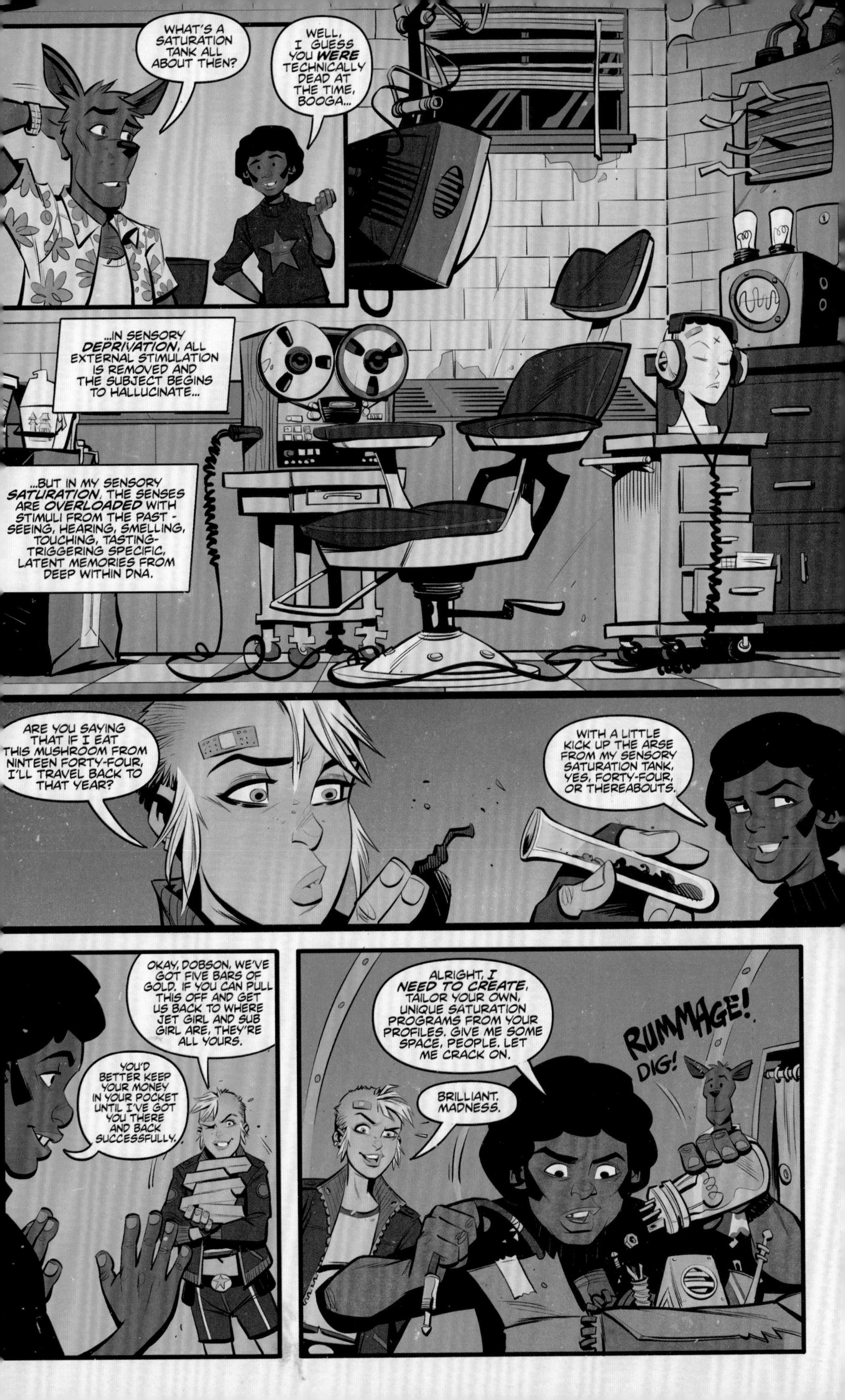
WHAT'S A SATURATION TANK ALL ABOUT THEN?
WELL, I GUESS YOU WERE TECHNICALLY DEAD AT THE TIME, BOOGA...
...IN SENSORY DEPRIVATION, ALL EXTERNAL STIMULATION IS REMOVED AND THE SUBJECT BEGINS TO HALLUCINATE...
...BUT IN MY SENSORY SATURATION, THE SENSES ARE OVERLOADED WITH STIMULI FROM THE PAST - SEEING, HEARING, SMELLING, TOUCHING, TASTING- TRIGGERING SPECIFIC, LATENT MEMORIES FROM DEEP WITHIN DNA.
ARE YOU SAYING THAT IF I EAT THIS MUSHROOM FROM NINTEEN FORTY-FOUR, I'LL TRAVEL BACK TO THAT YEAR?
WITH A LITTLE KICK UP THE ARSE FROM MY SENSORY SATURATION TANK, YES, FORTY-FOUR, OR THEREABOUTS.
OKAY, DOBSON, WE'VE GOT FIVE BARS OF GOLD. IF YOU CAN PULL THIS OFF AND GET US BACK TO WHERE JET GIRL AND SUB GIRL ARE, THEY'RE ALL YOURS.
YOU'D BETTER KEEP YOUR MONEY IN YOUR POCKET UNTIL I'VE GOT YOU THERE AND BACK SUCCESSFULLY.
ALRIGHT, I NEED TO CREATE, TAILOR YOUR OWN, UNIQUE SATURATION PROGRAMS FROM YOUR PROFILES. GIVE ME SOME SPACE, PEOPLE. LET ME CRACK ON.
BRILLIANT. MADNESS.
RUMMAGE!
DIG!

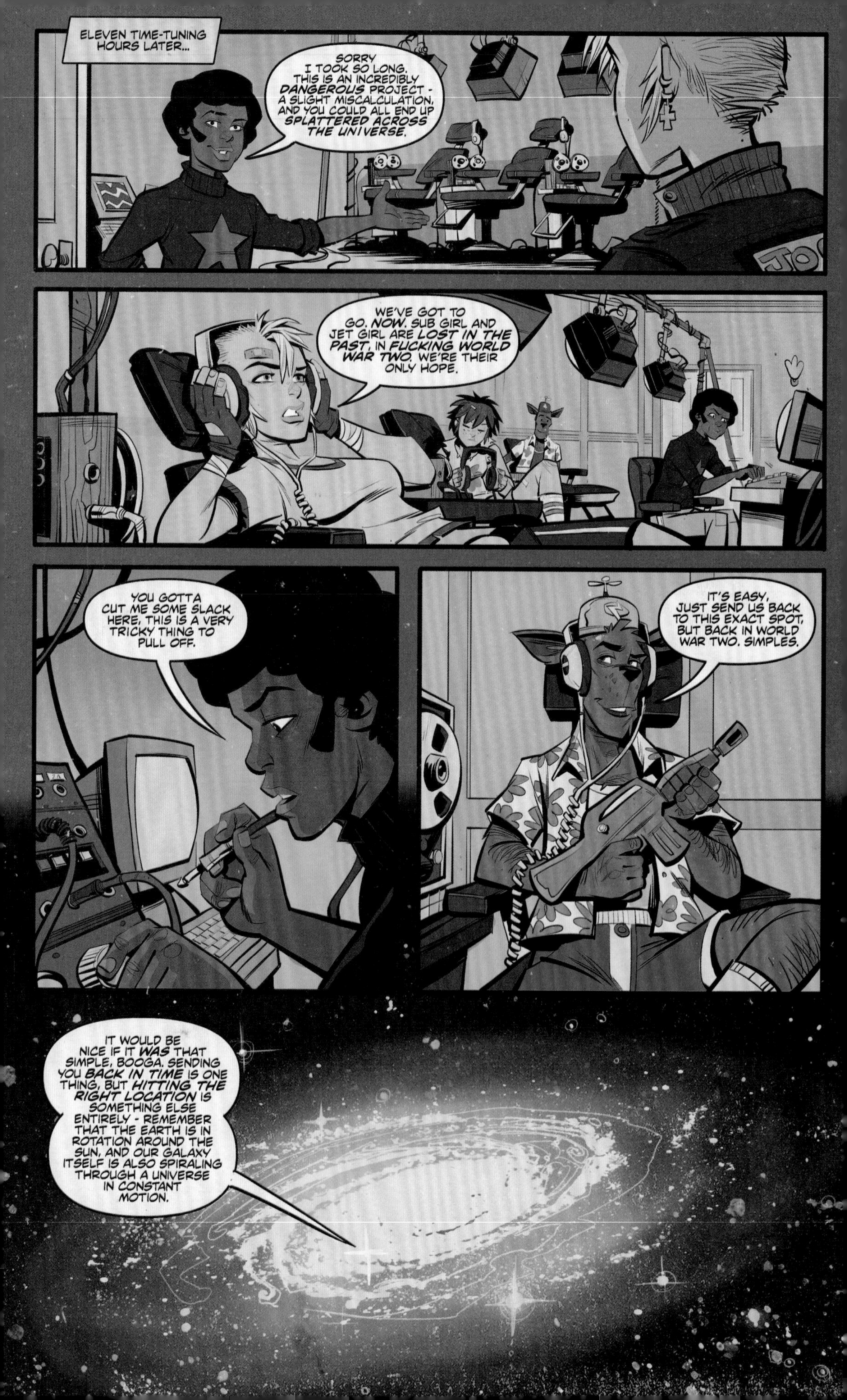
ELEVEN TIME-TUNING HOURS LATER...
SORRY I TOOK SO LONG. THIS IS AN INCREDIBLY DANGEROUS PROJECT - A SLIGHT MISCALCULATION, AND YOU COULD ALL END UP SPLATTERED ACROSS THE UNIVERSE.
WE'VE GOT TO GO. NOW. SUB GIRL AND JET GIRL ARE LOST IN THE PAST, IN FUCKING WORLD WAR TWO. WE'RE THEIR ONLY HOPE.
YOU GOTTA CUT ME SOME SLACK HERE, THIS IS A VERY TRICKY THING TO PULL OFF.
IT'S EASY, JUST SEND US BACK TO THIS EXACT SPOT, BUT BACK IN WORLD WAR TWO. SIMPLES.
IT WOULD BE NICE IF IT WAS THAT SIMPLE, BOOGA. SENDING YOU BACK IN TIME IS ONE THING, BUT HITTING THE RIGHT LOCATION IS SOMETHING ELSE ENTIRELY - REMEMBER THAT THE EARTH IS IN ROTATION AROUND THE SUN, AND OUR GALAXY ITSELF IS ALSO SPIRALING THROUGH A UNIVERSE IN CONSTANT MOTION.

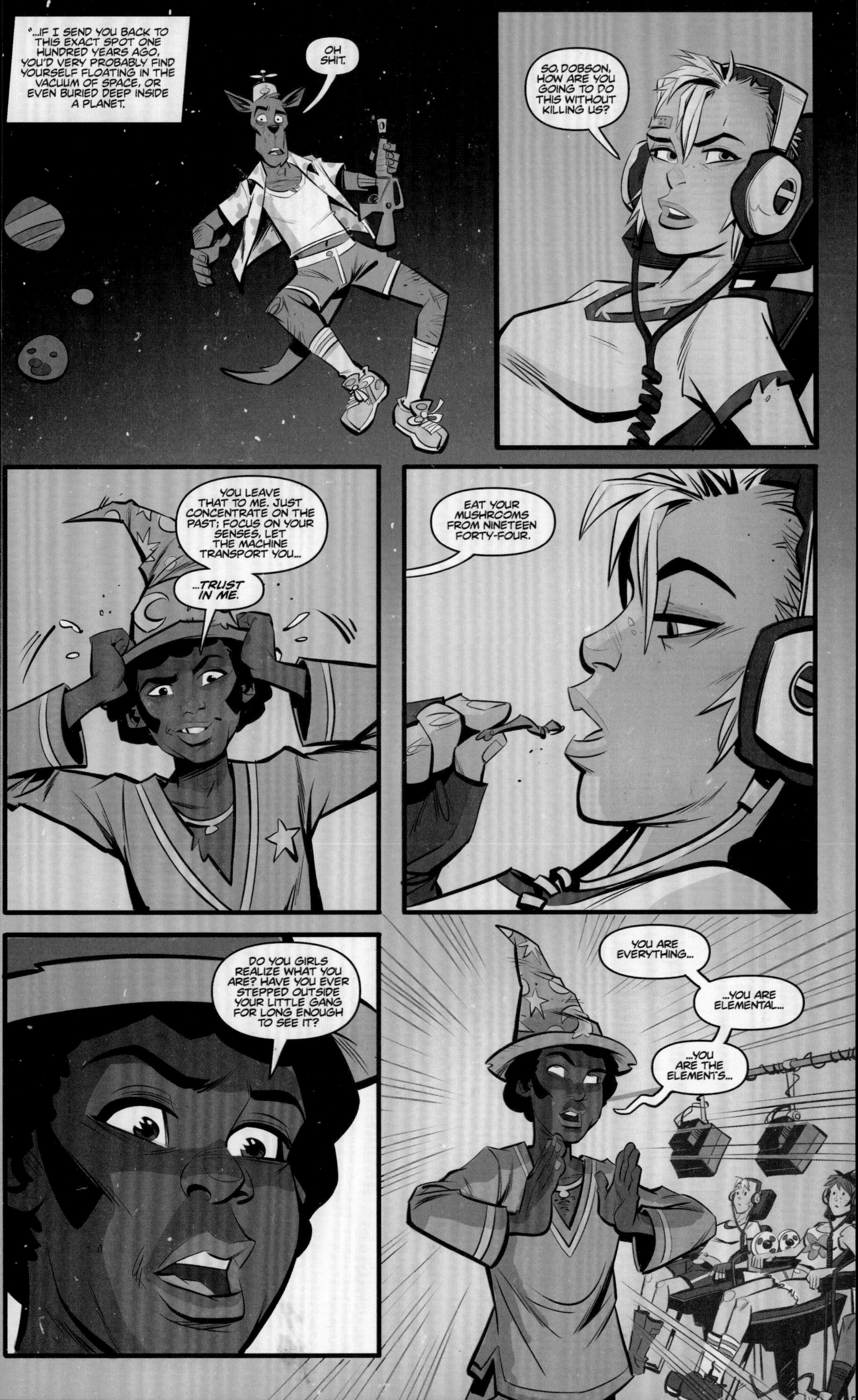
"...IF I SEND YOU BACK TO THIS EXACT SPOT ONE HUNDRED YEARS AGO, YOU'D VERY PROBABLY FIND YOURSELF FLOATING IN THE VACUUM OF SPACE, OR EVEN BURIED DEEP INSIDE A PLANET.
OH SHIT.
SO, DOBSON, HOW ARE YOU GOING TO DO THIS WITHOUT KILLING US?
YOU LEAVE THAT TO ME. JUST CONCENTRATE ON THE PAST; FOCUS ON YOUR SENSES, LET THE MACHINE TRANSPORT YOU...
...TRUST IN ME.
EAT YOUR MUSHROOMS FROM NINETEEN FORTY-FOUR.
DO YOU GIRLS REALIZE WHAT YOU ARE? HAVE YOU EVER STEPPED OUTSIDE YOUR LITTLE GANG FOR LONG ENOUGH TO SEE IT?
YOU ARE EVERYTHING...
...YOU ARE ELEMENTAL...
...YOU ARE THE ELEMENTS...

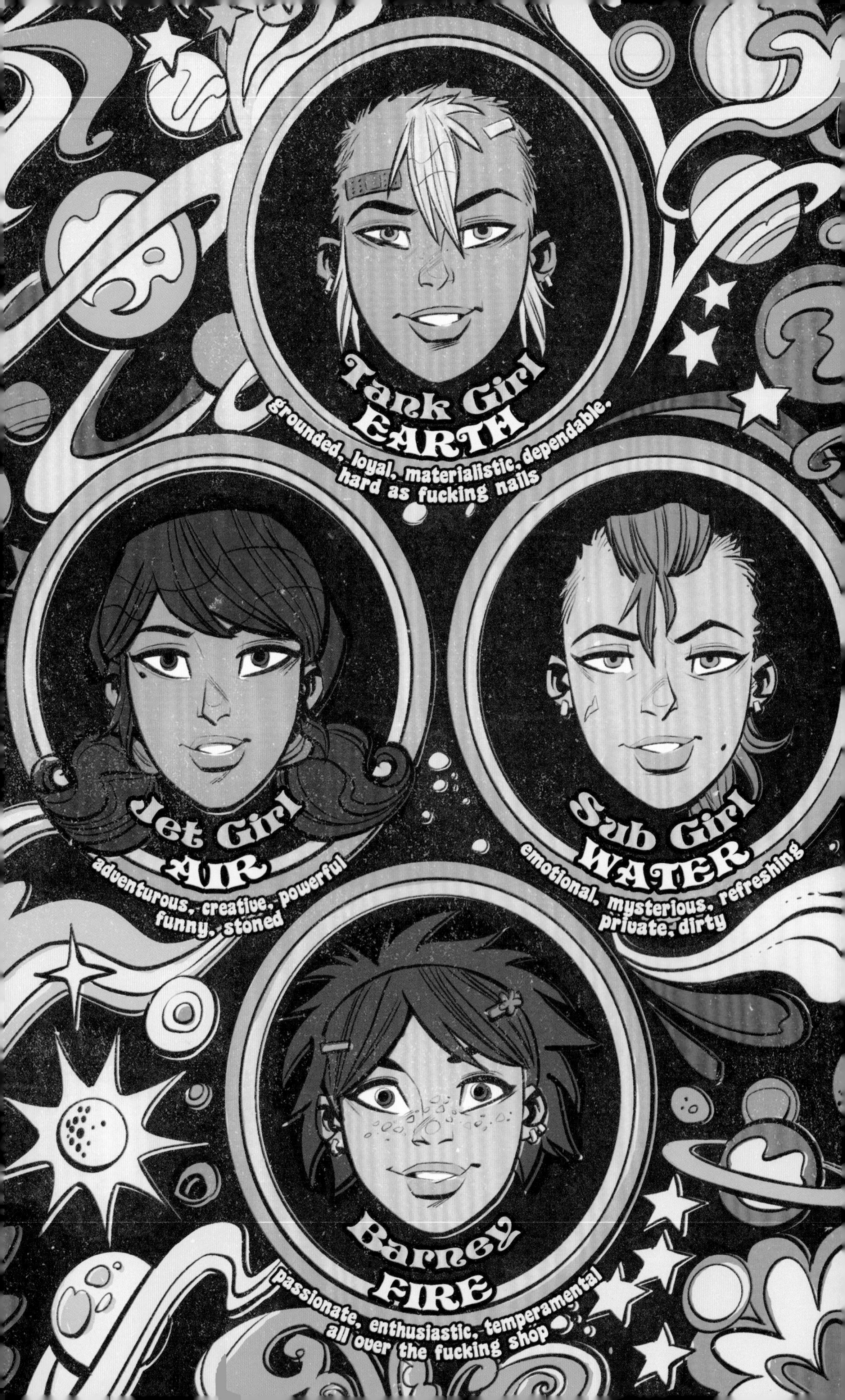
Tank Girl
EARTH
grounded, loyal, materialistic, dependable,
hard as fucking nails
Jet Girl
AIR
adventurous, creative, powerful
funny, stoned
Sub Girl
WATER
emotional, mysterious, refreshing
private, dirty
Barney
FIRE
passionate, enthusiastic, temperamental
all over the fucking shop

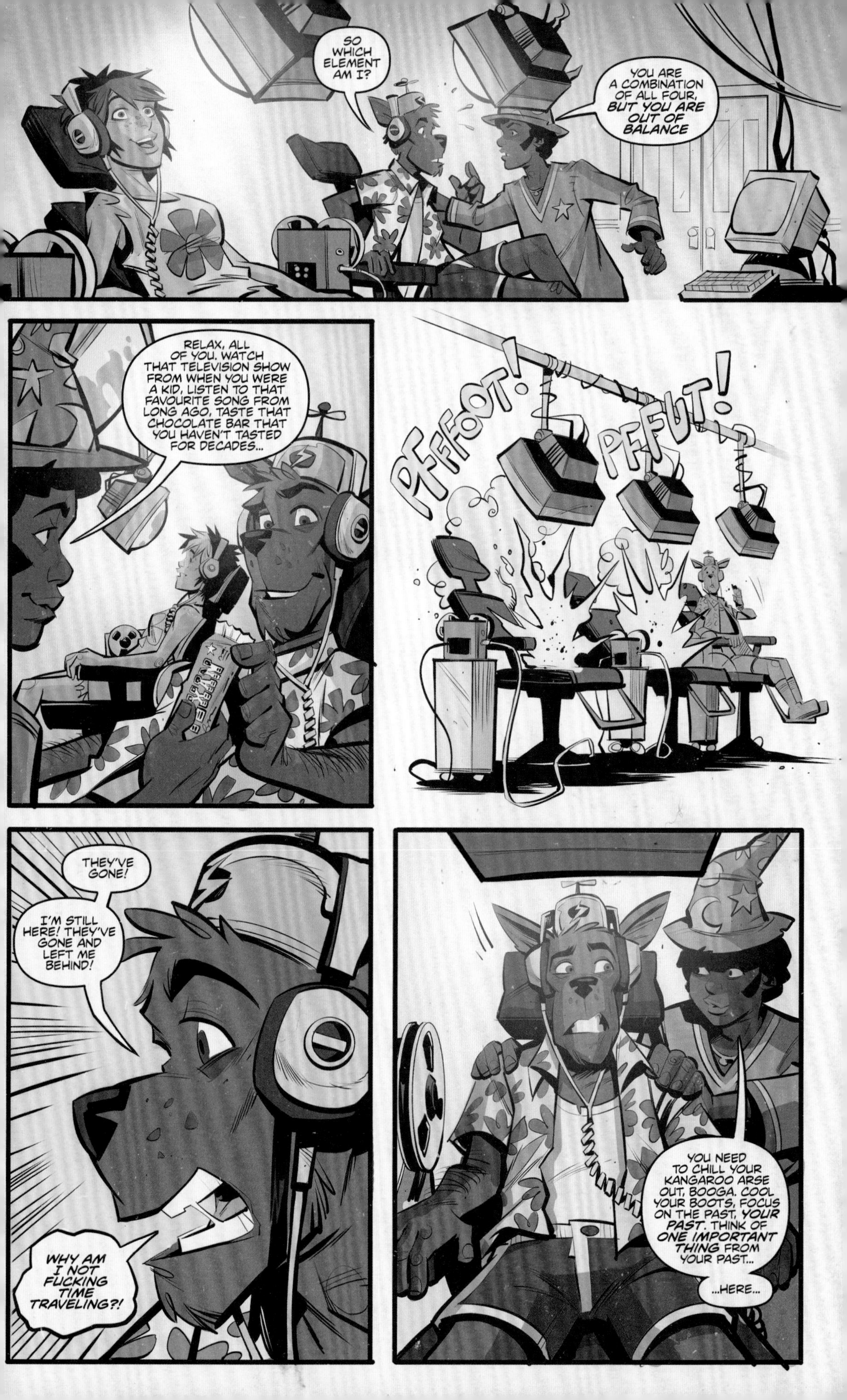
SO WHICH ELEMENT AM I?
YOU ARE A COMBINATION OF ALL FOUR, BUT YOU ARE OUT OF BALANCE
RELAX, ALL OF YOU. WATCH THAT TELEVISION SHOW FROM WHEN YOU WERE A KID, LISTEN TO THAT FAVOURITE SONG FROM LONG AGO, TASTE THAT CHOCOLATE BAR THAT YOU HAVEN'T TASTED FOR DECADES...
PFFFOOT!
PFFUT!
THEY'VE GONE!
I'M STILL HERE! THEY'VE GONE AND LEFT ME BEHIND!
WHY AM I NOT FUCKING TIME TRAVELING?!
YOU NEED TO CHILL YOUR KANGAROO ARSE OUT, BOOGA. COOL YOUR BOOTS, FOCUS ON THE PAST, YOUR PAST. THINK OF ONE IMPORTANT THING FROM YOUR PAST...
...HERE...

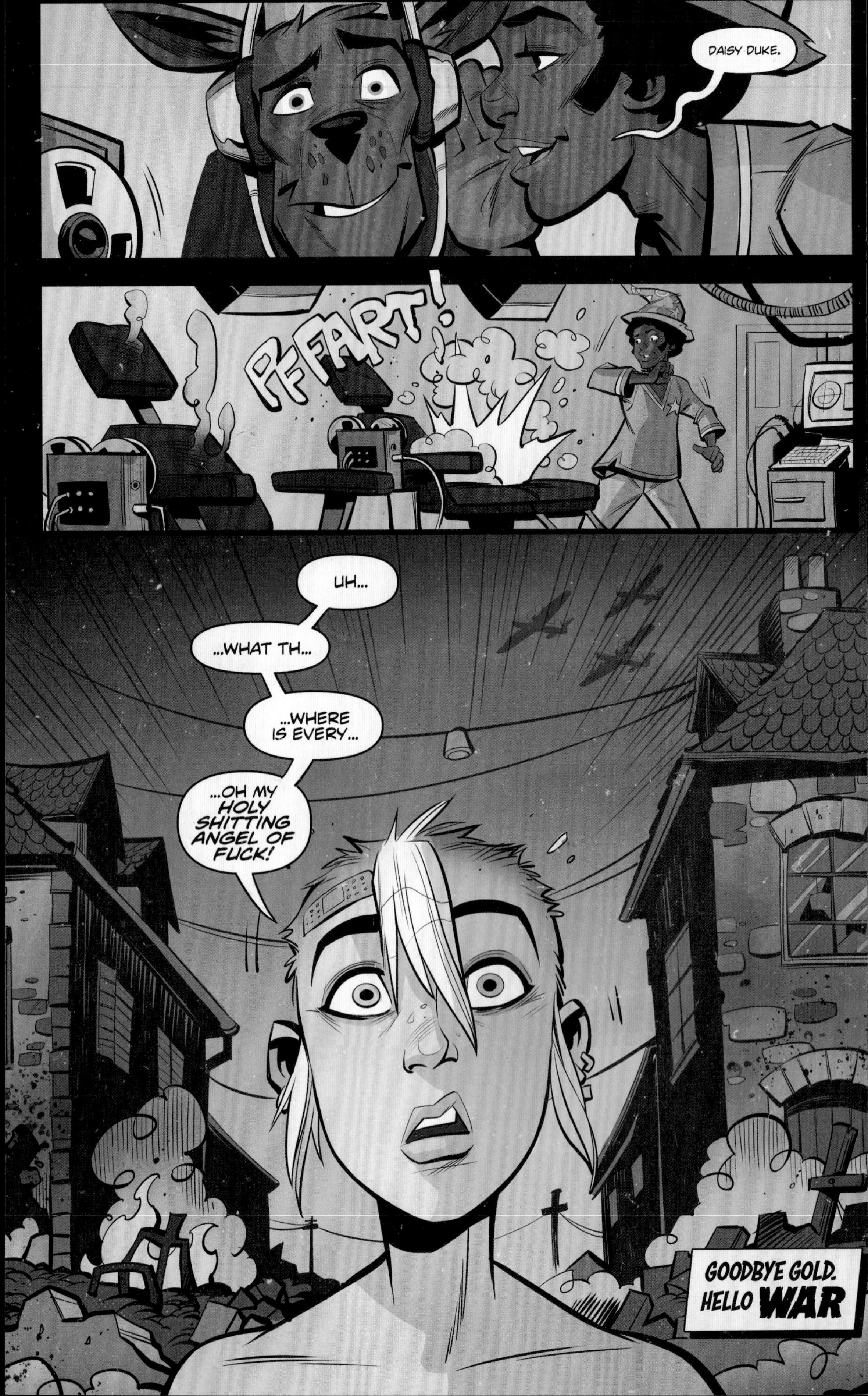
DAISY DUKE.
PFFART!
UH...
...WHAT TH...
...WHERE IS EVERY...
...OH MY HOLY SHITTING ANGEL OF FUCK!
GOODBYE GOLD. HELLO WAR

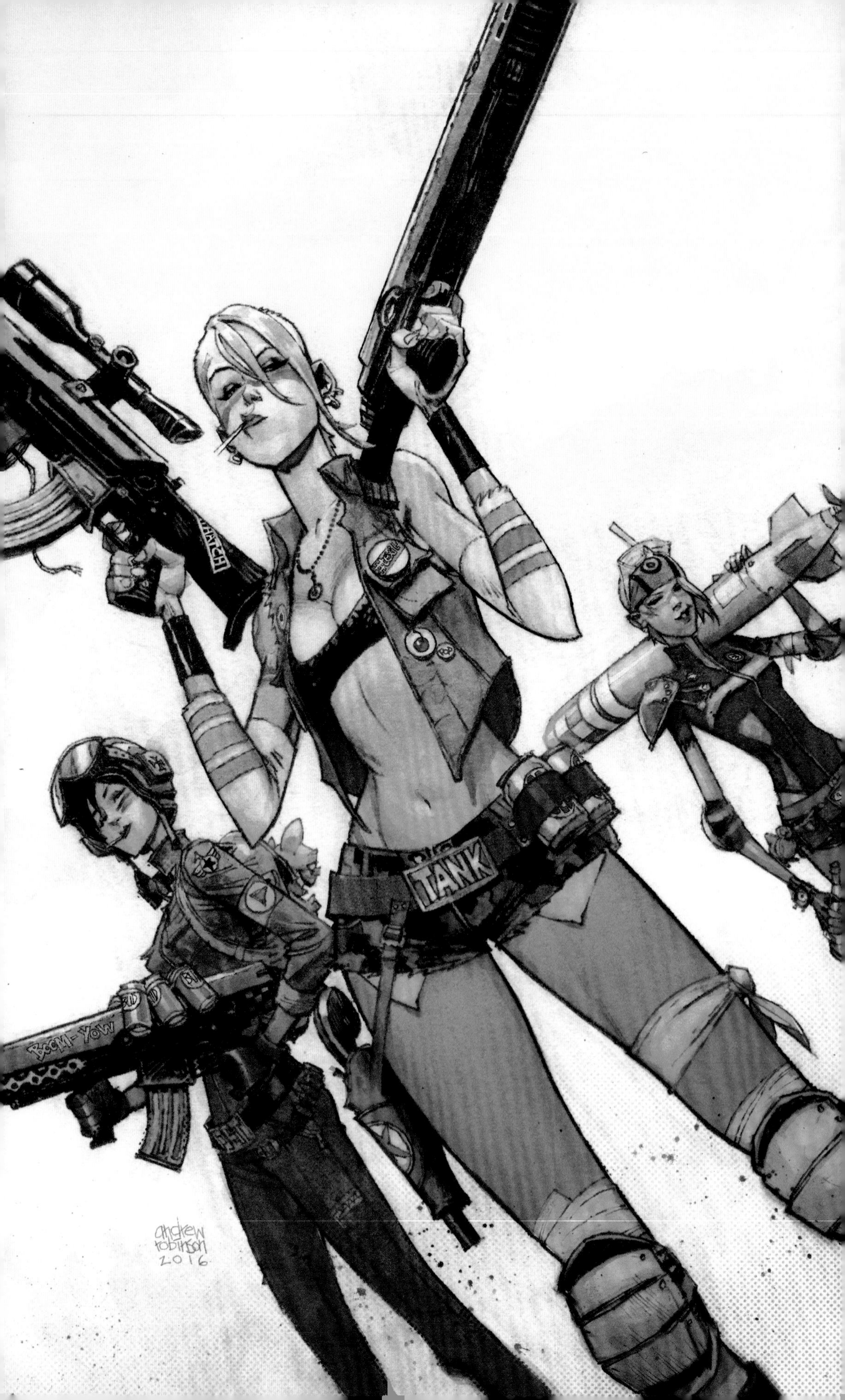
TANK
BOOM-YOW
andrew robinson 2016

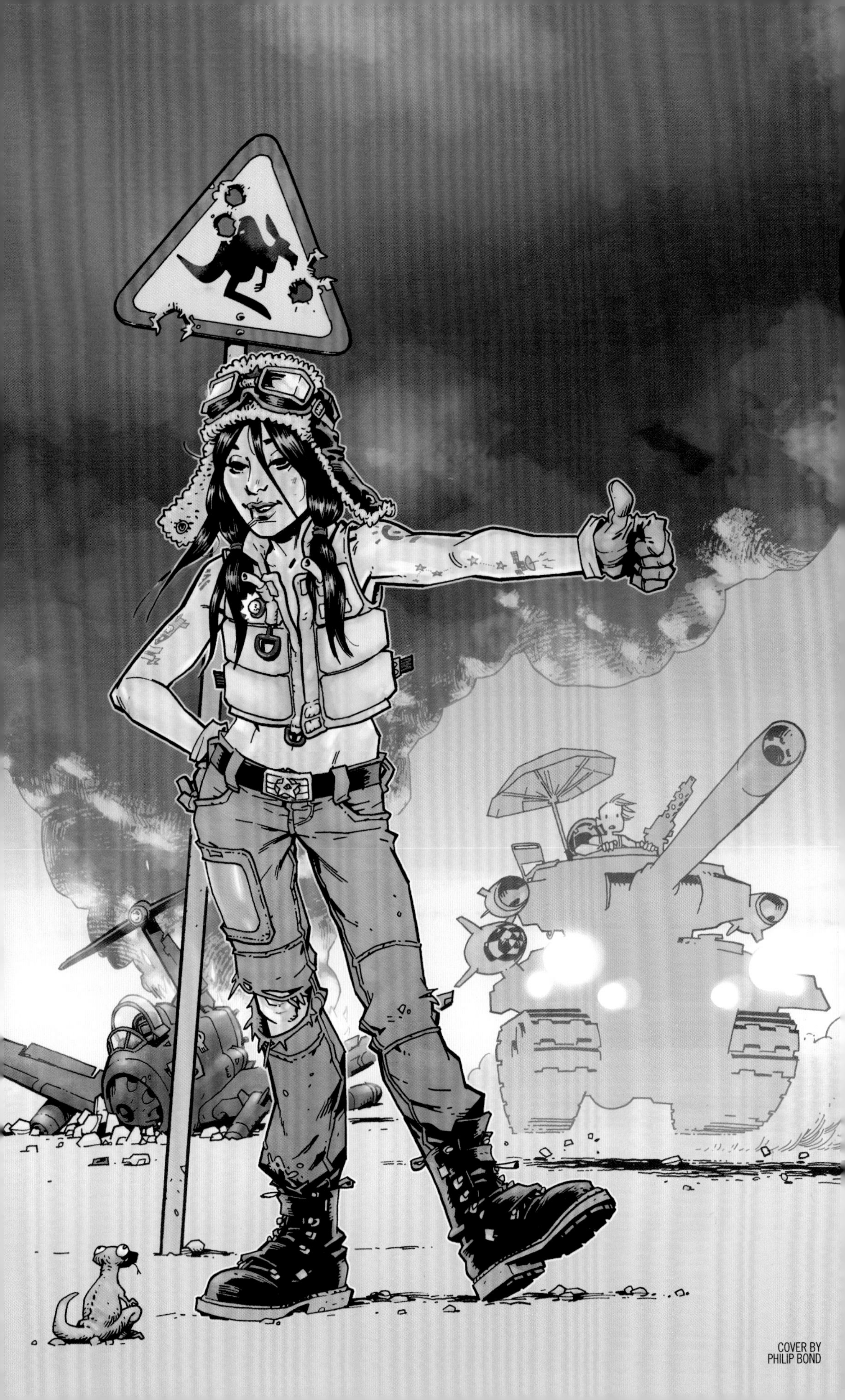

COVER BY
PHILIP BOND

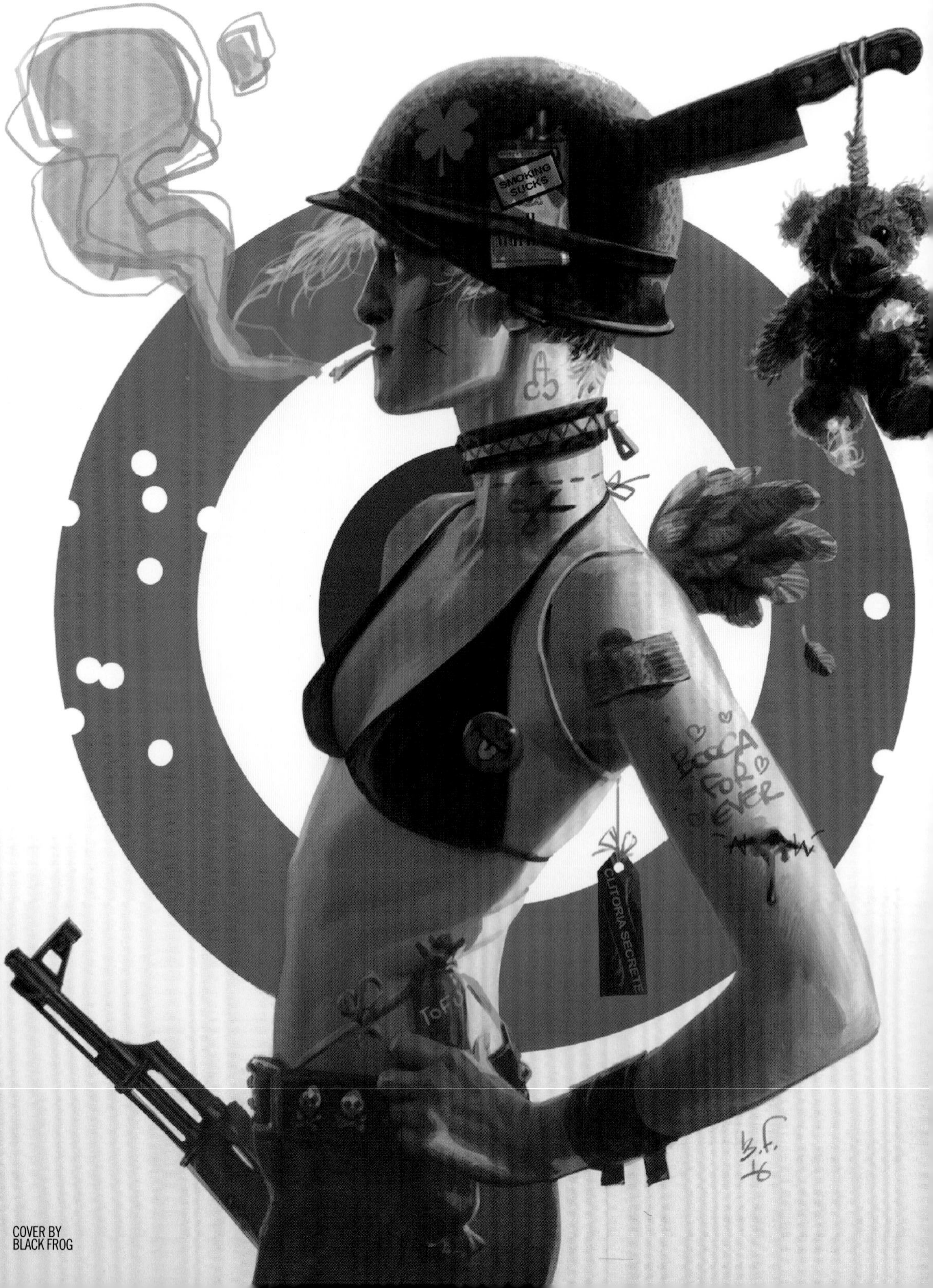
SMOKING SUCKS
BOCCA FOR EVER
CLITORIA SECRETE
TOFU

COVER BY
BLACK FROG

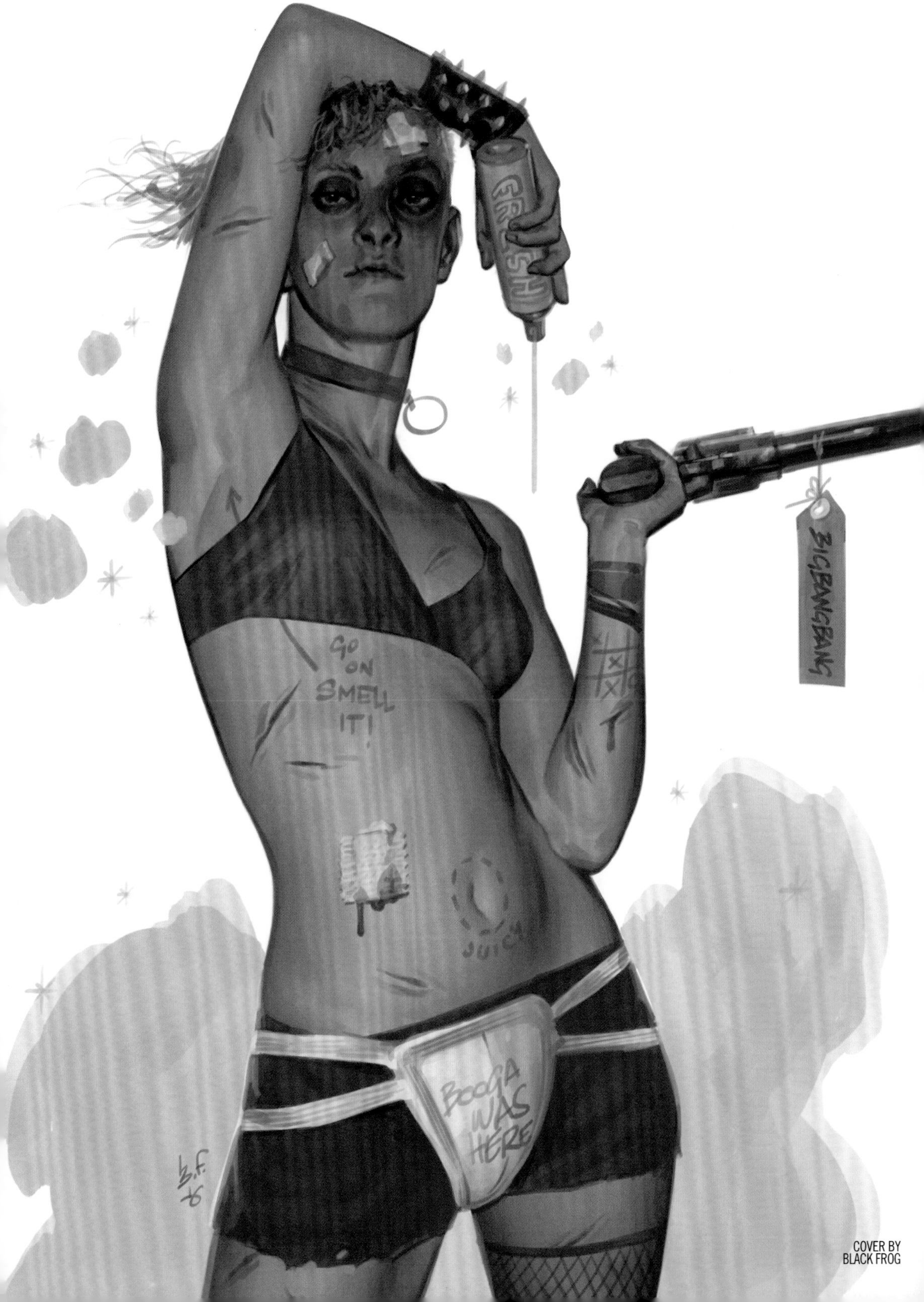
GRESH
BIGBANGBANG
GO ON SMELL IT!
BOOGA WAS HERE

COVER BY
BLACK FROG

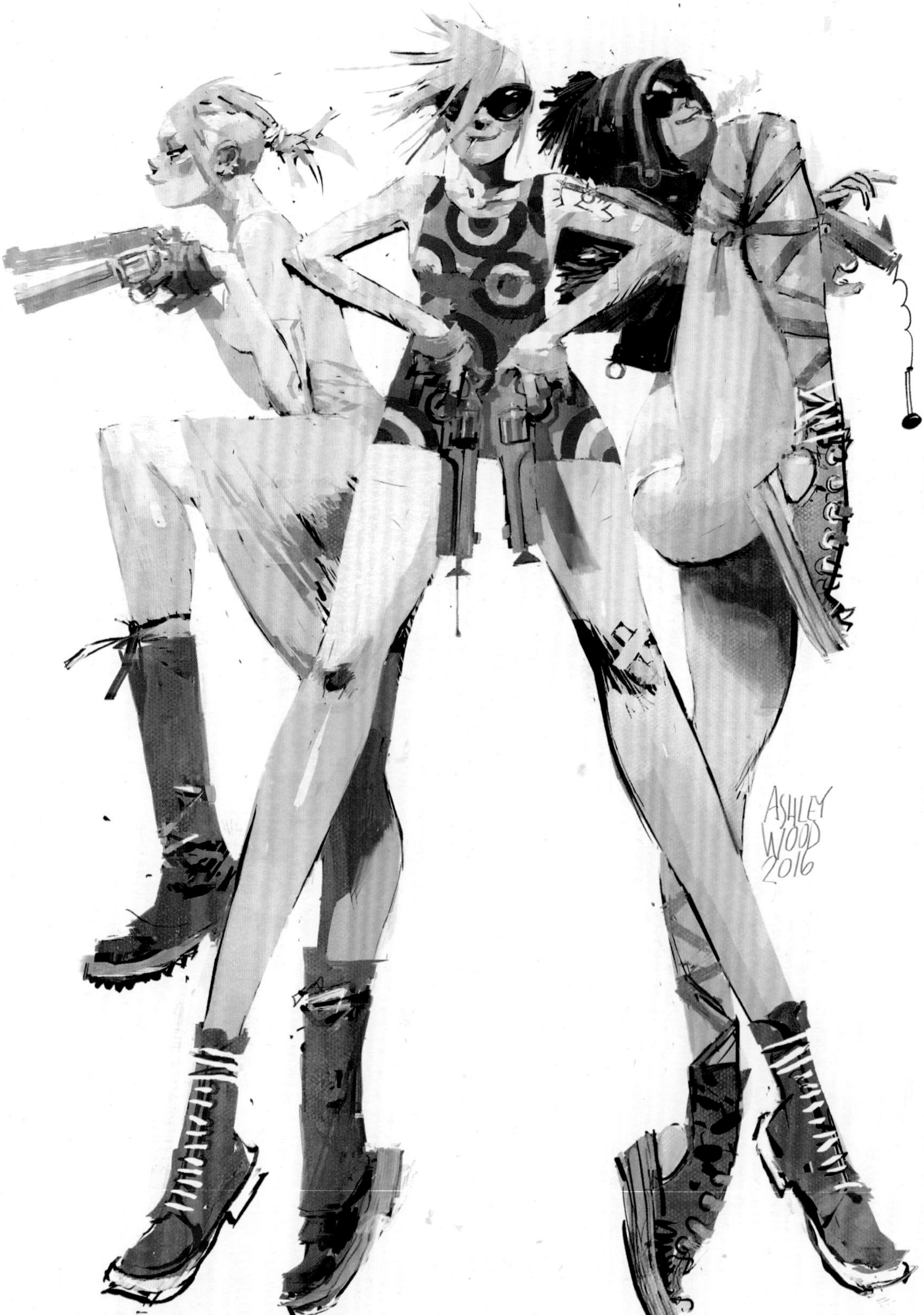
ASHLEY WOOD 2016

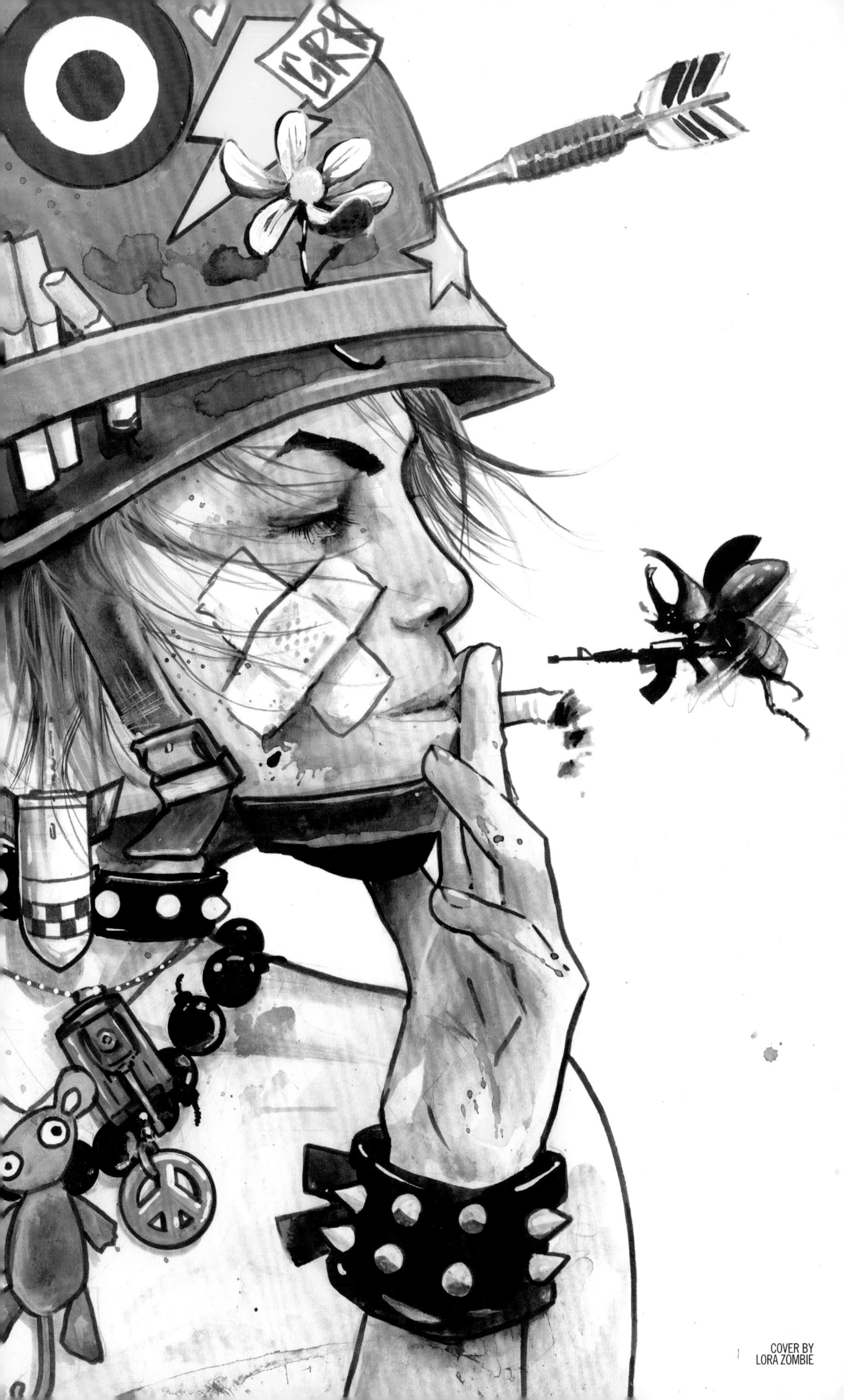
GRR

COVER BY
LORA ZOMBIE

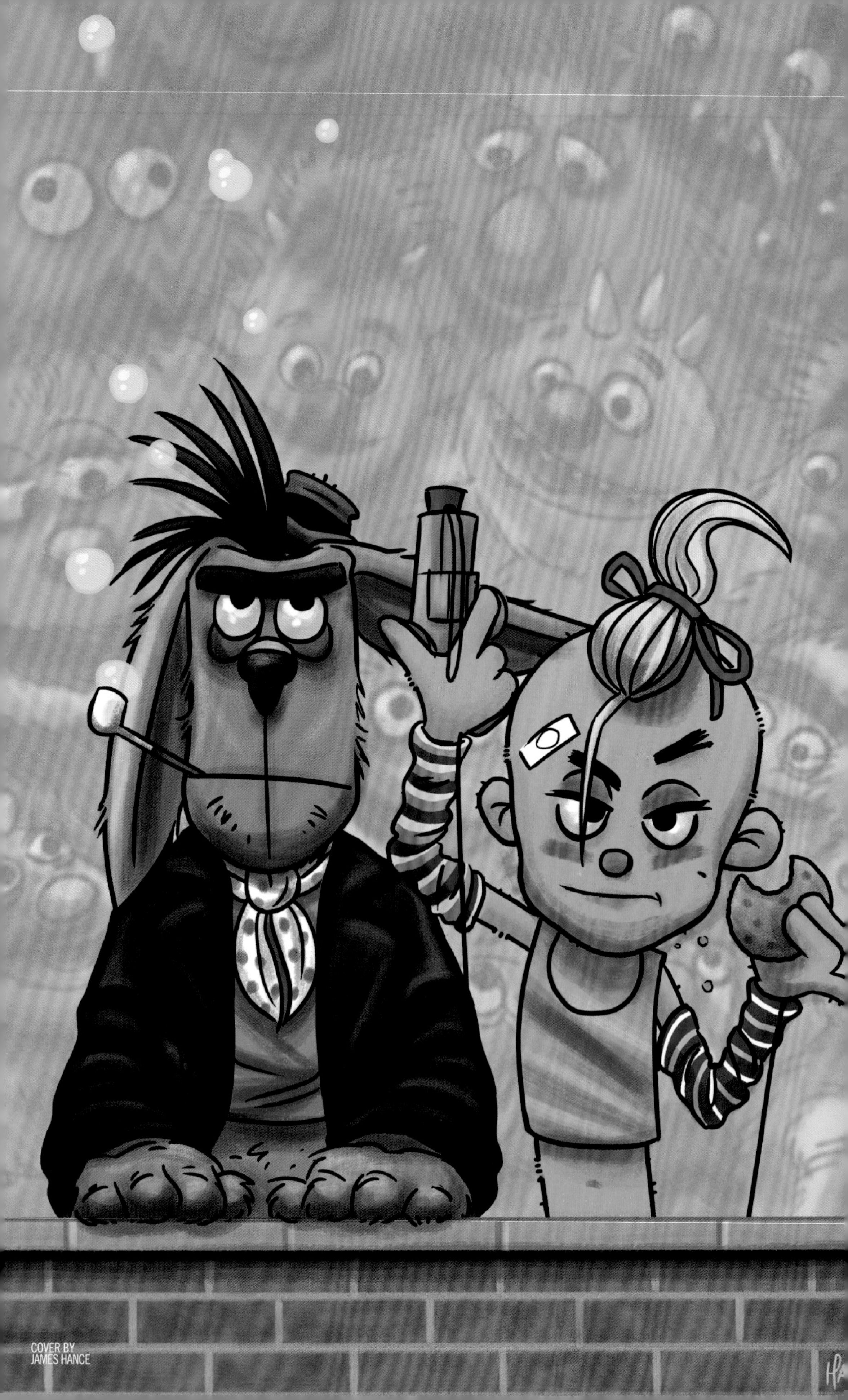
COVER BY
JAMES HANCE

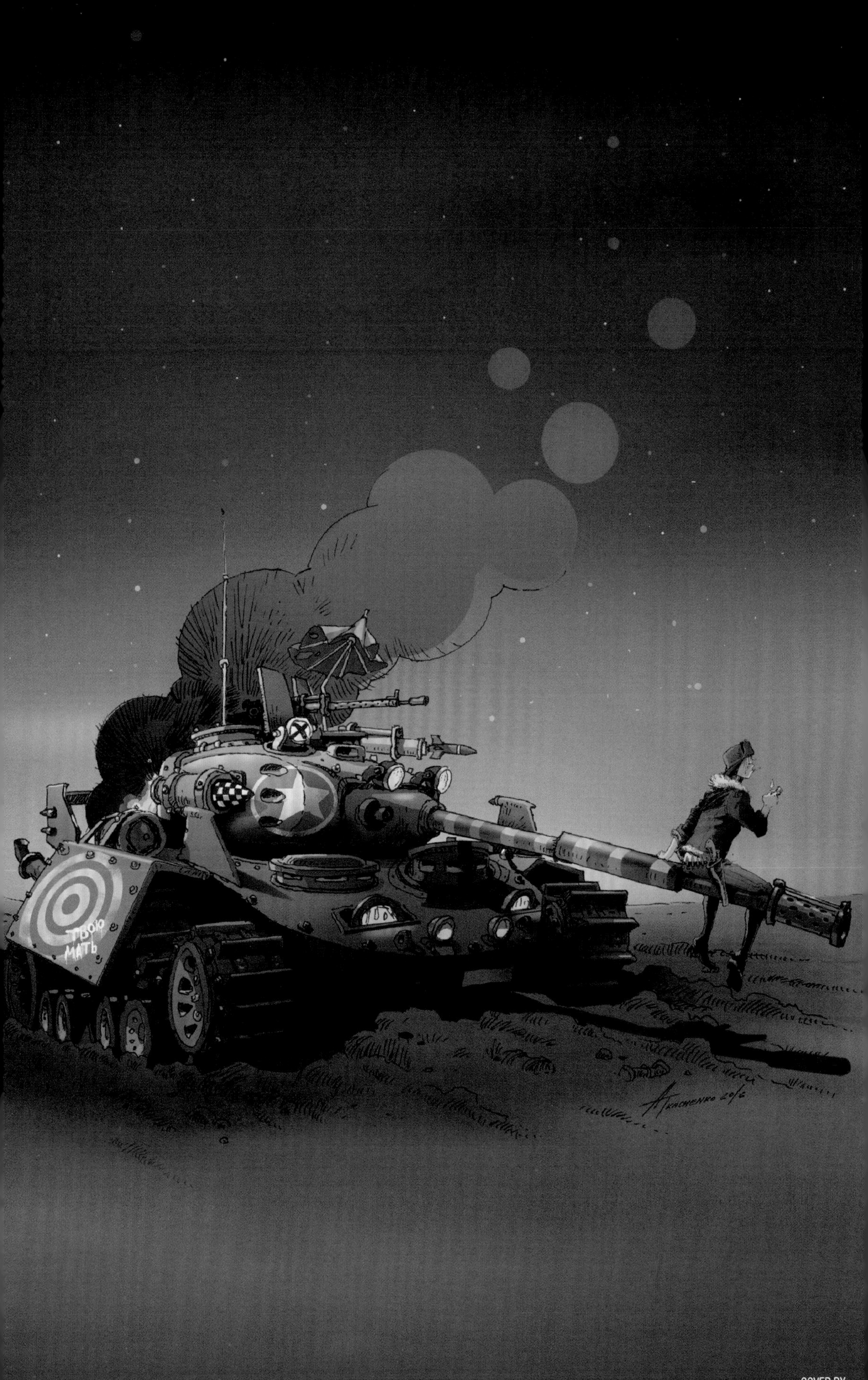
ТВОЮ
МАТЬ

COVER BY
ANDREY TKACHENKO

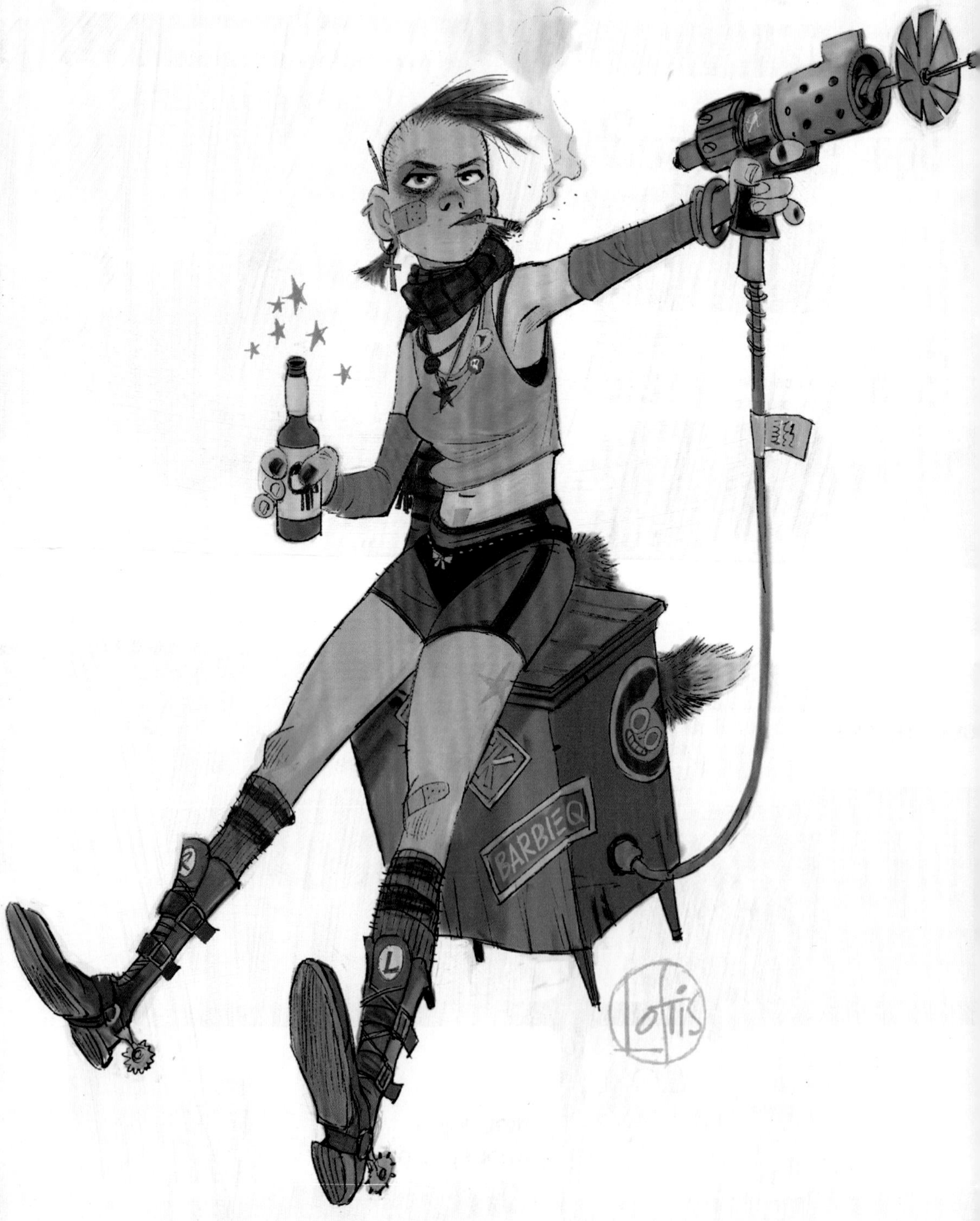
BARBIEQ
Loftis

COVER BY
COREY LOFTIS

21st CENTURY TANK GIRL

JAMIE HEWLETT RETURNS TO TANK GIRL!

JAMIE HEWLETT (GORILLAZ) IS LEAPING BACK ON THE TANK GIRL WAGON, RE-TEAMING WITH SERIES CO-CREATOR ALAN MARTIN TO BRING YOU A WHOLE NEW TAKE ON THE FOUL-MOUTHED, GUN TOTING, SWILL-SWIGGING HELLION!

ALSO AVAILABLE

- THE POWER OF TANK GIRL
- EVERYBODY LOVES TANK GIRL
- CARIOCA
- SOLID STATE
- TANK GIRL 1-3
- BAD WIND RISING

ALSO AVAILABLE TO PURCHASE ON YOUR DIGITAL DEVICE

ON SALE NOW AT ALL GOOD BOOK STORES
WWW.TITAN-COMICS.COM

Titan Comics